THE WORK OF CONFLUENCE

PSYCHOANALYTIC IDEAS AND APPLICATIONS SERIES

Madeleine & Willy Baranger

THE WORK OF CONFLUENCE
Listening and Interpreting
in the Psychoanalytic Field

Edited and with a commentary by
Leticia Glocer Fiorini

Foreword by
Cláudio Laks Eizirik

Psychoanalytic Ideas and Applications Series

KARNAC

Chapters 1, 2, 3, 8, and 9 first published in Spanish in the *Revista Uruguaya de Psicoanálisis*, translated by permission.

First published in 2009 by
Karnac Books
118 Finchley Road
London NW3 5HT

Chapters 1, 2, 3, 8, and 9 translated for this edition by Haydée Breyter.
Chapter 7 translated for this edition by David Alcorn.

British Library Cataloguing in Publication Data

A C.I.P. for this book is available from the British Library

ISBN: 978-1-85575-761-5

Edited, designed, and produced by Communication Crafts

www.karnacbooks.com

CONTENTS

PSYCHOANALYTIC IDEAS AND APPLICATIONS SERIES

IPA Publications Committee

The Publications Committee of the International Psychoanalytical Association continues, with this volume, the series: "Psychoanalytic Ideas and Applications".

The aim is to focus on the scientific production of significant authors whose works are outstanding contributions to the development of the psychoanalytic field and to set out relevant ideas and themes, generated during the history of psychoanalysis, that deserve to be discussed by present psychoanalysts. The relationship between psychoanalytic ideas and their applications has to be put forward from the perspective of theory, clinical practice, technique, and research so as to maintain their validity for contemporary psychoanalysis. The Publication Committee's objective is to share these ideas with the psychoanalytic community and with professionals in other related disciplines, in order to expand their knowledge and generate a productive interchange between the text and the reader.

With this collection of Madeleine and Willy Baranger's main significant papers, the Publications Committee achieves the aim of publishing and expanding the Barangers' *oeuvre* in the English language and, consequently, reaching a broader spectrum of read-ers. These contributions represent a pioneering and anticipatory work of great interest to the psychoanalytic world. Their proposals concerning the concepts of psychoanalytic field, "basic unconscious fantasy", bastion, and insight address the whole question of the analytic situation and anticipate current debates.

Special thanks are due to Mrs Madeleine Baranger for her in-valuable assistance and to Cláudio Laks Eizirik for his Foreword to this volume.

Leticia Glocer Fiorini
Chair, IPA Publications Committee

ABOUT THE EDITOR

Leticia Glocer Fiorini is a training psychoanalyst of the Argentine Psychoanalytic Association. She is the current chair of the Publications Committee of the International Psychoanalytical Association and of the Publications Committee of the Argentine Psychoanalytic Association, and is a former member of the Editorial Board of the *Revista de Psicoanálisis* (1998–2002, Buenos Aires). She won the Celes Cárcamo Prize (APA, 1993) for her paper, "The Feminine Position: A Heterogeneous Construction". She is the author of *Deconstructing the Feminine* (2007) and editor in Spanish of *El otro en la trama intersubjetiva* [The other in the intersubjective field], *Tiempo, historia y estructura* [Time, history and structure], *Los laberintos de la violencia* [Labyrinths of violence], and *El Cuerpo. Lenguajes y silencios* [The body: Languages and silences]. Among other contributions in psychoanalytic journals, she has also published: "The Sexed Body and the Real: Its Meaning in Transsexualism" in *Masculine Scenarios*; "Psicoanálisis y género. Convergencias y divergencias", in *Psicoanálisis y relaciones de género* ["Psychoanalysis and gender: Convergences and divergences", in *Psychoanalysis and Gender Relations*]; and "The Bodies of Present-Day Maternity", in *Motherhood in the Twenty-First Century*.

FOREWORD

Cláudio Laks Eizirik

Willy and Madeleine Baranger, analysts of French origin who
trained in Argentina and who had a decisive role in the development of Uruguayan psychoanalysis, are two of the most creative and
stimulating authors in Latin American psychoanalysis. Among their
many contributions, I would like to mention two main concepts
that can shed light on the therapeutic action of psychoanalysis.
Their concepts of the *dynamic field* and *unconscious fantasy* represent
the convergence of various contemporary schools of thought, such

Cláudio Laks Eizirik is currently the President of the International Psychoanalytical Association. He is a Training and Supervising analyst of
the Porto Alegre Psychoanalytical Society, as well as its former President
and Institute Director, and is also an adjunct professor of the Psychiatry
Department of the Federal University of Rio Grande do Sul, Brazil. He
was President of FEPAL, the Latin American Psychoanalytic Federation
and a former Dean of the Medical School at the same University. He is a
member of the Editorial Board of the *International Journal of Psychoanalysis*
and of several Brazilian journals. His main interests are in psychoanalytic technique: countertransference and neutrality; psychoanalytic training and supervision; the relation of psychoanalysis and culture; and the
psychodynamic perspective of the human life cycle. He has edited four
books on these topics and has undertaken research and published several
papers on them.

as the ideas of Kurt Lewin, Gestalt psychology, and elaborations of ideas first put forward by Klein, Isaacs, and Bion.

The Barangers described different aspects of the analytic field (M. Baranger & Baranger, 1961–62): its spatial aspect, resulting from the particular features of the physical environment of the consulting room and variations in distance or proximity between analyst and patient; its temporal dimension, as indicated by the rhythm and length of sessions and the separations or interruptions occurring within the analytic process; and its functional configuration, due to characteristics of the setting—that is, the different roles assumed by patient and analyst.

The main focus of the Barangers' interest, however, was the study of the unconscious dynamic of the psychoanalytic field. Their central hypothesis was that the regressive situation of the analysis gives rise to a new gestalt, a bipersonal or basic unconscious fantasy of the couple that is different from the fantasies of the patient or those of the analyst considered individually. This fantasy underlies the dynamics of the analytic field—whether it is in motion or in stasis. This notion was inspired by descriptions of the mechanism of projective identification (Klein, 1946) and of the concept of unconscious phantasy (Isaacs, 1948) as an expression of the totality of mental life, comprising both instinctual (libidinal and destructive) impulses and mechanisms of defence against these impulses.

The Barangers saw the analytic field as the stage for the *mise-en-scène* of the patient's primitive fantasies. The assumption that unconscious fantasies are brought into the present in the analytic field lies at the root of one its main characteristics: its radical ambiguity—in the sense that everything and every event in the field can be understood at the same time as being or meaning something else.

The Barangers' approach differs to some extent from those of Klein and Isaacs in its emphasis on the idea that the analyst needs to understand not only the projection of the patient's fantasies, but also the processes arising between patient and analyst. This shared unconscious fantasy is conceived as a new structure that

> This structure cannot in any way be considered to be determined by the patient's (or the analyst's) instinctual impulses, although the impulses of both are involved in its structuring. More importantly, neither can it be considered to be the *sum* of the two internal situations. It is something created *between*

the two, within the unit that they form in the moment of the session, something radically different from what each of them is separately. [M. Baranger & Baranger, 1961–1962, p. 806]

As a consequence, the words of the interpretation not only disclose the unconscious contents of the patient's psychic reality but are also a form of *doing with the patient*. The interpretation must fundamentally be directed towards the here and now of the relationship with the analyst. The analyst's attention must be focused on the present of the analytic situation, and not on the discovery or reconstruction of facts from the past, or on the regressive reproduction of the fixation points and libidinal stages of infantile development.

The importance assigned to the analyst's participation led the Barangers to examine the role of countertransference as an instrument of technique. The analyst, to the extent that he/she is the depository of different aspects and objects of the patient's self, assumes a multiplicity of varying functions. Thus, he must continuously observe his countertransference if he is to understand the successive unfolding of the patient's fantasies. In later formulations, the Barangers (M. Baranger, Baranger, & Mom, chapter 4, this volume; W. Baranger, chapter 3, this volume) stressed the importance of maintaining analytic asymmetry. Taking into account Racker's idea of counter-resistance, they showed that the link between the patient's resistance and the analyst's counter-resistance can contribute to either becoming chronic. This gives rise to the formation in the analytic field of a bastion, maintained by both patient and analyst. The Barangers defined this bastion as "a neo-formation set up around a shared fantasy assembly that implicates important areas of personal history of both participants and attributes a stereotyped imaginary role to each" (Baranger, Baranger, & Mom, chapter 4, this volume).

Madeleine Baranger (see chapter 5) suggested that the attitude of analytic listening—an important part of the way psychoanalysis acts therapeutically—is diametrically opposed to the mental position of the observer or experimenter in the physical and natural sciences. The scientific observer plans his observations and experiments on the basis of his expectations, which depend both on his general knowledge of his discipline and on the idea or discovery that he considers may cause his science to progress. He works with prior concepts that organize the same observation in order to verify

or falsify them. However, the psychoanalyst must beware of mentally obstructing access to the unforeseen; or to the experience of
surprise, which is precisely what he hopes for as a characteristic of
the emergence of the unconscious.

But, as Madeleine Baranger stresses, analytic listening is not a
passive or naive form of listening. It is, in fact, guided by the analyst's full listening resources, among them the analytic theory that
provides him with an implicit framework with which to accommodate his discoveries. According to Madeleine Baranger, each analyst
develops a scheme of reference that is made up of his theoretical
allegiances, his knowledge of analytic literature, his clinical experience (especially his failures), what he has been able to learn about
himself in his personal analysis, and his identifications with his own
analyst and clinical supervisors, as well as the theoretical fashions
that periodically sweep through the psychoanalytic movement. My
own approach to analytic neutrality (Eizirik, 1993) attempts to include an emphasis on the difficulty of—and yet the unavoidable
need for—keeping a certain critical distance from analytic theories
that might impair our listening.

What does the analyst listen to? Madeleine Baranger proposes
that what defines analytic listening and distinguishes it from any
other kind of psychotherapy is that it attempts to listen to the unconscious. In other words, the analyst listens to something other
than what he is being told. But to imagine that he seeks a latent
content that exists behind the manifest content would be to reify
something dynamic. The unconscious is not *behind*: it is elsewhere.
Instead of referring to the well-known spatial metaphor of the structure of the mind, Baranger suggests that we seek out unconscious
meaning that appears somewhere in disguise—as a sort of riddle
that the analyst is challenged to solve. The listening of the analyst
consists, then, in decentring the patient's discourse and stripping
it down in order to find a new centre, which at this moment is the
unconscious.

Three factors are involved: (a) the patient's explicit discourse;
(b) the unconscious configuration of the field (the conscious fantasy
of the field), which includes the transference/countertransference;
and (c) what corresponds at this point to something unconscious
in the analysand, which must be interpreted. It is by virtue of the
mediation of the unconscious configuration of the field that the pa-

tient's unconscious can express itself and the analyst can compose an interpretation. These are, in my view, the main elements that make up the therapeutic action of psychoanalysis as formulated by the Barangers (Eizirik, 2007).

These ideas on the analytic field strongly influenced the way many analysts work at the present time and stimulated new and creative developments, such as those advanced by Antonino Ferro.

Despite their prolific contributions, well known by analysts who read Spanish, the analytic thinking of the Barangers can only be found in papers published in the main analytic journals. In 1999, Kancyper edited a valuable book in Buenos Aires in which several analysts from different countries described the influence of the Barangers' ideas on their own approach to the theory and practice of psychoanalysis.

Now, however, thanks to the efforts of the IPA Publications Committee, we have, for the first time, a comprehensive view in English of the richness and depth of the contributions to psychoanalysis of Willy and Madeleine Baranger.

Beyond their views on the analytic field, we can also find in this volume papers on insight in the analytic situation, on infantile psychic trauma from us to Freud: pure trauma, retroactivity, and reconstruction; the ego and the function of ideology; the dead–alive: object structure in mourning and depressive states; the notion of "material" and the prospective temporal aspect of interpretation; bad faith, identity, and omnipotence.

Willy Baranger died in Buenos Aires in 1994; Madeleine Baranger keeps her active role in her own society, the APA, as well as at international analytic meetings, where her papers and valuable comments, as well as her lively and expressive presence, are always warmly welcomed.

I am sure that the readers of this book will join all those who have already had the pleasure of meeting the Barangers in person or through their writings and will gain, through this volume, a renewed interest in and fascination for the continuous expansion of analytic thinking.

THE WORK OF CONFLUENCE

1

"Insight" in the analytic situation

Madeleine Baranger & Willy Baranger

"What do they do? They dialogue."

Sigmund Freud

The necessary character of the rules that determine the particulars of the analytic situation, the goal of the study of its dynamics, the aim of the instrument of psychoanalysis, interpretation, the core of the specific process of cure: all this is insight.

Given the crucial importance of this phenomenon, we cannot help wondering why insight has not been the object of more systematic specific studies and why its concept has not yet been more clearly delineated.

Our purpose here is to examine the function of insight within the analytic situation, starting from the generally—albeit not

Official paper presented at the First Pan-American Psychoanalytic Congress, Mexico, 1964. Published in Spanish as "El 'insight' en la situación analítica" (*Revista Uruguaya de Psicoanálisis*, 6, 1964: 19–38).

universally—accepted tenet among analysts since Freud that insight is the essential goal of all analytic processes.

This implies, then, that the analyst acts through his interpretation and not through *"being"*, contrary to what some people think— erroneously, in our opinion. The analytic experience is built on a basis of natural communication, artificially modified and codified by the pre-established framework of the analytic situation, between two human beings with functions determined by the very structure of the situation. This communication is the matter of psychoanalytic knowledge and work in so far as it is interpreted, producing a new communication between both parties on a different, elaborate level, corresponding to the "logos". If this dialectic turn is missing, the psychoanalytic process fails, regardless of the "therapeutic" result.

In our study of insight, we start out from certain findings or a frame of reference outlined in a previous work (M. Baranger & Baranger, 1961–62). We will briefly summarize these points.

I. Characteristics of the analytic situation

(A)   The analytic situation is, essentially, a bipersonal situation. All that takes place in it, all that can be formulated about it, is anchored in this basic fact.

This artificial situation has a determined frame in space, in time, in the asymmetric functional structure (an analyst, a patient).

Even though this situation comprises two people, a third, absent–present one is immediately introduced, thus reproducing the oedipal triangle "crucial in neurosis" and also in normal evolution. Particular states turn this triangular relationship regressively into an actually bipersonal situation or into a multipersonal relationship. In any case, the triangle is the basic situation from which all the other situations are structured.

(B)   The analytic situation is essentially ambiguous. It functions in an "as if" condition (as if the analyst were my father, etc.). If it loses this ambiguity (if the analyst is my persecutor, or if he is just my analyst), the process stops functioning. It is also ambiguous in time (to experience past or future situations in a present situation), in space (to be there and, at the same time, here), and in a bodily sense (the analyst's and the patient's body sensations can erase the real physical limits—the patient may experience the analyst as a foetus inside his own body, etc.).

(C) The bipersonal field of the analytic situation is structured according to three basic configurations—the structure determined by the analytic contract (fundamental rule, commitment to understand and not to judge, etc.), the structure of the manifest material (the patient tells his analyst, presumably gratifyingly, the frustrations his wife makes him suffer, for example), the unconscious fantasy that gives rise to the emergence of this manifest content: the latent or unconscious material (such as a fantasy of homosexual union with the analyst–father).

The point of urgency of the interpretation is determined by the significant intersecting of these three configurations. They converge at this point.

(D) This point of urgency does not depend on the patient alone (although the analyst strives not to suggest or impose *anything*). Via his interpretation and the selection of the material, the analyst gives direction to the process (Lacan, 1958). The point of urgency is an unconscious fantasy, but a *couple* fantasy. Despite the analyst's "passivity", he is involved in the patient's fantasy. His unconscious responds to it and *contributes to its emergency and to its structuring*.

The point of urgency is an unconscious fantasy of the couple (which is *created* within the couple as such). This fantasy can be defined as "the dynamic structure (of the couple) that at any moment confers meaning to the bipersonal field".

(E) The analytic situation can be defined as "a couple situation in which all the other imaginable situations of the couple (and others) are experienced, but none is acted". So its mobility and indefiniteness are essential.

The analytic couple is defined by the reciprocal projective identification (Amado Levy-Valensi, 1963) of its members, that is, by an interplay of projective identification on the part of the patient and of projective identification and projective counteridentification (Grinberg, 1956) on the part of the analyst. This process has special characteristics in the patient and in the analyst.

(F)   The dynamics of the analytic situation—or of the primary structure that we later define as transference/countertransference—depend on two things: the primary field structured as a common "gestalt" with the analyst's and the patient's unconscious material and the analyst's interpretation. The analyst, in turn, because of his orientation, partly conditions the dynamics of the field by selecting the material. A common language develops between analyst and patient, which is different in each analytic situation, although it takes place with the same analyst. The dynamics of the analytic situation depend on the analyst, on his personality, his technical modality, his tools, his framework, as well as on the patient and his conflicts and resistances, his whole personality.

(G)   What has, since Freud, been called "transference neurosis" and also, later, "transference psychosis" is, in fact, a transference/countertransference micro-neurosis or micro-psychosis. It is a pathological process not within the patient, but in the bipersonal field. Every analyst is aware of how much he is involved in the process.

It is in the essence of the analytic process that the patient tends to repeat the vicious cycles of his life in the analytic situation and that the analyst does the same. The analyst's function consists in allowing himself to be involved, partly, in a pathological process specific to the field in which he finds himself—and in which he is already involved because of his relationship with the patient—but also in trying to rescue himself as well as the patient, since both are on the same boat.

(H)   The dual rescue can only occur by interpretation. This allows—if it is adequate—the passage from the primary couple community of the bipersonal field to another kind of community, in which some of the field neurosis or psychosis has been overcome or elaborated. The analyst's training is essentially used to enable him to be involved in the field pathology and at the same time to provide him with the elements to elaborate it. The previous aspects and remnants of his personal neurosis are of great importance. Hence the desirability of a determined patient to be in analysis with a determined analyst.

(I)   The concept of the patient's "neurosis" or "psychosis" does not have any operational value in itself (this does not rule out the importance of the diagnosis or the patient's structure), but only in connection with his future analyst and the predictable phenomena in the bipersonal field.

Insight may be defined as a trait of an individual gifted with an easy access to his intrapsychic processes, and there are several varieties. Here we regard it as bipersonal, correlative to interpretation, and specific to the analytic situation.

(J)   The process of elaboration of the field consists in the analyst's interpretation and the patient's "understanding". If we delve deeper into this we realize there are not two processes, but only one. An interpretation that does not reach the patient is useless and can be dispensed with. The patient's single understanding has no bearing on the analytic process. The specific analytic insight is the process of joint understanding by analyst and patient of the unconscious aspect of the field, which permits it its pathological present content to be overcome and the respective involved parts to be rescued.

II. Processes underlying the analytic situation

What is the analytic field composed of? What does it constitute as such? At first sight, it is a field of communication, where things are said and listened to, and where other things are transmitted and received in a nonverbal way. It makes sense to think, with Liberman (1962), that intrapersonal communication in the patient, with its impediments, is reproduced in the interpersonal communication in the field. The same can be said about the analyst, although to a different extent.

The field is structured by the interaction of communications to and from both centres: analyst and patient. However, communication is established at very different stratified levels, which interweave or separate according to the vicissitudes of the dynamic processes

taking place. Beneath the verbalized "material" there is a rich interchange, the transmission of multiple experiences, sometimes
even in the body (transference and countertransference somatic
reactions to the nonverbalized aspects of the communication).

That which structures the field is unconscious fantasy, which can
be conceived by analogy with what we know about unconscious fantasy in the individual psyche. In fact, this definition should be stated
in an inverse sense, from the immediate object of our knowledge,
the fantasy of the analytic situation, towards fantasy as it works in
the psyche of each one of the members considered in isolation. The
bipersonal unconscious fantasy of the field is what gives it meaning
at any given moment of its functioning and what conditions the
emergence of the manifest verbal content. It includes a distribution of roles between analyst and patient, the activation of diverse
impulses, the presence of danger for the patient (and perhaps for
the analyst as well), the use of defence mechanisms, reciprocal projection and introjection of objects and of parts of both "selves".

Field fantasy tends by its essence to erase the individual boundaries between analyst and patient, including the space between their
respective bodies (this is one of the reasons why patients stay in a
position from where they cannot see the analyst: looking, as a way
of establishing and controlling the distance, would work in a sense
inverse to that of communication). In this manner, the analytic situation lends itself to facilitating projective identification. The field
is constructed and functions from projective identifications, with
their natural corollaries, introjective identifications (Klein, 1952a,
ch. 6 and 9; Klein, Heimann, & Money-Kyrle, 1955, ch. 13).

Nevertheless, the nature of the processes of projective and introjective identification in the analyst is different from that in the
patient. This difference accounts for the asymmetry in the field.
They are not merely quantitative differences. On a certain level,
projective and introjective identification phenomena are of the
same nature in analyst and patient. The analyst can view the patient
according to some aspects of his "self" or of his internalized objects
or react with "projective counter-identification" (Grinberg, 1956)
to the projective identification unconsciously accepted from his
patient. But, on another level, the analyst keeps—normally—these
phenomena under control to avoid invasion by the patient. This

difference led to countertransference being regarded at first as a disturbing phenomenon in the analytic process instead of an integrating part of its essence, and it contributed to maintaining the myth of the analyst as mirror. On this second level, the analyst uses introjective identification to let himself be penetrated to a certain extent by the patient's projections and his own projective identification, in order to recognize himself in what has been introjected by the patient. These two phenomena can take place in the analyst in a correlative and communicated form or in an isolated way. In the first case, the spontaneous introjective–projective situation provides food for interpretation. In the second, the analyst's understanding and interpretation run close to the analytic situation without penetrating it, and so an obstacle or an aspect of field neurosis appears. We do not think that the second situation can be completely avoided, as that would mean that it is possible to avoid the bipersonal field reflecting the neurotic areas and the patient's neurosis becoming neurosis in the transference.

To put this into metapsychological terms, this means that the observer ego of the analyst may or may not be communicated with his own spontaneous processes in relation to the patient. From this perspective, the observer ego is not merely a pure observer, but an interpreting ego with the analyst's own theoretical framework, his fantasy and his concept of the analytic work, his fantasy and his concept of what is happening in the field and in the patient, and with the knowledge he has gained about himself and with his capacity for clinical work obtained from his training and his personal analysis.

Conversely, in the patient, because of the regression induced by the analytic situation itself, the observer ego generally stops functioning and sinks into the less differentiated functioning of psychic organizations. There are two exceptions: "resistance" states (corresponding to states when the analyst suffers from lack of communication) in which the subject, threatened by an unconscious danger, refuses to regress and maintains a defensive schizoid splitting that isolates a part of his ego, with the intention of monitoring the nearness of danger and protecting his frontiers with his inner world and with the analyst. In this case, he can use false insight as a way of defending himself against interpretation, reducing it to abstract terms and emptying it of any experienced content. When this situation arises, the analyst feels that all his efforts have failed at this point.

The other exception to the patient's undifferentiated functioning is found in the true insight. We shall come back to this.

These considerations only attempt to develop what Freud described (1913c, 1916–17) as the analytic situation: the fundamental rule and evenly suspended attention.

III. Stereotype in the field and the paralysing of insight

Both the regressive aspect of the analytic situation and the importance of repetitive phenomena combine to render it necessarily pathological. On the other hand it is the basic condition for it to achieve its aim and help the patient. A really "terminable" analysis, if such were possible, would be one in which the field functions freely, without pathological crystallizations. The analytic process can be conceived as the successive resolution of all the impediments that time and again hinder communication and the mobility of the field.

If, as Freud thought in one of his unfinished works (1940e [1938]), every defence mechanism implies a certain "Spaltung", some splitting within the ego, then every pathological construction of the field implies a splitting of one of its sectors, which then escapes the general dynamics and creates a more or less marked paralysis. Even if there is some mobility in the field, the splitting functions to isolate the split sector, so that it remains out of the dynamics of the situation. This splitting does not mean repression: some parts of the split sector are conscious or can easily become conscious. Others, on the contrary, are repressed and correspond to more archaic splits that support the present splitting (M. Baranger, 1960; M. Baranger & Baranger, 1961–1962).

In the bipersonal situation, this process becomes really detrimental when the patient's attempted splitting meets the analyst's unconscious complicity or a blind spot. A restriction in the analytic process can be observed. The process continues, there is elaboration of part of the material, but something very important is left out of the process and remains crystallized.

And this, of course, places too great a limit on the result of the analysis.

This bastion (M. Baranger & Baranger, 1961–1962) hinders progress. There are bastions the patient is determined to keep out of the contract. It may be an object relationship, a pleasant activity the patient considers "perverse", some information concerning his economic situation, an ideology, and so forth. If there is no complicity on the analyst's part, then the patient's bastion is just a difficulty for the analytic work or a "resistance", but it is not a bastion in the field. The patient tries one way or another to breach the fundamental rule, and the analyst strives to reintegrate into the general movement the content avoided by the patient. However, when such complicity is present, communication is divided: a sector of the field crystallizes, comprising the patient's resistance and the analyst's counter-resistance, unconsciously communicated and operating together, while on another separate level an apparently normal communication goes on.

Yet the disadvantages of such situation are immediately felt, and if the field bastion is strong, the general dynamics tends to be paralysed. This is what happens in those analyses that "do not work". Freud (1916–17) described the process in a rather different way but along the same lines when he compared analysis to the re-conquest of a territory invaded by neurosis and noted that the invasive army could fight at any point it chose, and not necessarily at the same points at which it had fought to achieve the conquest. We can add that if the analyst counts on allies in the invaded territory, the invader also has agents working for him in the liberation army, which brings about the paralysing of some of its forces and may even cause failure of the conquest.

Very often this resistance/counter-resistance collusion transforms the dynamics of the field, which Pichon-Rivière (1956) has compared to a "spiral process", into a uniform and monotonous circular movement—like walking a treadmill, to use a frequent metaphor. Both analyst and patient keep walking the treadmill or the bastion that both have unwittingly built.

The most extreme example of field pathology is when the patient lives on the analyst as a parasite. If part of the analyst's task is to be penetrated by the patient's projective identifications or serve as depository of the patient's feelings, the session finishes in general with the restitution of what has been deposited. But there are times when this reparation does not take place (perhaps because the penetration has been too violent and invasive?), and the analyst remains "inhabited" by a part of the patient after the end of the session. If the process turns chronic, the situation becomes parasitism exercised by the patient.

Subjectively the analyst feels impotent, invaded by the patient; the analytic situation loses its temporal framework and overflows out of the sessions, and concern about the patient appears between the sessions. This type of situation is often produced by the threat of a self-destructive acting-out on the part of the patient (suicide, self-inflicted accidents, psychotic breakdown, etc.). This parasitism on the analyst can sometimes be perceived in a material form in the active participation of people related to the patient (relatives, friends, physicians, etc.) who burst into the analyst's life and try to make him act too (admission to hospitals, psychiatric treatments, etc.). When this happens the analytic situation has exploded, and the analyst and the patient's environment act as carriers of fragments of his own "self", as actors in a play in which the director is the patient.

At times a clear sequence between the paralysing phenomenon in the field by a bastion and the explosion of the analytic situation can be observed. The bastion, in these cases, conceals and defends a "psychotic nodule" in the patient which, when it is activated, provokes a sudden explosion, and the analyst is caught in a parasite relationship. The analyst's impotence in the field gives way to impotence before the parasite invasion of a part of the patient and the spreading of many others on many people.

It often happens that the patient is parasited by the analyst, and this, too, is the result of an interplay of projective and introjective identifications. This is to a certain extent a general situation—this is why the analyst has been described as the patient's "parasite superego" (Radó)—and can in some cases become massive. The patient feels like a puppet directed by the analyst, lives for the analysis, and behaves as if the analyst is constantly commanding him. If this happens, there is a transitory impoverishment of the patient's ego as he empties himself on behalf of the analyst whom he idealizes; consequently, he feels empty or as a recipient of all his dead or useless objects.

Any phenomenon of parasitism, in so far as it means a stereotype function of the two real participants of the field out of the basic reciprocal function stated in the analytic contract, belongs to field pathology. This is not necessarily a symbiotic situation. It can even be said that the analytic situation is in itself symbiotic. First, because it reproduces regressive situations of the child's symbiotic dependence on his parents and, second, because it is oriented towards the production of projective identifications. By a symbiotic situation we understand one in which the individual borders are blurred at certain points and to some extent, where processes of projective identification prevail, and where, therefore, there is a sharing of functions between the symbiotic persons. We think that necessarily there is some degree of symbiosis in any couple (and even much more in a lasting couple) and in any human group functioning as such. "Strictly speaking", states José Bleger (1961), "we can refer to symbiosis when there has been crossed projective identification and each of the depositories acts responding to the complementary roles of the other and vice versa". In a way, the analytic situation corresponds to the definition (the analyst is the analysand's "adult", "healthy ego", etc. and the analysand is the "child", the "neurotic", etc. who lies inside the analyst). Although there are moments when the roles are changed and the analyst is the sick child and the analysand is the healthy adult.

Strictly speaking, the analytic situation is also a partial and artificial symbiosis, even though it is constantly being corrected and "de-symbiotized" by the analyst. It is bound to produce and reduce symbiosis. When due to the characteristics of both members, the symbiotic situation goes beyond the limits of reductiveness, a true symbiotic situation is produced, and a bastion appears. If attempts to reduce the bastion fail, then instead of a limited symbiosis a bursting symbiosis is produced and quickly turns into parasitism.

IV. The function of insight

The abovementioned considerations lead us to regard insight as a phenomenon of the bipersonal field. We have to draw a strict distinction between insight as a personal quality or instances of self-discovery from insight as it happens in the analytic situation.

It is the same word: however, the phenomena are not comparable as regards their results, in addition to being totally different in essence. Analytic insight is the work of two people.

In general, it is the result of the interpretation given by the analyst. If so, the moment of insight has been prepared by previous material, and the analyst has given partial interpretations. A dialogue has been established, reaching a point at which the analyst formulates the "mutative interpretation" (Strachey, 1934) that elicits insight.

In other cases, it is the patient himself who puts an end to the dialogue and arrives at a formulation that clarifies the situation of the bipersonal field and the inner situation that has structured it. When this happens, it is the analyst who learns from what the patient has taught him. Freud's "opus magnum" may perhaps have been to allow himself to be taught by his patients (by Dora, or by the "Wolf Man", by Little Hans) and to teach us how to allow patients to teach us. Even today, any theoretical progress in psychoanalysis is the result of the collaboration of an analyst with his patients.

The discovery—insight is always that, even when for the analyst it means facing familiar and experienced situations—always entails surprise. That is why Freud considered that when a patient uttered "this would never have occurred to me", it was a confirmation of his interpretation.

Insight is not produced by just any interpretation given by the analyst, nor at any given moment of the evolution of the field. There must be a previous mobilization in the field. Paralysis, one of the basic phenomena of the field pathology, is an anti-insight condition *par excellence*. Insight implies the reintegration of paralysed situations in the "bastion" into the general dynamics of the analytic situation, to recover what has been alienated and make it "one's own". In this sense, it means overcoming the splitting and agrees with what Melanie Klein called the "depressive position". It means the reparation of a field situation endangered or damaged by dissociative processes. It is a re-association. To accomplish this reparation, the analyst never acts alone. He can repair the situation if the patient agrees momentarily with him to do so—that is, if both share the need to do it.

That is to say, insight is something that takes place within a symbiotic situation. It is a second look of the field that allows a dual interior vision. It is between these two faces, strictly speaking, that insight is produced and the symbiotic situation ceases to be. Insight is the moment when the conjoined efforts of analyst and patient reach awareness and formulation of the symbiotic situation as such. This runs parallel to a discrimination process in time as well as in space: "I am repeating that infantile situation in a context that does not justify it; this does not belong to me, it belongs to the other—this of the other only belongs to me." Insight therefore allows a redistribution of parts, of both the analyst and the patient, placed into the field in consequence of the establishment of the symbiotic situation. Both become aware of the previous situation of the field, of the specific way in which it was hampered, and then they individualize themselves and find a new place in the recipro-cal situation as determined by the basic contract. But in-between something else has taken place: an obstacle has been surmounted, something that was split has been integrated, the patient's inner object situation—and, to a lesser extent, that of the analyst—has been modified.

The touchstone of insight and of the validity of the formulation that is one of its essential moments is the change in the kind of communication felt in the transference and in the countertransfer-ence. The bond between analyst and analysand relies no longer on complementarity but on sharing the same experience—of discovery and enrichment, of free communication, of non-erotized affection, and, without denying the aggressive tensions that have been pro-duced and will be produced again, the possibility of a future in the field and in life, since the latter depends on the former. It is to ex-perience the shared analytic work as something positive and worth while. This appreciation has nothing to do, qualitatively, with the "blissful" moments present in any analysis that reproduce the happy moments of union with the breast, with the mother, with the ideal-ized object. This is not contemplation, but life, with a projection into the future. The moment of insight, thus defined, amounts to the essential, specific, authentic gratification the analyst may derive from his work, apart from others that are not so fundamental.

When they find themselves communicating in the field and be-tween themselves at the moment of insight, analyst and analysand feel that they communicate within themselves and enjoy a wider access to the various areas of their psychic life. This is a moderate

inner communication that takes into account the differences between regions and functions—neither invasion nor confusion, but
discriminated unification. The observer ego, or the ego in an observation function, that in the patient had plunged into regression
and had lost autonomy and that in the analyst had been reduced
to the impotent contemplation of the bastion, re-emerges in both
in full swing.

In the analytic situation two clearly differentiated extreme types
of functioning can be seen in the observer ego. At moments of difficulty because of the bastion, the patient's observer ego functions
in a defensive way, watching the field. The patient may occasionally
resort to false insight (Richfield, 1954) (transcribe the situation
into abstract words, with more or less success), but this formulation
does not mean the least progress in communication. The same may
happen with the analyst. When this occurs, the analyst's observer
ego and the patient's observer ego cannot collaborate, since both
stand in a defensive position against the other. Both intellectual-
ize in order to separate. Conversely, at the moment of insight, the
patient's observer ego and the analyst's observer ego differentiate themselves from the rest of the intrapersonal field, to come
together in the interpersonal field. It is not fusion but coexisting
and collaborating, working, even intellectually, to unite. At such
moments, analyst and analysand share the analytic task.

This means that the patient's and the analyst's fantasies of illness
and cure correspond. At the beginning, regardless of all rational
concepts about the subject, the patient expects magic responses
from his analyst. He comes to analysis with a fantasy of what is happening to him, of his "illness", and also with a fantasy concerning
the analyst's efforts towards his cure. The analyst, too, has a general
fantasy of his work and a particular one about the patient's structure, his disorders, what his treatment will be like. In both of them,
these fantasies start building once the bipersonal field has been
established, and they evolve with the dynamics of the field. Thus a
fantasy of the bipersonal field is created as well as one of its evolution, of the role both participants have in it, of the pathology and its
possible cure. In general, these fantasies of patient and analyst do
not correspond (the analysand may expect from the analyst something he can never give him—e.g. a penis from a woman analyst).
Evolution in the field produces a gradual approximation of the

fantasy of illness to the fantasy of the cure, on the one hand, and of the analysand's fantasy to that of the analyst, on the other hand.

This fantasy of the field pathology and of the kind of work to be accomplished determines to a great extent the patient's behaviour and whether or not he is going to cooperate in the analytic task, and it also determines the analyst's attitude, his choice of interpretations, the direction he gives to the process. The moment of insight is when the two fantasies correspond as regards the understanding and formulation of the present state of the field and analyst and patient are both aware simultaneously of the exact nature of their mutual work at a given point. After that the field reverts to a pathological structure, though different, and the patient's and the analyst's fantasies drift apart, one from the other, reintegrating another part of the history, other conflicts, until analytic work makes it possible to surmount the new impediment and there is a new insight.

Conclusion

Analytic insight is a process through which it is possible to emerge out of a situation of paralysed, parasitic, or symbiotic communication, to progress, by way of a process of discrimination, to a situation of object communication. Insight is characterized by:

1. a previous mobilization of the bipersonal field, which brings down the pathological bastion;
2. a redistribution in the field of the symbiotically mixed parts of analyst and patient;
3. a discriminating re-individuation of both and the emergence of the ego in its observing and discriminating function;
4. an intra and interpersonal union in the shared task;
5. an integration of the fantasy of illness in the field and the fantasy of its cure, both in analysand and in analyst.

2

The notion of "material"
and the prospective temporal aspect
of interpretation

Willy Baranger

In psychoanalysis we very often use concepts that "are self-explana-
tory" and do not seem at first sight to need further explanation or
clarification. They imply underlying theories and have a direct influence on our technique. Therefore, any technical interpretation
or action responds, in the analytic dialogue, to the "material" the
patient brings. Once it has been stated that this material comprises
the patient's verbal manifestations as well as facial expressions, attitudes, silences, omissions, and so on, the concept is thought to be
clear enough, and attention is focused on other issues.

However, this concept presupposes a whole theory about the
nature of the material as something "already existing" or "already
present", previous to our understanding and to the interpretation
we give the patient. In other words: term and concept of material
imply a retrospective attitude in the analytic work, similar to the

Presented on 31 March 1959 at the Argentine Psychoanalytical Association. Published in Spanish as "La noción de 'material' y el aspecto temporal prospectivo de la interpretación" (*Revista Uruguaya de Psicoanálisis, 4,*
1961–1962: 215–251).

discovery of something buried. The "latent content" present in the material or manifest content unveiled by interpretation (communicated or not) seems to be more *real* than the manifest content—since it determines the manifest content and means the same, but undisguised.

That is, interpretation consists in revealing or discovering something present or past that is somehow made present by repetition.

When we interpret, our intention is *"to do something for"* the patient, to bring about change in our bipersonal field, and, in the end, to facilitate his access to a certain goal. Even when interpretation is formulated in the past, it carries a future meaning.

On a temporal level, there is a contradiction between our concept of material and our concept of interpretation. The former is retrospective and looks to the past; the latter is prospective and looks to the future.

If this were an absolute contradiction, material and interpretation would never meet, and analytic technique would be ineffective.

The only feasible solution to this seeming contradiction is to think of an intrinsic relation between material and interpretation and that both are placed in a completely temporal perspective that includes the three time dimensions (past, present, and future).

This introduces an important change in our concept of the analytic material and a greater awareness of the prospective aspect of interpretation.

I. The concept of "material" and the fantasy of analytic work

With his first great psychoanalytic discovery—"hysterical people suffer mainly from reminiscences" (1895d)—Freud gave a certain direction to psychoanalytic activity and framed a specific concept of analytic material. The direct material provided by the patient (associations, dreams, etc.) appeared as the visible manifestation of more important hidden material, which could be reached through its conscious extensions. The reappearance of repressed unconscious material, with the cathartic discharge corresponding to affects previously detached from emotional expression, would lead to the resolution of symptoms. Thus analytic work was oriented towards the search for repressed memories. The early discovery of resistance and the new function of interpretation (that of resolving resistances) implied a phenomenon that could not be fully account-ed for by memory theory. Yet Freud always stuck to his definition of the therapeutic psychoanalytic treatment as the "suppression of infantile amnesia" (1905d).

Therefore analytic work was linked to an archaeological fantasy quite clearly described in *Civilization and Its Discontents* (1930a). Analysis consisted in unearthing overlapping memory traces cov-ered by superficial layers of psychic phenomena. Similarly to ar-chaeological ruins of different cities built in the same place at different times, memory material could be mixed regardless of time, with the advantage over archaeology that in analysis buried material is not spoilt by time but remains unchanged until it is retrieved.

Analytic technique consists, then, in digging up, gradually and with care, the overlapping layers of memories, and as the treatment progresses, new memory material emerges.

But at the same time, Freud and psychoanalysis discovered other phenomena, which took this concept further and which they in-cluded in their technique. The theory of instincts developed with a stress on the structuring aspects of psychic life (ego and then su-perego) and on the importance of introjected objects, and so forth, while holding on to the first concept of material as memory traces and to the fantasy of the archaeological technique. Even today it is difficult for us to avoid confusion between what is "deep" and what is archaic in psychic evolution. When we refer to a "deep interpreta-tion", we mean at times an interpretation in oral or anal terms, for example. When we refer to a "deep nucleus" in a patient's conflict, we mean that it is something that is very difficult to change in the patient or something that belongs to his remotest past.

The theory of symptoms as expressing a forgotten memory, though not wrong, proved to be insufficient—hence the attempt to go deeper and deeper into the past, searching for the ultimate root of neurosis. This process grew with the progressive awareness of the importance in the evolution of the first years, then the first months of life. There was a parallel between the reconstruction we made of human psychosexual evolution and progress in the opposite direc-tion, from present to past, carried out in psychoanalysis.

Of course, facts never present on a technical level the logical determinism that organizes them in theoretical reconstruction. In fact, analysis is a movement to and fro, going toward and away from present and past. The reappearance of repressed memory material was part of this process but did not wholly explain it.

The theory of pathogenic memory was shaken when Freud realized that the traumatic experiences the patients thought to be the cause of their disorders had sometimes never happened. In many cases patients remembered episodes of infantile seduction that could never have occurred as they reported them. Freud confessed that for a moment he doubted psychoanalysis, until he was able to face this difficulty and overcome it. He realized that in a way he had been deceived by his patients because what they described to him as a real traumatic event belonged not to the patient's objective history but to his subjective history—and that fantasy could be as pathogenic as memory. He gave less importance to the characteristics of the traumatic event, whether real or phantasied.

And with this the technical importance for psychoanalysis of the past changes significantly and the need to find a parallel, even an approximate one, between the retrospective technical course of an analysis and the genetic course of the evolution of a patient disappears. Amnesia and repression are no longer synonyms, and the concept of material changes its content.

Besides, this discovery carried the germ of a new theory of memory, which Freud never developed systematically and which he believed compatible with the psychological ideas of his time about the nature of memory. These ideas were based on the concept of memory trace framed by psychological empiricism. Memory was viewed as a registration apparatus and the traces as accumulated impressions on it. Although there was no search for a brain corollary of these traces, their psychological conception was a mere translation on the level of consciousness—or later, with Freud, on the level of the unconscious—of the material addition of the brain traces. The study of the first drawing of the psychic apparatus in *The Interpretation of Dreams* (1900a) leaves no doubts about this.

This theory did not prevent Freud from making concrete and valid discoveries concerning memory that, had they been systematized, would have led to quite a different theory. Memory may have been regarded as a function of the past, rather than regarding the past as a function of memory. The poles of memory would have been splitting and assimilation instead of traces and consciousness.

In any case, the archaeological fantasy fails to translate the analytic process adequately. Material cannot be conceived as a series of superposed layers of memory traces, the oldest being those at the bottom.

Interpretation ceases to be the translation of an unconscious text that exists by itself and independent from it. In fact, the validity of an interpretation does not depend on its correspondence with the material brought by the patient, since this material does not exist without our interpretation and we cannot be sure that it exists in reality. The difference between an adequate interpretation and an inexact one, in our experience, is provided by the noticeable change in the patient that takes place or fails to take place after it. The emergence of memories is one way, among others, of assessing whether the interpretation is valid. The appearance of fantasies has the same value of confirmation as even a simple change in mood or in the position of the body, as long as they are intelligible to us.

We know, with the patient's confirmation, that something is happening inside him, that we were able to understand part of it, and that the sharing of this knowledge has modified something in the patient—his past has been changed. We often say that the patient has become aware of more elements from his past. But it may be too early to say this now. This implies that the patient's past has an absolute existence, by itself, that we know this objective past, that it can be compared with the memory the patient has of his past. In truth, one of the elements of comparison is missing, since we only count on the patient's conscious memories. It is true, however, that in a sense we know more about the patient's past than the patient does himself. For example, a dream may lead us to think of the existence of some past situations the patient has never mentioned—experiences related to anal eroticism, for instance. If an interpretation fails to produce an effect, we know in any case that this kind of feeling exists in everyone and corresponds to universal infantile experiences. Perhaps when similar material emerges in a different situation, we give the patient an analogous interpretation, and this time it works. The patient retrieves past experiences or fantasies related to anal eroticism. It can be said that we knew the patient's unconscious dimensions, of which he became conscious after our interpretation. We never know whether these are true memories, but it does not really matter, because the important thing is that the patient has added to his conscious and unified experience something he had kept detached from it.

I shall not address the problem of why we experience some memories as true, as really having happened in the past (although this feeling of the authenticity of a memory is not an absolute criterion at all, since there are historically false memories), and, conversely, we may have doubts concerning true memories.

This may help us to define better our concept of material. Material is, in a broad sense, all that the patient conveys by way of multiple languages. But if this is said in Japanese to someone who does not know this language, he will only understand the intention but will be unable to grasp its meaning. Therefore, material becomes meaningful because the analyst understands it.

In other words, material is produced by either expressed or silent interpretation.

There is no doubt that patients' material—in this second sense—has varied in different eras of the progress of psychoanalysis. In 1910 patients did not speak of their superego, but now we know that they certainly often referred to it.

That is why we find the archaeological fantasy of the encounter with the past so inadequate.

There is an intrinsic relation between material and interpretation: there is no material without meaning for interpretation, there is no interpretation that cannot be confirmed or refuted in the patient's existence.

Therefore, to focus analytic technique on the past means to overlook the concrete nature of the material and the basic relation between material and interpretation in the bipersonal analytic situation. If this situation is viewed in a complete temporal perspective covering past, present, and future, both the neurotic conflict, which is its object, and interpretation, the technique used to bring about improvement, will have to include not only the past and the present but also the future.

II. Temporal dimension of the conflict

Most of the concepts elaborated by Freud to account for neurotic phenomena are temporal concepts due to their historical and genetic perspectives. Stages in psychosexual development, fixation, triggering situations, regression, transference, repetition are all time-related—at times in the past, at others in the present, though the future is always missing in these descriptions.

Neurosis, perversion, or psychosis, as well as character, denote some kind of confinement in the individual past. The more pathological the state, the greater the confinement, while at the same time the future disappears. Thus, the future appears in negative terms through its absence.

But is this absence of future a mere consequence of the conflict? Or is it one of its intrinsic aspects, suggesting active processes that are meant to erase this dimension?

Clinical experience leads us definitely towards the second option: not all patients lack future in the same way or have the same attitude with regard to this absence. The structure of temporality depends directly on the structure of the conflict: it is part of it. To each type of neurosis, psychosis, or personality corresponds a particular absence of future. I will only refer here to two fundamental examples: the loss of future in the paranoid–schizoid structure and in the depressive structure.

The nonexistence of time in clinical schizophrenia has often been observed in psychiatry; psychoanalytic experience has also described a very special kind of anxiety in schizophrenic personalities when confronted with time (for example, they react with massive regression when there is a break in the analytic process: weekends, holidays, etc.).

This absence of a future dimension is also found in autistic schizoid personalities, but side by side with the temporal cycle of routine there is a hidden feeling of eternity in the contemplation of the marvellous inner object. I observed this in a patient who entertained this fantasy: he spoke about a novel by Jules Verne he had read as a child, which had struck him: *The Antarctic Mystery, or the Sphinx of the Ice-Fields*. This happens to be a magnet mountain in the Antarctic that attracts with irresistible force all metallic objects.

Arthur Gordon Pym (Edgar Allan Poe's hero in his short story "The Mystery of Arthur Gordon Pym", who was missing in the story) is found dead, stuck to the sphinx by the gun he was carrying on his shoulder. Pym had died years before, but his body was perfect because he was frozen. This magnetic sphinx, which bewitches men and arrests time (by freezing), conveyed a very archaic fantasy of the mother—or the breast—as an object for contemplation. Similar fantasies turned up in dreams in the shape of fabulous treasures but unreachable, which the patient could only contemplate.

In depressive personalities, time awareness is equally deprived of future but in a different way from the one just described. Here time is structured at a certain point: a moment of loss, death, or destruction of the object. Time is orientated backward, from present to past. To be sure, the present is not experienced as a real present, as this would imply present anchorage and future perspectives, and here it is only a weak emanation from the absolute crucial moment of the death of the object. In order to go forward and have a future, the ego must be able to overcome its guilt and carry out the assimilation of the destroyed object, thus opening the way to reparation. These temporal depressive feelings appeared in a 22-year-old woman patient in a fantasy of old age. She felt that her life was over, that she had no hope of ever experiencing love or maternity because "it was too late". Paradoxically, she saw in single women fifteen years older than herself more possibilities of life and of having children. She saw herself in terms of wrinkles and the menopause. Time had stopped after her mother's death a couple of years before, and she felt deeply guilty about it. She could not live her own life but identified with her mother's destroyed aspects (old age, menopause, wrinkles, etc.) in a vain attempt to bring her back to life.

Just as there are countless combinations between schizoid types and depressive types, so there is a large number of possible combinations between schizoid experiences and depressive experiences of time.

Freud implicitly noted this lack of future when he ascribed to the repetition compulsion a decisive role in psychic life and particularly in neurosis. Repetition hampers all possibilities of having a future.

Destiny is perhaps how the repetition compulsion is more clearly manifested. Seemingly new situations are only repeating essential traits of childhood patterns, leaving no room for change and progress. It is very interesting to observe patients' attitudes when they become aware of their destiny. Mostly they consider destiny as something alien to them, because they cannot change it freely, but only in a very limited way—and they regard it as part of the external situations that have determined it. "I am not lucky. I am not to blame." They may also consider it an inherited "burden", occasionally quite heavy one (in families with suicides, for instance, there is, apart from constitutional and identification factors, the idea of a destiny of suicide, which is sometimes accepted with resignation). It may also be located in the body: "it's physical, there is nothing doing", "the past is the body"—meaning that the body has been shaped by phylogenetic evolution and individual history. This use of the body to keep the past as alien—which seems to be essential in hypochondria—was clear in the session of a patient suffering from a fibroma. She had had it for months, and the doctor had advised her to wait and have surgery later. Then she lost both her parents in an accident, and she found it very difficult to work through the mourning. Shortly afterwards, she started experiencing some discomfort caused by the fibroma, and she wanted to be operated on as soon as possible. During the session I am discussing, the patient expressed her wish to be operated on, giving various contents to the fibroma, together with the fantasy that this surgery would mean a turning point in her life. She would be able to get rid of her subjection to her parents, something she had experienced all her life (the fibroma came to stand not only for this subjection and this fixation, but also for the dead parental couple not assimilated in the mourning. And surgery meant getting rid materially of her past, thus evading the process of mourning). Afterwards, she associated with putting an end to a frustrating triangular love relation (confirmation of the interpretation of the fibroma as the combined parental couple). She commented that the surgeon had told her that she would have a greater chance of getting pregnant with her husband after the surgery (on this level, the fibroma stood for the dead child she had phantasied having with her father and which prevented her from having real, live children). She finished the session in a rather paradoxical way, saying she might die during the operation. (In fact, she was afraid of the positive aspects the opera- tion, of the liberation it would bring about, of the future it would open up, as all this was experienced as unknown and threatening because her parents would not allow it and would punish her, drag- ging her with them into death.)

In this session, we can see how she placed the past into her own body because she could not assume either the past or the future, and this, as well as the mechanisms mentioned before, point to a process that is present in any pathology of splitting or temporal splitting. This is no different from the splitting mechanism Melanie Klein describes, but it denotes the temporal part of any splitting. Splitting in its broader sense—and not only as a basic mechanism of the paranoid–schizoid position—is understood as the active separa- tion by the ego of a part of an experience. It may be of an object, of something experienced, of an aspect of the ego or the superego, and so forth. A depressive position may be split off and projected when the ego cannot bear it (when by projective identification the patient places on the analyst the sadness he cannot feel).

The split-off part is withdrawn from the whole experience and consequently from time. If this happens to be an object, it remains forever a persecutory or idealized one; if it is an experience of mourning, it remains present in spite of time passing. The split-off part is kept out of psychic circulation, out of any possible change. Time splitting is found in all pathologies. Therefore, bodily, intra- psychic, perceptive, social, ideological areas remain out of circula- tion, are crystallized, have no time or future.

This may be what Freud meant when he referred to the uncon- scious being atemporal: something that happened a long time ago is felt as present as when it took place, and it is manifested on the pathological level. We have known since Freud ("Splitting of the Ego in the Process of Defence"—1940e [1938]) and Melanie Klein that processes of repression are supported by processes of splitting. That is why repressed unconscious processes are atemporal (out of time).

Therefore, since all pathological processes are based on repres- sion and other defence mechanisms, they find expression neces- sarily through various forms of temporal splitting. When they are very strong, they unsettle temporality as they unsettle the person (schizophrenic suppression of time, retrospective general orientation of depressive time). When they are more limited, they erase temporality from certain sectors of individual existence, but other sectors continue living and progressing, just as relatively integrated persons can also show serious disintegration in some areas of activity (for instance, those having a perverse aspect).

These facts confirm our knowledge of the principles of psychic structure concerning the genesis of temporality. In childhood under the paranoid–schizoid position there is no temporality, as there is no structured inner or outer world. The very intensity of the processes of splitting prevents the structuring of temporality. Objects have absolute characteristics (persecutory or idealized) and are therefore unchangeable. In fact, if the aspects found in the objects are split off or denied, their possibility of evolution is likewise barred. Frustration is experienced as an attack from the persecutory breast and is resolved by the optional hallucination of the idealized breast. When this is not enough to neutralize the growing anxiety, despair and utter helplessness arise because subjectively there is no possibility of having the real breast again—it has "gone for ever".

Melanie Klein described the progressive passage from the paranoid–schizoid position to the depressive position: that is, the form in which temporality can be possible. As the need to have an absolutely good or absolutely bad object diminishes, it is also less necessary to have an immutable object. If the subject is capable of unifying to some extent the good and bad aspects of the object, he can endow it with an existence of its own: that is, the object has permanent elements underlying its successive and contradictory appearances.

The infant needs the idealized breast less when it ceases to be his only protection against persecution. He is then in a position to accept that the same breast could be source of gratification and of frustration and accept too the disappearance of the breast, because he is confident it will appear again. The acceptance of this temporal alternation of absence and reappearance and the possibility to anticipate the reappearance coincide with the first access to temporality. It follows that the depressive position cannot be reached without this first appearance of temporality. This is a process of reciprocal conditioning: the depressive position conditions the appearance of temporality, and temporality, in turn, facilitates the structuring of the depressive position.

Even though Melanie Klein did not deal specifically with the onset of the structuring of temporality in individual evolution, some passages in her works lead us to the concept I have just stated. In "Envy and Gratitude" (1957) she stresses both the relation of temporality to the depressive position and the dialectic process by which the progressive structuring of temporality and the elaboration of the depressive position by reparatory processes condition each other:

> When the infant reaches the depressive position and becomes more able to face his psychic reality, he also feels that the object's badness is largely due to his own aggressiveness and the ensuing projection. This insight, as we can see in the transference situation, gives rise to great mental pain and guilt when the depressive position is at its height. But it also brings about feelings of relief and hope, which in turn make it less difficult to reunite the two aspects of the object and of the self and to work through the depressive position. This love is based on the growing unconscious knowledge that the internal and external object is not as bad as it was felt to be in its split-off aspects. Through mitigation of hatred by love the object improves in the infant's mind. *It is no longer so strongly felt to have been destroyed in the past and the danger of its being destroyed in the future is lessened; not being injured, it is also felt to be less vulnerable in the present and future.* The internal object acquires a restraining and self-preservative attitude and its greater strength is an important aspect of its super-ego function. [Klein, 1957, p. 196; emphasis added]

A greater contact with reality gained at the beginning of the depressive position corresponds to the infant's better knowledge of the rhythms of daily life (time for eating, time to be taken care of, time for the mother to be with him, etc.). That is why regularity in these rhythms is so important.

Temporality is definitely structured with the elaboration of the depressive position. If the depressive position is too intense, if the fantasy of destruction of the object by the subject's aggressive drives prevails, then temporality is structured mostly in reverse (it focuses on the past event of destruction of the object). This is split-off temporality: one part goes on progressing and structuring the future, the other remains fixed to events of the absolute past.

The depressive position is overcome through reparation, which gives way to the possibility of a future. Future is the most fragile dimension of temporality, because for a human being the hardest task is the elaboration of the depressive position by reparative mechanisms. True reparation implies radical relinquishing of omnipotence and the acceptance of real conditions. It opens the way to the future, but always to a mediate and difficult-to-attain future. The paranoid–schizoid position must be successfully resolved and the depressive position free from guilt. Provided these conditions are met, reparative mechanisms work relatively freely, the future is structured normally, and many temporal splittings are avoided.

III. Prospective temporal aspect of interpretation

If the retrospective aspect of material falls short of covering the whole concept, if the neurotic conflict has a prospective temporal dimension as the inevitable corollary of its retrospective temporal dimension, interpretation cannot remain, in fact, in a retrospective attitude.

The aim of interpretation is to bring about change, even when the form is purely objective and refers to the patient's past. The temporal dialectic of interpretation has been pointed out by several authors.

The prospective temporal aspect of interpretation can be seen in the formal listing of the different types of interpretation used in psychoanalysis. Sigfried Bernfeld mentions five types of interpretation frequently used in psychoanalysis.

1. Interpretation according to the intention: for example, interpretation of a slip to refer to the unconscious intention implicit in it and which transforms the intention of the conscious expression.

2. Interpretation according to the function: for example, we can interpret a dream, taking into account its function of protecting sleep.

3. Interpretation according to diagnosis: this interpretation con-
    sists in applying a general relation between two phenomena to
    a phenomenon delivered by the patient now. The structure is
    the following: X means A; X' (the element considered as present
    material) is like X. Consequently, X' stands for A. Example:
    avoidance behaviour is a signal of phobic anxiety.

4. Interpretation according to symbolic translation.

5. Placing the element for interpretation in the patient's whole life
    experience [*in dem Gesamtzusammenhang der Person einordnen*].

The first two types obviously directly imply a complete temporal
dimension of interpretation, because of the direction of the intention and of its function oriented to the future. The third type of
interpretation is not placed on a temporal level: it is a technical
indication previous to interpretation rather than an interpretation
in the strict sense, since it overlooks the intentional meaning of the
phenomenon to be interpreted.

Symbolic interpretation is not used in isolation, but within the
context of a broader interpretation or to pave the way for other
interpretations.

With regard to the fifth type, which Bernfeld mentions last as being the most synthetic, it is what might be called global situational
interpretation and comprises the complete temporal perspective
with its prospective aspect.

This is as far as the formal aspect of the interpretation is concerned. But a more careful examination of the mechanism of the
action of interpretation teaches us that, quite often, it has been
approached as a temporal dimension, even when its prospective
aspect has been overlooked. This temporal dialectics appears, for
example, in Strachey's work on mutative interpretation (1934).
Mutative interpretation—that which brings about a real change to
the patient—comprises two phases (which can be simultaneous):
in the first phase the patient, assisted by the analyst's "auxiliary
superego", "is aware that he has sent a certain amount of id energy
directly to the analyst". If this phase is not completed by the following one, it is of no use for the cure. In the second phase the
patient understands that such energy is directed towards an archaic
phantasied object and not towards a real one. The second phase

opens a way out of the neurotic vicious cycle in which the patient has been confined. This second phase is essentially temporal: it is a confrontation and discrimination between a past situation and a present situation, which had, before interpretation been undifferentiated for the patient.

If the second phase of the mutative interpretation is successful, the patient introjects a new modified object, and in this way he needs less to repeat archaic situations and project old phantasied objects on various people. The cycle of repetitions is opened, and temporality comes in.

Strachey does not formulate this last conclusion explicitly, but I believe it can be inferred from his work. The crucial moment of interpretation is when temporal dimensions, up to now fused, can be discriminated. Interpretation structures the past and the present reciprocally in time and space, thus introducing new possibilities of future.

Recent works (Henry Ezriel's, 1951, in particular) have drawn our attention towards the "here and now" of the psychoanalytic situation in contrast with the retrospective attitude (for us only apparently) of the first years of psychoanalysis. This attitude may lead to confusion.

Neither the "here" nor the "now" can be defined without an exhaustive system of time–space parameters. The "here", the room where the session takes place, does not exist as an absolute system of reference. It can disappear from the patient's experience (for example, when he feels himself as being inside the analyst, or when he feels the analyst inside him). It can be split (some areas in the room, some objects as good or bad inner objects, areas that do not exist for the patient). Above all, this room is part of a house, in a street, in a city, in the country where we live. "Here" can also mean at a certain moment of the analysis: "in America", or on this planet, or "among the living", in opposition to "the afterlife".

The "now" does not refer to the very infinitesimal present or the length of the analytic session, since during a session there can be many "nows" that are markedly different one from the other ("at the beginning of the session I felt restless, now I am better"). The "now" is not a well-defined temporal unit or, and this is worse, a unity of feeling. The "now" gains meaning only in a wider emotional context. The difficulty a patient has in one session to contact

the analyst may derive from the fantasy of giving up analysis, something he mentioned the previous week and which up to this moment has not come up in today's material, or it may be related to
a date he has tomorrow with a woman, and he imagines that the
analyst forbids this.

Or the "now" can be the whole session, and it is difficult to
understand why it is separated from what came first and from what
follows next—that is, from the whole temporal dimension in which
the session takes place and which gives it meaning. Or else to insist
on the "now" means that interpretation has to stem from a situation the patient experiences now, "a point of urgency", integrating
past repeated situations and future feared situations. Yet this idea
of the "point of urgency" to choose the adequate interpretation
at a given moment has governed the analytic practice for the last
thirty years or more.

If the "now" is considered in its strict and exclusive sense (provided it has one), analytic work is reduced to a mere phenomenological description of what is happening in the session. Whereas
if the "now" is considered as the need to insert interpretation in
temporality around an "urgent" centre, integrating past and future
elements, thus facilitating the re-structuring of the patient's emotional world, then we agree.

An interpretation confined to the "now" becomes merely descriptive, and it can only be a remark because it lacks the temporal
dialectic that is the essence of interpretation.

The analytic situation is a bipersonal field structured in time
and place. The temporal dimension of this field is as fundamental
as it is in the life of patient and analyst. This field is filled with the
"outside" of the patient's life, with his past and his future. It is like
a screen without projections. In this field the patient's objects from
the past and future and his imaginary objects are called forth by the
word. Their appearance and their projection on the analyst are not
by chance: they condense the patient's temporality. This temporality is, by definition, split off: some dimensions are missing or are
invaded by others, and it is in general badly organized.

Reciprocally, any modification in this privileged field brings
about changes "outside", in the past and the future of the patient.
What is projected onto the screen is transformed and influences
the projector. To put it in temporal terms: the temporal structure

of the field reflects the temporal structure of the patient's existence and modifies it.

Interpretation is meant to modify the structure and, in particular, the temporal structure of the field by reducing temporal splitting in the patient. This transformation is produced by a progressive discrimination between the ego and his objects, between phantasied objects and real objects, between inner world and outer world, which runs parallel to discrimination of temporality in all its dimensions. The past merged with the present is successfully separated from the present, if the archaic object is differentiated from the present object, if the ego differentiates its past aspects from present reality, and in so far as the ego assumes the future. When the patient accepts the split-off parts of temporality, they become part of it again.

In addition, interpretation acts in a specific temporal field delimited at the onset of the treatment. Both patient and analyst know that their cooperation will last for a long time and that there will be many crises between them. The patient expects something very important from his analysis, and the analyst also expects something from his patient. Interpretation stands between a dual fantasy of the cure: the patient's, to reach a certain goal, and the analyst's, to help the patient to be cured, to find relief from suffering, or to overcome serious difficulties.

Interpretation can be given or received in several ways, but always within the mutual basic analytic commitment. It is true that sometimes the two fantasies of the cure do not correspond at the beginning, that the patient's unconscious fantasy may be to receive omnipotence from the analyst, and his conscious fantasy may be to reinforce his neurotic difficulties. Unconscious and conscious fantasy of the cure evolve as the analysis progresses, as the analyst's fantasy concerning his patient's cure likewise changes as he gets to know him better. But this fundamental aspect of the transference—the hope that both patient and analyst share—is always there, otherwise there is no analytic treatment.

Paradoxically, a patient who considers himself "done", hopeless, envisages the future from the moment he starts an analysis.

This is why the states of hopelessness or of no future are of great importance in the analytic technique. Quite often a patient gives up the treatment because of hopelessness. If he cannot attain his goal, what is the use of going on? These states of hopelessness are the result of marked temporal splitting and an increase of dissociation mechanisms against anxiety.

However, the feeling of hopelessness is *in itself* so important that it may be the cause of a premature interruption of the treatment. Interpretation is inserted into temporality in two ways: in the patient's split-off temporality and in the basically hopeful temporality of the analysis. And one of its essential functions is to bring about a dialectic movement of temporality aimed at recovering the future dimension. Temporality has essentially a prospective temporal aspect. The question is to know how and to what extent this aspect has to participate in the formulation of the interpretation.

IV. Interpretation and temporality: technical consequences

If interpretation means much more than merely re-discovering or bringing to the present something from the past—"material" in the most radical retrospective meaning of the word—if it is intended to open a partially or totally closed field in one of its temporal dimensions, that of the future, should we include this dimension explicitly in it? And if so, how? And to what extent?

This inclusion immediately appears very dubious to psychoanalytic minds. We know that all the attempts in this direction have misled the analytic technique. The essential difference between analytic technique and other psychotherapeutic techniques is that these techniques use the future dimension of the patient systematically, as if he had an open future (as if he were not caught in a neurotic cycle). The psychotherapist then acts as the patient's "kind superego", allowing him "more instinctive gratifications", and finally uses, in a rather shameless way, some kind of suggestion.

We have all learned through experience that this behaviour proves to be harmful in the course of an analysis: it heightens repression and reinforces resistance, contributes to a greater concealment of the conflict, and makes its real solution more difficult. Let this be enough.

The future is used as a threat or as a promise by the psychotherapist—both absolutely pointless, since they do not help the patient to integrate the unconscious aspects of his conflict.

Leaving aside these crude forms of suggestive psychotherapy, we find more "subtle", more analytic ways of the same behaviour. One of them is called "active". Ferenczi (1920) called "active technique" the imposition of certain "duties" on the patient, such as "performing certain unpleasant acts" or "avoiding some pleasant acts". He thought that this was likely to favour free association, since the duty imposed on the patient facilitated the emergence of important parts of repressed memory material. The use of the active technique was intended to shorten the length of the analytic treatment, in those cases in which avoidance of a dangerous situation or the search for erotic satisfaction meant an obstacle to the progress of the analysis. It arises in response to a feeling of impotence of a purely interpretative attitude in the face of the patient's neurotic cycle, which leads the analyst to adopt a position of omnipotence, forcing the patient to break that cycle. It means managing the transference relationship under the threat of the analyst breaking up that relation (withdrawal of affect, interruption of analysis, etc.). Experience has shown that such behaviour arouses intense and justifiable resentment in the patient, which is very difficult to overcome later on.

Another form of suggestive psychotherapy is interpretation that is psychoanalytic in form and pedagogic in substance, which indirectly invites the patient to give up or to adopt certain ways of acting or feeling. This means imposing on the patient *our* fantasy of cure and closing down his own possibility of a future.

If these were the only forms of including the future dimension in interpretation, I would not even mention the problem.

If we examine the analytic bipersonal situation carefully, we become aware of the prospective dimension and that it should be interpreted. To interpret is to act with the thought, on the symbolic level, to search for something in the future, and to include explicitly the temporal dimension.

One way to do this is to note and systematically interpret temporal splitting in patients. We have already mentioned that this splitting is always present and can even become crucial with some patients. Due to the nature of temporality, there cannot be any problem in the past that is not correlatively linked to the patient's future. Freud already noted this fact when he perceived the temporal dimension of anxiety: that is, a dread of something happening, an impending catastrophe, a threat of danger, and the ensuing rejection or flight from the immediate or distant future.

It is understood that the future is absolutely unknown. This is why the future dimension of temporality is so distressing—and this is why it is so difficult for patients to accept their own temporality. It not only arouses the most archaic, terrifying fears, but it is felt as worse than anything that has ever been experienced. Unconsciously, it is equal to the total insecurity of an ego that is entirely helpless in the face of terrible dangers.

The first thing the patient does to save himself from this dreaded unknown is to split off the future and regard it as non-existent, to look for shelter in a conflictive and unsatisfactory past but one that is at least known and partly tamed, thus choosing to be stuck in futile repetition instead of facing new situations.

This is expressed in the transference by a very frequent: "What should I do under this or that circumstance?" On the surface, this kind of question is no problem for us. First we do not answer, and then we try to interpret the content. But it also gives us the opportunity to bring temporal splitting to consciousness. The patient tries to put in us his capacity for anticipation, the task of evaluating and foreseeing what may result from a decision: he wishes to deposit in us his responsibility, because he feels unable to bear it. The patient fears succumbing once again to his compulsion to repeat the neurotic past and deposits in us the task of deciding what he should do to avoid the confusion he feels between his past and his future. Of course, in order to do so, he has to split his personality. He may lay on us the reasonable and adapted aspects of his personality, which he fears may be invaded by his conflicts, or else he may try, by presenting the situation in a special way, to extract advice from us according to his rather unconscious desires (then, if the decision turns out to be inadequate, we will be the one to blame for the failure). In this request for advice there is always, together with projective identification on the analyst of a split-off part of the self (superego, reasonable part of the ego, instinctive desires), an attempt to maintain temporal splitting and flee from the future. Similar situations happen in everyday life between a person and his confidant.

In this case and in other similar ones, the aim of interpretation is to bring temporal splitting to consciousness. Second, interpretation aims to clarify the reasons for the permanence of temporal splitting, caused by the fear of independence, the fear of the unknown, the lack of capacity to assume responsibility for the future. And, lastly, interpretation aims to achieve a re-introjection of the future dimension in the patient's experiences and feelings.

Therefore, the formulation of interpretation should include in an explicit way the prospective temporal aspects split off by the patient, so as to open the neurotic cycle and transform it into a dilemma. This becomes evident in the interpretation of a dream. We are already used to essentially not interpreting the mechanics of dreams, the mechanisms of elaboration that have dictated its genesis, but, rather, to interpret the situation—that is, the repeated traumatic situation and the dreamer's attempts to elaborate it or find a solution to it (Garma). The dream is interpreted in its two dimensions: the past, the repetition of the traumatic situation, and the future, the attempt to modify or elaborate such a situation, without forgetting, of course, what unites this past and this future, the present transference situation, which is, at the same time, repetitive and hopeful.

The metaphor of the neurotic vicious cycle conveys a well-defined temporal feeling in the patient as well as in ourselves when we focus on it. It is certainly the feeling of an insoluble contradiction or a snake that bites its tail. But it is mostly the feeling that time does not unfold and keeps on spinning around itself—a repetitive circular time with no future.

Alongside this, there are a large number of cases in which the neurotic cycle is broken and there is movement towards the future. This is, in my opinion, the general rule.

Take, for example, a case of a young woman who suffered from a phobia of being deflowered. Analysis revealed that this phobia stemmed from an intense fixation on her father (with adolescent fantasies in which the father had to deflower her) and from more archaic feelings (her mother's death while giving birth: a consequence of sexual relations; a fantasy of "becoming a nun" so as to be bound to her mother, who was watching her from heaven; a strong erotic fixation on her mother, which was confirmed by memories and death feelings associated with the primal scene). I used to worry about this person's future. If she failed to overcome her phobia, she was doomed to frustration and to the resentment

found in single women, to misfortune and loneliness. I often realized that I was more worried about this predictable destiny than
she really was.

This phenomenon became more evident when the patient started a love relation and was about to overcome her old phobia. She
first showed conversion symptoms that had been long overcome
in the past (nausea and inability to eat in the presence of desired
men), and she let me know through a friend that she had arranged
to meet her boyfriend, so that they would not be left alone (to avoid
the phobic situation). When I learnt this, I was very angry, and I
thought this girl was wasting her life, that she would never progress,
that I was wasting my time. I could not help realizing how absurd
my reaction was (why get angry with a symptom?). Unexpectedly,
in the following session she told me that she had succeeded in
overcoming her phobia and was going to get married.

At that point I recognized the phenomenon Grinberg (1956)
calls "projective counter-identification". I had absorbed the patient's feelings of "wasting her life", "having no future", of being
impotent before her fate. Meanwhile, the patient felt relatively free
and was confidently building another destiny. As her anxiety about
destiny had been previously re-introjected and elaborated, she was
able to be open to the future. As long as this anxiety remained split
off and projected, deposited on me, she was able to open partially
to temporality while putting on the analyst the part that was not
opened yet.

These examples illustrate the breaking of the neurotic cycle and
its transformation into a dilemma. Some, purely verbal dilemmas,
do not resolve the condition that may arise in real life because
they lack a basic condition: a good enough ego–object union that
facilitates the structuring of the depressive position. The present is
a partial reintegration of destiny, which, with the help of a partial
placing of the neurotic cycle on the analyst, facilitates recovering
the future. Thus the neurotic cycle is transformed into a dilemma
experienced as partially solved (the neurotic cycle was: "I fear the
sexual contact that I desire with the object" . . . "I avoid all possible objects" . . . "I keep the object away so I will never satisfy my
desire" . . . "frustration increases my fears"; the dilemma was: "I
choose a destiny of fear and frustration and waste my life or else
face life and dare to confront fear").

If temporality is only structured in individual history with the depressive position, we assume in technical terms that interpretation facilitates the repetition of this process. The building of the future dimension is produced at the same time and in the same measure as the elaboration of the depressive phase. Time is blocked both in the paranoid–schizoid position and in the depressive position until the latter is overcome by reparation.

Hence the importance that feelings of hope and despair have in life as well as in the analytic situation. Technically, the appearance of an authentic feeling of hope means an excellent test for the modification of the patient's inner object situation. By authentic hope I mean the opposite of hypomanic hope (an omnipotent feeling that the future is certain, that everything is within easy reach) and the opposite of the negation—actually schizoid—of the future (when the patient has no concern for the future because it does not exist for him, although this is worrying for the analyst). Authentic hope is coextensive with effective processes of reparation and sublimation—that is, the subject's capacity to recover, repair, or merely replace his objects through his own creative activity. This means that the objects may be lost or destroyed (death of the objects), and the patient is aware of the effort he has to make to maintain them or to reconstruct them but feels confident about it.

Despair, in contrast, appears in two forms: as the impossibility of breaking free of the cycle of immutable objects and establishing temporality (paranoid–schizoid despair) or as the awareness of being the prisoner of destroyed or irreparable objects, which works as a magnet and pulls all temporality back into the past (depressive despair).

That is why Melanie Klein has underlined explicitly the importance of feelings of hope in analysis. Hope, in analytic technique, appears when the patient can feel deeply the depressive position:

> It can be observed in the analyses of adults and children that, together with a full experience of depression, feelings of hope emerge. In early development, this is one of the factors which helps the infant to overcome the depressive position. [Klein, 1952a, p. 214]

This combination of hope and depression may sound paradoxical at first. But we have to take into account that progress of insight elicited by the establishment or the recovery of the depressive position facilitates reparatory processes:

> Omnipotence decreases as the infant gains a greater confidence both in his objects and in the reparative powers. He feels that all steps in development, all new achievements are giving pleasure to the people around him and that in this way he expresses his love, counter-balances or undoes the harm done by his aggressive impulses and makes reparation to his injured loved objects. [Klein, 1952a, pp. 214–215]

Increase in reparatory actions facilitated by the elaboration of the depressive position leads to the opening of temporality. If Melanie Klein does not use this word, she at least expresses this concept quite clearly:

> The pain the patient experiences during the analysis is also gradually lessened by improvements bound up with progress in integration, such as regaining some initiative, becoming able to make decisions he was previously unable to reach and, in general, using his gifts more freely. This is linked up with a lessening inhibition of his capacity to make reparation. His power of enjoyment increases in many ways and hope reappears, though it may still alternate with depression. I have found that creativeness grows in proportion to being able to establish the good object more securely, which in successful case is the result of the analysis of envy and destructiveness. [Klein, 1957, p. 233]

Once temporality is opened and there is access to the future, different feelings appear: of continuity, of life, of counteracting the knowledge of inevitable death:

> Those who feel that they have had a share in the experience and pleasures of life are much more able to believe in the continuity of life. Such capacity for resignation without undue bitterness and yet keeping the power of enjoyment alive has its roots in infancy and depends on how far the baby had been able to enjoy the breast without excessively envying the mother for its possession. [Klein, 1957, p. 203]

Despair about the past (the consciousness or fantasy of having an absolutely terrible past) negates the feeling of being and having been in life and impedes the belief in its continuity, whereas the awareness that present and future hold still unexpected possibilities, which can emerge during the analytic process, gives a different and better image of the past (by definition, no human being alive has had an absolutely bad past).

I think I interpret Melanie Klein rightly when I hold that the analytic process is basically a dialectic between an inhibiting past and a closed future. Interpretation has to consider all the dimensions of temporality because it is a mediator between past and future and facilitates their integration and attendant modification.

The comparison between an interpretation focused on the past and a situational interpretation helps us to understand this dialectic process better. It often happens that after an interpretation related to the past, the patient responds with a question: "And so what?" Suppose that we have told him: "You are repeating with me a situation from the past." Meaning: "But we can break free from this situation because your past is different from your transference present." But the patient does not grasp this, because he is caught in the past and he is bound to repeat it. He does not feel released from this tie to the past and asks: "And so what?" This question, first of all, disregards the interpretation ("This is what you say, but what's the use of knowing this?") and also expresses the hope that the analyst may magically change the past ("It is so, but you have to change my past"). Perhaps this is an authentic awareness that something is missing in the interpretation. The patient feels he is caught in his neurosis: "The analyst has a future; I don't."

I do not mean to criticize this kind of interpretation, which is an indispensable moment in the structuring of a situational interpretation, but I would like to point out the need to complement it with its temporal aspect and to integrate into it the exclusion of the future by the conflict and the avoidance of the dilemma. For example: "You think that this interpretation is useless because you prefer to be caught in your past, otherwise you would have to face situations that for some reason are dangerous to you".

The formulation of the dilemma itself does not bring about any special therapeutic effect: such an effect depends on re-introjection and re-projection processes and on the ensuing modification of the objects and the ego, but I do consider it important for the *elaboration* of the situation to include those future perspectives when they appear in the field and to connect them to the development of reparatory attitudes and inner unification.

To sum up: It is not my purpose to suggest perspectives when they are not present, as this would mean leading the patient into intellectual constructions that he does not feel, that are not his, and which he cannot accept due to his conflict, but to remark and interpret temporal splitting and each progress in the opening to the future when it really appears in the patient.

This concept of interpretation as a dialectic process between the past—the transference situation—and the future is closely related to our concept of insight. A technique essentially focused on the past is bound to consider insight as the contemplation of figures in a wax museum, because the material that is the object of insight is ultimately regarded as a group of wax figures. In contrast, figures and look condition each other: the act of insight structures what is seen and "vision" itself. Therefore the inclusion and the splitting of the future dimension in the act of insight are of utmost importance.

The past is not univocal. It is structured together with a particular future, or lack of future. To conceive the past as univocal and unchangeable obstructs the therapeutic action of interpretation, as this works retrospectively on a gestalt that endows the past with meaning. Therefore the past is not a privileged dimension of interpretation but, rather, a dimension that gains meaning only within a whole made up of all dimensions. Anticipation in the patient and in the interpretation is as important as reconstruction: the future is as "material" as the past.

The interpretation that elicits insight produces a dialectic movement: reintegration of the past through modified transference repetition, reintegration of a possible split-off past, retroactive modification of the past in relation to this global situation.

In other words, psychoanalysis acts basically on a person's destiny (including his symptoms, his character, his structure, etc.). If we picture destiny as a curve, the purpose of analysis for both patient and analyst is to achieve the reconstruction of the total curve. The first part of the curve, the part already lived, does not mean much in itself, but it does so as a part of multiple possible curves. If Napoleon had died on the bridge at Arcole, if one of his men had not leapt in front of him to shield him and died in his place, he would have been remembered as an ambitious general with some talent, and his previous life, instead of being understood as the first steps of a future genius, would be only a part of a completely ordinary destiny.

The same is true in an analysis about premature birth, bad breast-feeding, too early weaning, witnessing the primal scene, and so on. No matter how many of these traumatic situations may have happened, they do not act in a mechanical, causal way, but as elements of a destiny that can or cannot be overcome, according to what comes next and to the analytic process. Occasionally these elements may have an extremely great weight. What the patient has already lived can be regarded as the beginning of a multiplicity (quite large, but not infinite) of possible destinies.

The common concept of material leads us to conceive destiny as already outlined and, in the same way, to approach vocation as the encounter with something existing in the patient's eternity. But, in fact, we can only find in the patient elements that acquire meaning when structured in a vocational gestalt.

The analysis of the patient's ideology is also important to make him aware of his destiny and guide him towards his future.

Analysis is not an encounter, but a construction. Interpretation aims at transforming the burden of fate into an element of creation.

3

Spiral process and the dynamic field

Willy Baranger

It is difficult—but worth while and even necessary—for any human being to know where he is standing in relation to who his father was—whether it is paternity strictly speaking, in a familial sense, or symbolic paternity. I was linked to Enrique Pichon-Rivière by an analyst–analysand and teacher–disciple relation and later by a close friendship with a very talented and admired older friend. This is the framework for my present thoughts, a very personal backdrop to a work that is neither a story of a part of my life nor a eulogy for him.

Pichon-Rivière's formulations concerning the analytic process as "spiral process" date back to the years between 1954 and 1958 in the intellectual evolution of the author. We shared with the founding group of the Uruguayan Psychoanalytic Association the elaboration of some of Pichon-Rivière's ideas through many long "seminar" meetings. What did we study in those meetings? Freud's letters to Fliess (Masson, 1985), Freud's last works—"Analysis

Published in Spanish as "Proceso en Espiral y Campo Dinámico" (*Revista Uruguaya de Psicoanálisis, 59*, 1979: 17–32).

Terminable and Interminable" (1937c), "Constructions in Analysis" (1937d)—and also other authors, such as Henry Ezriel ("The psychoanalytic Session as an Experimental Situation": 1951), Melanie Klein, and Paula Heimann.

But Montevideo meant to him affectively something more than to any of us, and it can be summed up in "Maldoror"—or "Lautréamont" or "Isidore Ducasse".[1] Enrique Pichon-Rivière shared with us the aim (a myth?) of striving for a freer psychoanalytic institution—a more creative one, one more open to the understanding of madness and less closed in conceptual orthodoxy and petty rivalries. Maldoror, as model, was not too bad. "Mal d'aurores", we used to say. And this does not rule out the "Mal d'horreur" of *Les chants*. We all had both: good things and bad things, dawns and horrors, with a clear predominance of dawns. Now we can take stock.

I believe in those years Pichon-Rivière reached the climax of his development in psychoanalytic theorization, before the movement that would lead him later on to social psychology and to leave us.

But let us come back to those years full of creativity and enthusiasm. In Buenos Aires, around Pichon-Rivière, there was an important school of thought as well as other equally active and creative trends. Many of us—Jorge Mom, David Liberman, José Bleger, Edgardo Rolla (to quote just a few does not mean forgetting the others)—were in permanent interaction with him. In such a fervent atmosphere, each of us at times contributed his thoughts, and these would contain a remnant of an idea Pichon-Rivière had planted. It seems impossible to tell—and it does not really matter—who produced or who received those ideas, the fact is that Pichon-Rivière gave each of us much more than he received from us.

* * *

Pichon-Rivière's conception of the analytic process as a "spiral process" is the synthesis of a body of ideas that includes his study of psychoanalytic technique and especially his studies on transference (quite new at the time of its publication, since Paula Heimann's first work on the subject was the only antecedent). It is then that Pichon-Rivière conceived the idea of approaching the analytic situation as a unity, as an object for study.

Paradoxically—and the reference to Paula Heimann points to this curiosity—this is his most "Kleinian" period. At precisely the

same time when Paula Heimann left the Kleinian movement because of her disagreement concerning the function of countertransference in the analytic process, Pichon-Rivière drew closer to
Paula Heimann and to Melanie Klein. This paradox is only superficial if we bear in mind his totally independent spirit as regards
adherence to schools and internal quarrels.

Why, then, am I talking about his "most Kleinian period?" In
those years the progressive discovery of child analysis was developed, following the Kleinian line, by Arminda Aberastury de Pichon-Rivière, so through her—at that time she was his wife—this
discovery reached us all, including him.

If you approach it without prejudice—I mean, without the prej-
udices of later years—the theory of the "spiral process" agrees to a
great extent with basic Kleinian concepts. But it disagrees with later
concepts, such as those by Donald Meltzer in his 1967 book *The
Psycho-Analytical Process,* as these could reasonably be questioned
from a correct Kleinian perspective.

"Spiral process" does not depend on the depressive position
for the direction of the analysis. Meltzer's conception is lineal, in
one direction only (from the paranoid–schizoid position to the
depressive position, which *ideologically* is the goal), whereas the
spiral model can include the depressive position as a moment that
is not necessarily more positive or more advanced than the previous one. At least, Pichon-Rivière's model gives us the possibility
of keeping the phenomenological variety and the complexity of
progressive and regressive phenomena (and regressive disguised
as progressive) that appear in the analytic process. In his description of the analytic process, Donald Meltzer seems to forget that
Melanie Klein, in her fundamental work on the emotional life of
the infant (1952b), describes the depressive position on the basis of
two different dimensions: first, the "infantile depressive position",
from a genetic perspective at approximately between three and six
months and, second, the depressive position, in the dialectic of the
evolution–involution that characterizes psychic life in all its temporal development, as one of the poles of this dialectic. From this
perspective the analytic process cannot be described as "a natural
process" (Meltzer) similar to the growth of a plant that is bound to
follow certain stages to arrive at the adult plant. The really important part of the "growth", to continue with the botanical metaphor,

comes *after* the establishment of the depressive position: Melanie Klein calls the third part of the abovementioned work "Further Developments and the Modification of Anxiety".

This theoretical misunderstanding (between Klein's formulations and those of Meltzer, as the latter do not explicitly disown Klein's theory) would not exist if the concept of a "spiral process" were accepted.

* * *

The reason why this concept of Pichon-Rivière carried further some apparently more orthodox "Kleinian" developments lies in his differentiation between what belongs to history and what belongs to genetics. And this is nowadays accepted by the most lucid trends in current psychoanalysis, in my opinion. Here we encounter one of the problems that was our concern in those years in Montevideo: the problem of psychoanalysis as a science and how it is related to the experimental sciences or to the sciences of man.

The problem Henry Ezriel posed in his works about the analytic situation was of utmost importance for Pichon-Rivière. This "ideal", which we now consider as absolutely wrong, defines the analytic situation as an experimental situation in which a specific constellation (or Gestalt) of manifest elements is understood and formulated by the analyst to the analysand, and this brings about a restructuring of the initial situation for the patient. Although this does not translate accurately what happens in a concrete analytic situation or account for the process, it does point out something important. Given an analytic situation, the analyst interprets: if his interpretation is confined to the present situation, whatever the elements of the interpretation, he does not get out of the present situation. It happens to be the translation of what the patient says, does, or manifests. In Ezriel's description the historical dimension implied in the process of interpretation appears blurred. If interpretation fails to include history, it cannot reach the subject, because the subject is history. He is his individual history, the mythical history of his family, of his religious or ethnic group, of his country, of mankind. The subject exists by virtue of his background. Everybody is now familiar with these ideas, especially Freud's readers. However, there was a time when this "rehabilitation" of the role of history in our technique sounded quite unusual. Herbert Rosenfeld's visit to

Buenos Aires in 1975 comes to my mind, when he referred to an overlooked aspect of Melanie Klein's thought (which she expresses several times throughout her work) when she insists on the role of history in the analyst's task.

In Meltzer's work this seems to be blurred or almost erased, whereas in the theory of the "spiral process" this is underlined and comes to the fore as it should. Pichon-Rivière's thought is dialectic. By "dialectic" I am not referring to any of the specific Hegelian forms—with which he was, of course, familiar—but, rather, to that line of thought started by Socrates, which Hegel developed into a method. I find Pichon-Rivière's comments on Freud's and Melanie Klein's works more fruitful than other current ones and more open to further expansion.

Spiral process designates a specific dialectic of the analytic approach to temporality. "*Hic et nunc*" ("here and now"), Ezriel says, translating wrongly Melanie Klein's tendency to maintain the validity of the subject's historical dimension, although she does not clearly differentiate it from the acquired knowledge about his psychogenetic evolution. "*Hic et nunc et mecum*", Pichon-Rivière says—here, now with me—but he adds "as far away and long ago" and also "as in the future and somewhere else". The dialectic of the spiral process comprises all temporal dimensions, both the past, which is repeated in the present analytic situation, and the future, which opens in a prospective way.

The specific impact of psychoanalytic interpretation lies precisely in the repetition, produced at the transference level, that is broken by interpretation. This opens the possibility of temporality, which now breaks out of the vicious cycle of repetition and gives way to the prospective dimension of the future rescued from the repetition compulsion. Thus the comings and goings of the analytic process, in one sense and another, return to the past and go forward to the future—different spiral movements without an absolute beginning (not even the subject's birth, of course) and without a predetermined end (except the inevitable, though not determined, death). The superposition of the curves in the spiral shows this mixture of repetition and non-repetition observed in the characteristic events of a person's life; this movement of deepening into the past and construction of the future defines the analytic process. The repetitive structures that govern an individual destiny lie one over the other at different moments in his history, at different levels of his constitution, wavering between the repetitive spelling of the same word—that written on the back of the guilty man in Kafka's *In the Penal Colony*—and making out of these letters a new word: to repeat and to elaborate. The tri-dimensional model of the spiral is directly on the same line as Freud's "Analysis Terminable and Interminable" and as the concept of temporality Freud developed in this work.

* * *

Spiral movement starts from a point in the present—with a configuration given by the analytic framework—which is the point of access to the dialectic of the spiral. Pichon-Rivière called this the "urgency point". Even though this term is borrowed from Melanie Klein, it is easy to see that Pichon-Rivière meant something quite different and more complex by this. For Klein the urgency point depends on what it is necessary to interpret for the movement of the analysis to proceed, and it is signalled by anxiety, manifest in the session or latent, hidden behind an inhibition or a lack of associations, or of play when dealing with children. By urgency point Pichon-Rivière understood the emergence of something, a situation, rooted in the past, which often invades the present. The horrors of madness emerge from the past: if one does not want to plunge into them, one remains caught, and no dawn shines. The urgency point lies in the emergency of madness. Pichon-Rivière was well acquainted with this through his psychiatric practice before and during his analytic experience. He used to place himself on the dangerous edge of madness—not altogether there, neither completely here—hence his participation in the surrealist movement, which expressed in literature what he was doing then. His whole life and teachings lie on this dangerous fringe and nowhere else.

Spiral process recovers, in the framework of the analytic situation, the various sides of a person's destiny that change with each turn in the spiral. This process has its roots in archaic configurations predating the differentiation for the subject of his existence in mind, body, and world, his interrelated and constitutive "areas".

A subject's destiny is constructed between an initial configuration that confers on him the basis of his individuality and a final configuration with the resolution of the enigma put forward by the starting point—hence the concept of "single illness", a unity of the individual beneath the phenomenological divisions through which it finds expression, at times in psychological symptoms, at times in the organic area, at times in relation to others, to groups, to society or to culture. In other words, the analytic spiral process stems from a "fantasy of illness" and heads towards a "fantasy of cure". This path is embodied in concrete events in his history, which add different traits in the evolution of the subject, the way different photographs of the same person, taken at different ages, can show us how features change with time, while the person remains the same. In Montevideo we searched for the traces of Isidore Ducasse—Comte de Lautréamont—in old files, but only found his father's tomb in an old cemetery in this city. His mysterious and dangerous fate had a paradigmatic attraction for Enrique Pichon-Rivière.

Lautréamont's birth is uncertain and no one knows exactly when or how he died (a storm in 1871?). His destiny is marked by a particular uncanny streak, which all those close to him seemed to have felt strongly. There are no traces of his real existence, not even portraits or photographs: consequently, all we count on concerning his physical appearance are imaginary pictures.[2] Enrique Pichon was always, from the time I first met him, thinking, writing, planning to publish his work on Lautréamont. The title was to be something like "The Uncanny in Lautréamont's Life and Work", and Enrique was convinced that the sinister potential of his destiny and those "*chants*" was such that it might turn very dangerous for those who became too involved in them. Beneath the magic formulations or black humour he used to express this, one could read the danger Lautréamont conveyed as an object of identification for certain people.

Lautréamont's destiny—everyone's destiny—corresponds to an unconscious organization similar to Freud's discovery of destiny neurosis, myth of origin, family romance. It is also what begins to be unveiled in the first session of a psychoanalytic process for those willing to receive it.

This concept of fantasy of illness as an originary unconscious construction sounds quite familiar now, and this is naturally so on account of the latest developments in analytic thought—for example, Leclaire's stages about primary narcissistic representative, its vicissitudes and metamorphosis.

The fantasy of cure as the *unconscious* goal of the analytic process emerges from the same fantasy as that of illness, as an option either to transform it or to avoid it. A person's desire for "cure", if it does not come from the deepest part of his individuality, cannot be granted by any decalogue of mental health, or any handbook of adaptation to a kind of existence determined from outside. It has archaic, omnipotent, unreal forms, but it also has elements that can be integrated into other configurations open to invention in the turnings of the spiral.

"Dynamic bipersonal field"

The concept that Madeleine Baranger and I formulated in "The Analytic Situation as a Dynamic Field" (1961–1962) stems from the same theoretical and technical interest we shared with Pichon-Rivière during the years of his elaboration of the theory of spiral process. Ours is an adjacent concept, introduced after that of spiral process; it does not contradict it, but nor does it derive from it directly.

It happens to be a line of thought close to it, stemming from the same point, but along a different trajectory. Spiral process aims essentially at addressing the temporal development of the analytic process, its coming and going, repetitions, elaboration, alternation between regression and progression, the dialectic of history and temporality. The "bipersonal field" attempts to describe more accurately the structure and dynamic of the analytic situation, focusing not on the whole of its development throughout an analytic treatment, but on smaller temporal entities: one session, or a part of it, or a group of sessions. It was never our intention to propose an alternative theory to that of Pichon-Rivière but, rather, a complementary one that could be articulated with his, with a different approach.

Looking back now, we do not believe that our "narcissism of the little differences" has influenced this distinction of approaches: our reference in this work to Pichon-Rivière is not a formality, but something we deeply feel we owe him.

Why introduce the concept of field in the description of the analytic situation? This concept has its origin outside psychoanalysis, in the Gestalt theory, to denote a group of interacting relations among a plurality of elements in a structure; in phenomenology, to denote the reciprocal constitution of the subject and the object in a specific function (the perceptive field, for example), and here we draw on Merleau-Ponty's *Phenomenology of Perception* (1945); in Kurt Lewin's psychology, although it differs from analytic psychology in some fundamental aspects. Our experience in analytic group psychotherapy concerning role-playing, functions, feelings among the members of a therapeutic group and the changing of roles also had a concrete influence on the formulation of this concept.

We thought then and we still think now that neither the analyst nor the analysand, once involved in the analytic situation and in the process, can be taken in isolation: they have to be approached as one functioning with the other. The analytic situation itself has to be understood as a structured whole whose dynamic derives from the interaction of its parts and from the effect of the analytic situation on both, in reciprocal causation.

As this changing structure develops within an agreed pre-established and relatively stable setting—even though this stability may be modified by changes that take place within the process—we found it was evident and necessary to use the concept of field to denote the framework of the situation, the functional configuration that determines its goal and procedure, the changes in the configuration that are produced, and the effect they have on both members.

* * *

To apply the concept of field to the analytic situation—along the lines of thought of "two-person psychology" put forward by Balint (1968), meaning this is about two people actually present, but with more people "absent and in effigy" involved—means bestowing full theoretical status to what Freud and, much later, Paula Heimann (1950) and Enrique Racker (1948) described as "countertransference". Racker's view of countertransference as a constant normal dimension that can be used (except in some extreme and paralysing forms) for the development of the analytic process, meant that the analyst was involved as an integrating part in the field, not only because of his framework, but also because of his personal and analytic experience, his present and past conflicts, his unconscious.

This does not mean, as it is sometimes believed, that the analyst is involved in the field in the same way as the patient. The field works on the basis of a radical asymmetry between the analyst's function and that of the patient. This functional asymmetry is manifested at a large number of points. To mention just a few: the analysand has to associate freely, as Freud has already stated; the analyst also associates freely, but concerning the analysand's associations: this is what Freud defined as "evenly suspended attention"; the analyst does not allow his attention to wander: if it does, he does not blame himself for lack of professional commitment but tries to find out why he this was so. What has caused this brief detachment from his connection to the patient? Does the content of his "evenly suspended" thoughts have to do with what the analysand says or hides? There must be a reason for evenly suspended attention to appear, and this may be found in the underlying processes in the field.

Asymmetry is also found with regard to the verbalization of free associations: the analytic contract expects the analysand to report them to the analyst as much as he can. The analyst, on the other hand, *should not* report his to the analysand. He has, instead, to frame them in a very special way as the result of the understanding of his association in connection with what concerns the patient. We were always absolutely convinced that any other use of countertransference—what is usually called countertransference confession—is almost always harmful and confusing to the analysand. An exception to this rule is when the analyst admits he had a slip when this is perceived by the analysand, and he then proceeds to examine it (as far as it is possible to understand it, but always for the analysand's sake).

Likewise, it is generally agreed that the analytic situation generates a certain degree of regression in the analysand, and sometimes in the analyst as well. This regression in the analyst is useful if it helps to perceive some tensions or concealed aspects in the field. When regression becomes too intense or acquires some qualitative forms, it may be counterproductive due to the blurring of the boundaries between analyst and analysand. When the analyst is aware of such a regressive state, he can take it as a warning signalling pathology in the field and use it to give a positive turn to the process.

In our description in 1961, we addressed the ambiguity of the analytic situation. We might have marked there the differences in ambiguity between analyst and analysand. When the latter accepts his inclusion in the field and the atemporal temporality of the process, he stands in an area of reality–unreality where there are events and feelings that may tend to erase the limits between the analytic process and "real" life. Provided the analyst re-imposes those limits, a moment of transference psychosis can prove to be very useful. However, if the analyst is not able to preserve the necessary ambiguity, the process deteriorates.

There are plenty of examples of points at which asymmetry in the field becomes evident and indispensable. The analyst is responsible for the "direction of the cure" and for the necessary conditions for the process to unfold.

* * *

Therefore the dual inclusions of the analyst in the field merit serious consideration. On the one hand, it is he who sets the rules of the game, the limits and functioning of the field, and is in charge of keeping them. The analysand has to comply with them, not only verbally, but also in his behaviour. On the other hand, the analyst is included in the field as a present interlocutor, as *object* (and not as a screen) for the analysand, as a resonant receiver of the analysand's reports, as an instrument performing his own task.

This division of the analyst's function in the field is expressed in a dual vision, or second look, and although this is a well-known phenomenon, little has been done to examine it further because it leads to countertransference, which is what most analysts would like to avoid. There are in any analytic session two different looks: a first, simple one, which focuses on the associative material rendered by the analysand: we analyse a dream, for example, connecting the elements of the manifest content with the associations, uncovering the day's residues that went into the making of the dream, establishing connections with previous dreams, with memories brought by the patient earlier, with his present situation related to other people, and so forth. While this work proceeds without problems, we stay within this look. Yet if some kind of difficulty arises, if something strange comes up in us—a definite feeling, a corporal reaction, an odd fantasy—we feel the need to change the direction of our look and to focus not only on the analysand but on the whole field, including ourselves. This second look includes the analyst's self-observation.

This is somewhat similar to what Freud described as a signal of the emergence of the transference: the patient's report is arrested or interfered with. Associations stumble upon an obstacle, we become aware that the analysand is immersed in thoughts or feelings referring to the analyst, and this should make the analyst shift his look towards the transference situation, without abandoning the first look. For the analyst this is not an obstacle in his work but one of his key instruments.

A very different situation may also arise: the analyst feels that something is hampering his work: "I don't understand this dream at all", or "What can I tell my patient that is not a repetition?" This and various other signals prompt us to pass on to the second-degree look, to commit ourselves in the field and approach it as a whole—above all when this takes place in many sessions or during a long period of the analysis. This second-degree look responds to a temporary or chronic obstacle in the functioning of the field. If everything goes well, the driver looks ahead on the road; if the car stops, or makes a peculiar noise, or a red light goes on, he has to see to it, and only once the problem has been rectified can the journey go on.

It is a well-known fact that in any analytic process the patient's resistance must be resolved: an analysand who does not show resistance, hypothetically, would not be in need of analysis. Racker, with his concept of countertransference, threw light on the understanding of this problem. The patient's resistance generates some resonance in the analyst, and there is a "coupling" between resistance and counter-resistance that may paralyse or hamper the process. If this coupling becomes chronic, a "bastion" arises—that is, a protected zone that includes elements of both participants—which remains outside the mobilization of the field, outside verbalization and elaboration, and which creates a situation that restricts the scope of psychoanalysis and may even cause its failure. A good many of the phenomena described as "negative therapeutic reaction", "analytic impasse", "unanalysability", "limits of the analytic process", are in fact due to these bastions, and we think most of them could find a more satisfactory outcome if this second-degree look were applied in a more conscious and specific way.

This does not necessarily mean that we reject the existence of the negative therapeutic reaction, or that some patients are unanalysable or at the limits of analysis, but that our purpose is to examine a well-known fact and its consequences: an analysand is not the same with one analyst as with another: each analytic process is unique; if a person fails with one analyst it does not necessarily mean he is bound to repeat the failure with another analyst. This puts in relative terms the concept of unanalysability.

A detailed description of the typical structures of bastions and some training in the use of the second look to recognize them and to examine them thoroughly would contribute to the re-activation of many stuck processes or prevent the construction of such bastions. We have addressed these pathological field structures in various works and described the phenomenon of the "parasitism" of the analyst by the analysand, in which the symbiosis that normally appears in the field goes beyond its time–space boundaries and the analyst feels "inhabited" by the analysand during weekends, for instance. We found this phenomenon pathognomonic of de-structuring the field and of the invasion of psychotic processes into it (whether or not the patient is psychotic in the clinical sense). So this is a signal warning about a potentially dangerous situation for the analysis.

We have also dealt with the "perverse field", in which analyst and analysand establish a tacit complicity—unconsciously in most cases—in which the perverse activity (in the strict sense of the word) substitutes for the act of analysing or being analysed—for example, sado-masochism. In some cases the analysand assumes the sadistic role, feels it his right to say everything he wants in order to debase, insult, scorn the analyst and thus reduce him to a masochistic victim. In others, the analysand comes to a session to receive gladly his doses of flagellation. Not to mention the multiple forms of paralysed field by neurotic bastions.

* * *

This second-degree look is the same as occurs in any supervision, but in that case it is between two different people who discuss what one of them is doing in analysing a third one. Supervision itself is a second-degree look, and it teaches us, mostly, to get used to applying such a look to the field.

The introduction of the idea of the "second-degree look" leads us to modify, not the central idea of our work in 1961, which we consider still valid, but at least some concepts related to it. Most of the concepts we think should be modified result from an over-extension of these concepts. For example, we do not think now that the field can be defined by the transference–countertransference. This definition lay in an over-extended concept of the transference as everything the patient thinks, feels, and imagines about his analyst. Transference is, then, understood to be the analysand's global reaction towards the analyst and becomes a constant and omnipresent dimension in the analytic situation. To adopt this definition raises some inconveniences. First, not all the phenomena included are on the same level. Many of them are trivial and not a useful or privileged way for reaching the unconscious, although important and authentic transference phenomena may appear as trivial in the manifest content. Other elements of this global response have to do specifically with the analyst's function, such as his right to answer or not to answer the patient's questions. Others, on the other hand, correspond to transference as Freud defined it, in its strict sense, as the repetition in the analytic situation of past situations in the analysand's life. These elements should be enhanced and given priority for interpretation. Second, the over-extension of the term transference leads to forcing its technical use. Interpretation systematically formulated as transference turns out, most of the time, to be directly deceiving or to restrain the register of the analytic communication. At the same time, it diminishes the emphasis of what transference really is in the interpretation. And third, the "here, now, with me" technique is likely to erase the essential historical dimension in the analytic process. If everything is transference, if any interpretation has to go through transference, then historic exploration—one of the essential resources of the analytic procedure—seems to be unnecessary or even the analyst's flight from concrete, present situations. These exaggerations occurred frequently among us until a few years ago due to disagreements about the legitimacy of extra-transference interpretations, to lack of discrimination between interpretations "*within the transfer-ence*"—the fundamental rule establishes analysis as a process that takes place "within" the transference—and interpretations of transference meaning that the latter suppose to be an explicit reference to the analyst. In other words, a very important part of analysis takes place under the analyst's first-degree look focused on the analysand and on the various dimensions of his temporality, including his transference.

The process of over-extension was extended, later, to the concept of countertransference as well.

Here, when dealing with what can be observed in the atmosphere of the human relation of our task with the patient, attention should be drawn to the silent feelings it awakens in us, to its general tone and variations—as also to the fantasies aroused by some moments, to our understanding of what the patient is saying and what he is hiding, to the intellectual work we are doing for his sake and to the "couplings", minor and transient or important and chronic, that prompt us to use a second-degree look. These latter should be properly called countertransference.

* * *

The same kind of mistake as that with the concepts of transference and countertransference has been made with regard to the concept of projective identification and projective counteridentification. Between 1946 (the introduction of the concept of projective identification) and 1960, Melanie Klein enlarged the extension of this concept significantly: when in her work "Notes on Some Schizoid Mechanisms" (1946) she presents the mechanism of projective identification, she describes it as a particular mechanism that implies a marked splitting in the subject's self and a projection of the split-off part or aspect into the object to destroy it, to control it, or to ensure its possession, with the ensuing impoverishment of the subject. It is only later that she extends this process beyond the paranoid–schizoid position, describes non-violent forms of projective identification, and even presents it as essential for human communication, as fundamental to the empathy that allows us to get to know the other. It was tempting, then, to consider the analytic process as a succession of multiple projective identifications followed by re-introjections leading to a gradual modification of the analysand's world of internalized objects and their psychic instances. León Grinberg, along the same lines as Melanie Klein, calls projective counteridentification the analyst's reaction to the analysand's projective identification. The process of extension of the meaning of these terms comprises transference and counter-transference on the one hand and projective identification and projective counteridentification on the other and arrives at a point when transference is mixed up with projective identification and countertransference with projective countertransference. This serves as a very good example of how discoveries in psychoanalysis are gradually weakened and worn down, losing their legitimate use in a conceptual magma.

Our formulations proved no exception: although phenomena of projective identification and counteridentification take place in the analytic situation quite frequently, they do not define its structure or its dynamic and even less the task going on within it. Nor are they sufficient to define the pathology of the field.

In addition, our work came up against two important hurdles, the first concerning the subject, the second language.

A "two-person" psychology, Balint said, and this was useful to overcome various difficulties by keeping it on the most obvious level (two persons talking in a room). "Bipersonal"—to denote the field—does not resolve any difficulty either, since the most immediate and fundamental feature of the field is a situation of *three*, or a triangle.

In fact, we needed to be aware of the importance of Lacan's concept concerning the subject. It concerns not two bodies or two persons, but two divided subjects, whose division results from an initial triangulation. Consequently the correct term would be "intersubjective field", which avoids the temptation (one really far from our frame of mind) of objectifying it. However, we encounter other problems: to what extent does our concept of field depend on the classic temporal framework of psychoanalysis (four or five sessions a week, fifty-minute sessions, or three-quarters of an hour)? What would happen if we were to alter—as Lacan does—the fixed temporal framework? Does it make sense to introduce the concept of subject and talk at the same time about projective identification? These are unavoidable problems, which I will not address at this point.

The second difficulty is presented and unsolved in our first work on the field. This problem lies in the specific action of the word (interpretation) on the structure of the field. This is precisely Lacan's starting point in his landmark "Rome Discourse" (1953). How can the analytic word reach the subject if he is radically heterogeneous to it? And if, as it happens (otherwise psychoanalysis would not exist), the word reaches the subject, does not this prove sufficiently that the subject is not heterogeneous to it?

Another turn of the spiral is necessary. The paths of theorization are perhaps not disconnected from the analytic process itself, as the "*chants*" of Maldoror are not disconnected from the hero's love for the female shark. The intersubjective field flows into the law of language, the same as that used to write, from its beginnings, the destiny of Pichon-Rivière's analysands, and his own as well.

Note

1. [*Les chants de Maldoror* (Lautréamont, 1868–69) was written by Isidore Ducasse under the pseudonym Comte de Lautréamont.—*L.G.F*]

2. [This was no doubt the case at the time of writing, but since then much more information has now become available on the Internet, including some portraits of Comte de Lautréamont (Isidore Ducasse).—*L.G.F*]

4

Process and non-process in analytic work

Madeleine Baranger, Willy Baranger, & Jorge Mario Mom

The "talking cure", named by Anna O and discovered by Freud, has been widely expanded and diversified throughout our century. Our objective here is not to summarize the vast literature on the subject but to underline several points that seem to define the analytic process. We believe that progress in psychoanalysis must arise from the study of clinical experience at its frontiers, at its topmost limits, in its failures. For this reason, we have concentrated our search on the analytic non-process, in the very places where the process stumbles or halts. This has led us to propose the introduction of several terms: "field", "bastion", "second look". When the process stumbles or halts, the analyst can only question himself about the obstacle, by encircling himself and his analysand, Oedipus and the Sphinx, in a second look, in a total view: this is the field. The obstacle involves

Pre-published paper for the 33rd International Psychoanalytical Congress, Madrid, July 1983 (ms. received October 1982). Published in Spanish as "Proceso y no proceso en el trabajo analítico" (*Revista de Psicoanálisis, 39* [4], 1982: 526–550). Copyright © W. Baranger, M. Baranger, & J. M. Mom. First published in English in *International Journal of Psychoanalysis, 64,* 1983: 1–15; reprinted by permission.

the analysand's transference and the analyst's countertransference and poses rather confusing problems. The arrest of the process introduces us fully to the nature of its movement, its inherent temporality. If the process is to continue, then by what mainspring can we accomplish it? Finally, we can only resort to the word, which may lead to an "insight". This, in turn, enables us to describe this particular dialectic of process and non-process as a task of overcoming the obstacles that determine its success or failure.

I. Analytic field and bastion

Nothing that can happen in an analytic treatment may be considered independent of the analytic situation, which functions as a relatively permanent background in relation to changing forms (in Gestalt terms). This background is a contract or pact, explicit in various aspects, between analyst and analysand.

The analytic pact has its well-known formal aspects, functional aspects, and structural aspects. We could mention phenomenal and transphenomenal aspects of the situation established by the pact. The ranking of the formal aspects poses diverse problems. We also know that certain formal aspects affect function itself: for example, the fixed or variable length of the sessions produces two very different types of analytic process.

In terms of function, we must emphasize that the pact establishes a basic asymmetry: one of the members will be the analyst and the other the analysand, allowing for no possible interchange of functions.

In terms of structure, we insist that the "fundamental rule" defines the analytic process. The Lacanian concept of "subject supposed to know", implicit in the fundamental rule, would seem to be enlightening. The fundamental rule places the analyst not only on an imaginary plane of knowing beforehand who the patient really is and what his fate will be, but also as listener and interpreter, committed to the truth of all the patient will associate with or experience. Most of all, it fully opens the doors to transference.

In an attempt to differentiate the circumstantial phenomenal aspects of the analytic situation and its transphenomenal structure, we have already felt it necessary to include in its description the notion of "field", expressed in several of Freud's descriptions as battlefield or chessboard.

The structure instituted by the pact is intended to permit certain work tending towards a process: experience proves that, beyond the resistances, whose conquest the constitution of analytic work precisely is, situations of obstruction in the process inevitably arise: the idea of field seems appropriate to these circumstances.

In other words, within the functional structure of the process, difficulties arise which *involve each member of the pact differently.* When examined, they show that *other, contingent structures,* which interfere in the functioning of the basic structure, have been created.

Our experience supervising many colleagues (from beginners to the most experienced) has taught us that, at those times, the basic asymmetry of the analytic pact is lost, and *another,* far more symmetrical *structuring* predominates in which the unconscious attachment between analyst and analysand becomes an involuntary complicity against the analytic process.

This gave us the idea of applying our experience in supervision to the treatments we ourselves practise when they become obstructed. In fact, we all do so spontaneously whenever we encounter an obstacle that goes beyond the analysand's habitual resistances. At these times, we use a "second look" in which we see the analytic situation as a field that involves us in so far as we fail to know ourselves.

Each of us possesses, explicitly or not, a kind of personal countertransferential dictionary (bodily experiences, movement fantasies, appearance of certain images, etc.), which indicates the moments in which one abandons one's attitude of "suspended attention" and proceeds to the second look, questioning oneself as to what is happening in the analytic situation.

These countertransferential indicators, which provide the second look, lead us to realize that within the field there is an immobilized structure that is slowing down or paralysing the process. We have named this structure the "bastion".

This structure never appears directly in the consciousness of either participant, showing up only through indirect effects: it arises, in unconsciousness and in silence, out of a complicity between the two protagonists to protect an attachment that must not be uncovered. This leads to a partial crystallization of the field, to a neo-formation set up around a shared fantasy assembly that implicates important areas of the personal history of both participants and attributes a stereotyped imaginary role to each.

Sometimes the bastion remains a static foreign object while the process apparently goes forward. In other situations, it completely invades the field and removes all functional capacity from the process, transforming the entire field into a pathological field. We will mention a few brief examples to illustrate the concept of bastion.

A. *A manifestly perverse patient*
He behaves like a "good patient", complies with the formal aspects of the pact, manifests no resistances, does not progress. The sessions, over a certain period, seem to be a condensed version of the whole of *Psychopathia Sexualis* by Krafft-Ebing (1886). The analyst "has never seen anyone with so many perversions". The bastion here is set up between an exhibitionist analysand and a fascinated–horrified analyst, the forced "voyeur", complacent with regard to the perverse display.

B. *An analysand, veteran of a number of analytic treatments*
In appearance, each session bears the fruit of some "discovery"; in reality, nothing is happening. The analyst is delighted at the subtlety of the analysand's descriptions of his internal states, enjoying his own Talmudism—until he realizes that, while they are toying with their disquisitions, the analysand is monthly placing the analyst's fees at interest, speculating with his delay in paying. The analysis of this bastion reveals a shared fantasy set-up: the analysand's old, surreptitious vengeance on his stingy father and the analyst's guilt-ridden compulsion to set himself up as the cheated father.

C. *Example of a bastion that has invaded the field*
A seriously psychopathic patient. The analyst is terrified, fearing the analysand's physical, homicidal aggression without being able either to suspend the treatment or to carry it forward. The nodular fantasy of this bastion is the patient's as torturer in a concentration camp, and the analyst's as tortured, powerless victim. With the conscious formulation of this manoeuvre, the analyst's terror disappears. The two individual histories converge in the creation of this pathological field.

This series of examples could be infinite. They show not only the interaction between the analysand's transference and the analyst's countertransference, but also the creation of a field phenomenon that could only be produced between *this* analyst and *this* analysand. We could describe it metaphorically as a "precipitate". But we must first understand the nature of the transference and countertransference and their relation to projective identification.

II. A jungle of problems: transference–countertransference–projective identification

Naturally, Freud's discovery of transference led him to deepen and widen this concept, culminating in a representation of the analytic process that is nearly "pan-transferentialist"—that is, as a substitution of the patient's initial natural neurosis with an artificial neurosis in the transference, and its resolution in this place.

As for countertransference, we know that Freud did not by any means give it the sustained attention he did to transference. Even today, many analytic authors consider countertransference an unessential, rather perturbing phenomenon, an undue residue of the analyst's insufficiently "cured" neurosis. With Heimann's pioneering paper (1950) and with Racker's (1953), which is nearly contemporary with it, countertransference was seen not only as a universal phenomenon, just as constant as transference, but as an indispensable instrument of analytic work as well.

Melanie Klein's discovery of projective identification (1946) profoundly modifies the theory of transference. Although Klein herself did not seek to do so, the theory of countertransference is also consequently modified. Klein's tendency to overextend the concept of projective identification, to the point that transference finally becomes synonymous with a continually active projective identification, led her to define the movement of the analytic session as a succession of projective and introjective identifications, resulting from the analyst's interpretive activity.

It was a great temptation to try to arrive at a unified theory of transference, countertransference, and projective identification. It would suffice to allow that the field created by the analytic situation consists of a transferential–countertransferential field formed on the basis of crossed-over and reciprocal projective identifications between analyst and analysand. Thus, the asymmetrical function of this field would constantly aim to undo the symbiotic structurings originating in the projective identifications by means of interpretation. In fact, we realized that such a definition could only apply, and without great precision, to extremely pathological states of the field: a field characterized either by an invincible symbiosis between the two participants, or by the annihilating parasiting of the analyst by the analysand. The simplification and unification of the theory led, not to greater coherence, but to a flattening. Today, we consider differentiation of the phenomena indispensable, *since their correct technical management depends on this differentiation.*

In any case, we cannot content ourselves with defining transference as the set of thoughts and experiences of the analysand as related to his analyst, nor countertransference as what the analyst thinks and feels with respect to his patient, since such a definition would eliminate not only what is structurally determined by the analytic pact but also, beyond this basic structure, the transferential or countertransferential categories that indicate to us the *priorities and characteristics of interpretive management.*

For example, at a certain point, shadings in an analysand's transferential expressions indicate to us a nearly obligatory turn through his history—"I dreamt that I was four years old and you were my dad . . .", etc.—and another expression may set another course.

This is one of the many cases in which theoretical coherence works *against* coherent practice.

Within the set of phenomena that we could term as transferential in the widest sense of the term, we must differentiate a series of basic categories.

1. everything in the analysand that responds to the structural position and function of the analyst, which has essentially nothing to do with the analysand's projections and which may sometimes be erroneously construed as a process of idealization;

2. the momentary and changing transferences that correspond to successive structurings of the field and do not necessarily demand interpretation, unless transference becomes resistance;

3. the repetitious and structured, basically unconscious, transfer-

ence that Freud referred to with the concept of "artificial neurosis" (1916–17, p. 444), which is always a privileged objective of the interpretive clarification: in other words, the specific way the analysand positions his analyst in the structure of this Oedipus complex, or projects on to him the figures of his primary objects of love, hate, identification;

4. transference by projective identification (using Klein's term in the specific sense she gave it when she discovered this mechanism): this type of transference is distinguishable from the others by the very well-defined countertransferential expressions accompanying it, and intervenes determinatively in the constitution of the pathology of the field; it demands interpretation.

The categories that we habitually use to differentiate the forms of transference (positive transference–erotic transference–negative transference) are actually descriptive and are based on the affective shadings of love and hate (the love necessary to the pact whose aim is not directly sexual, directly erotic love concealing hate in erotic transference, the thousand forms of hate in negative transference). It will be noted that the categorization we propose is based not on the phenomenal level but on the structures involved, using Lacan's (1958) distinction between symbolic and imaginary transference, Freud's repetitious transference, and Klein's transference as the product of projective identification. The latter differentiation involves two schemes of reference: the first, Freud's, necessarily implies a reference to the subject's history, whereas Klein's does not place it in the foreground, though it does not reject it. We do not in effect consider these to be two alternative concepts for the same object but, rather, different forms and structures of transference. The apparent simplification suggested by Klein in her concept of transference as equivalent to projection–introjection or to projective and introjective identification leads to the idea of a parallelism between positive and negative transference with a greater urgency to interpret (which for Klein is equivalent to *dissolving*) the expressions of negative transference in so far as they reveal pathogenic nuclei. Klein's departure from Freud is immediately perceptible: for him, transference love as the very condition for analytic work implies a clear privilege—that is, a non-parallelism between these two forms, implying that they do not function in the same way and in opposition to each other, but in different ways: not as heads or tails of the same coin, but as two coins of different values.

As for countertransference, the problems are different, although discrimination becomes even more necessary. We must adopt the directive idea that countertransference *is not* the inverse of transference, not simply because Freud studied the former in depth and the latter very little, but for structural reasons.

If we consider the axis to be the place from which the analyst speaks as such—instituting and maintaining the setting, interpreting that is, in Lacanian terms, the symbolic register, and this other place (parting from Lacan this time) where the analyst is, with his attention evenly suspended and the door to his unconscious open as an apparatus of resonance, then we establish a principle of asymmetry that would seem to constitute the analytic situation. Countertransference is thus shown to be distinct from transference not only because it is less intense and more instrumental, but also because it corresponds to a different structural position.

Due to his function, and from the outset, the analyst is committed to truth and abstinence from anything *acted out* with the analysand. In the analytic process there is no formalized, computable operation but a situation in which the analyst is committed, flesh, bone, and unconscious. He is so intrinsically, not contingently, because of the fact that an analyst listens and reacts: this implies that countertransference will be prohibited in its expression and condemned to an internal unfolding in him. The analyst's structural position marks certain limits within which his attention is "suspended" without falling, and the analyst works with the first look without the field as such appearing. In our view, it would be erroneous to define this structural countertransference in terms of projective identification, since this would eliminate differences among extremely contrasting aspects having opposite consequences to countertransference.

In this process of discrimination, we can isolate various forms of countertransference:

1. that which arises from the structure of the analytic situation itself and from the placement and function of the analyst within the process;

2. transferences of the analyst on to the patient which, as long as they do not become stereotyped, are a normal part of the process (e.g., "I know that this patient is not my daughter and that I must guard against my tendency to treat her as if she were");

3. projective identifications of the analyst towards the analysand and his reactions to the projective identifications of the latter: these phenomena provoke pathological structuring of the field, require a second look towards it, also demand priority in interpretive management; they may also produce the frequently occurring phenomenon that we usually term "countertransferential micro-delusions".

In the jungle of the complex, sometimes mixed and confused phenomena of transference and countertransference, certain ideas enable us to mark out paths that may guide us. The first consists of placing the constitutive in opposition to the constituted aspects of the transference and countertransference. This opposition, marked by Lacan when he refers to the "subject supposed to know", is not at all foreign to habitual psychoanalytic thought, at least in certain aspects. It underlies all the descriptions Freud has left us of the technique he invented; it is implicit in all the papers underscoring the opposition between setting and process; it is the basis for the very idea of an analytic interpretation (if the interpretation did not come from a different place from that of the associative material, where would its power come from?); it is what we ourselves are attempting to express in the idea of the structural and functional framework of the analytic situation. Its momentary loss is what some Kleinians describe as "reversal of perspective".

Not all phenomena of transference or of countertransference correspond to the same model or to the same mechanisms, nor should they be treated in the same way.

III. The analytic process and its temporality

Among the multiple metaphors that Freud used to describe the analytic process, some refer directly to history—for example, the battle history of a territory invaded by an enemy (neurosis) and its re-conquest (psychoanalytic treatment), another, the archaeological metaphor of reconstruction by excavation of the superimposed layers of the remains of different cities built and destroyed in the same place in different epochs. Other metaphors have no direct connection with time or with history: the sculptural metaphor ("*via di porre*", "*via di levare*"), the telephonic metaphor, the surgical metaphor. And between these two series is the chess metaphor. Obviously, none of these metaphors, by itself, fills the concept that Freud had of the analytic process: the choice of one or several over the rest involves a simplification—that is, a limitation—of the original concept. Nor can we say that Freud changed his mind with respect to this problem, but that each of these metaphors describes a facet of a very complex problem.

In any case, up to and including his last two great technical papers, "Constructions in Analysis (1937d) and "Analysis Terminable and Interminable" (1937c), the subject's history constitutes an essential dimension of what psychoanalysis must uncover.

This originates in Freud's first discoveries on memory: Freud's tendency to define the unconscious as the repressed, the repression having effect basically on *forgetting traumatic situations*. The mainspring of the analytic process is thus defined as a transferential repetition whose interpretation permits a memory of the repressed and its eventual working-through.

What happens after Freud?

The sense of history tends to get lost in two, apparently opposite, ways.

The first is partly based on several Freudian metaphors (the telephonic, the surgical, etc.) and also on the Freudian idea that everything is played out in the transference—that is, in the present; and in Freud's (misunderstood) statement that, in the unconscious, the temporal category does not function. Aside from this Freudian groundwork, this position aims to equate psychoanalysis and the "natural" or experimental sciences, in which history has no place. The most radical exponent of this position would be Henry Ezriel (1951), who declares that psychoanalysis is an "a-historic science", but we can perceive the same tendency in Bion and others.

The second tendency, although it does not flatly reject the subject's individual history, aims to dilute it in developmental psychology. Here, a number of misunderstandings have arisen, either because analysts try to adapt the scheme of the developmental phases of the libido described by Karl Abraham (1924) (thereby making Freud's indications on it rigid) to the experimental observations of developmental psychology, or because they attempt to submit analytic hypotheses to the evidence of experimental observation (e.g., Spitz vs Klein). In both cases, the basic prejudice lies in believing that psychoanalysis is continuous with respect to developmental psychology and that descriptions must necessarily correspond if they are true. This prejudice totally sacrifices the Freudian concept of *"Nachträglichkeit"*, according to which, instead of an event constituting a determining cause for a series of ulterior events, this initial event only takes on its meaning *in virtue of* the subsequent events. If one takes Freud's expression *"Nachträglichkeit"* seriously, the discontinuity of psychoanalysis with respect to any developmental psychology cannot fail to be evident. This does not, of course, imply any basic criticism of the results of developmental psychology. It does, however, imply a criticism of the contradictory concept of the "historic–genetic" approach described by some authors (e.g. Gill, 1956; Rapaport, 1951).

Past and present discussions to determine whether the analytic process develops and must develop in the "here and now" of the transferential situation of the session, or whether it aims at recuperating memories, seem to us to overlook the genuine Freudian dialectics of temporality. If analytic work is possible, it is so because the subject and the analyst think that exploration of the past permits opening up the future; it is because the complemental series do not constitute a mechanical determinism; it is because it is possible to escape, by means of interpretation, from the eternal, atemporal present of unconscious fantasies. Progressive and regressive movements take place together and condition each other reciprocally.

We do not consider exploration of the past to be the same as regression, although the two phenomena are often simultaneous. To explore the past is in many ways to relive it, and this involves primitive ways of feeling and levels of psychic organization. Nearly all authors agree that regression is a necessary dimension of analytic work. For that reason, the regularity and uniform duration of the sessions create a fixed temporal framework that permits regressive phenomena to unfold. We consider that one of the most subtle functions of the analyst is regulating the level on which analytic work may take place without the analysand getting lost in regression. We know it is not always possible to achieve this regulation and that undue regressions in the form of psychotic outbreaks occur in spite of our efforts. Between the reefs of lack of regression that would tend to transform analysis into a merely intellectual process and those of excessive regression in which the analysand would sink into psychotic states lies the area of "useful regression" in which we can safely navigate.

It is for this reason that a correct appreciation of the function of regression in analytic work is so important. The idea exists, in certain analytic tendencies, that regression is *in itself* the essential therapeutic factor. These authors consider that the analytic situation, in a state of regression, is bound to call up ever more remote phases of the patient's existence. Theoretically, this attitude means searching for the determinant pathogenic factor farther and farther back in the subject's infancy, encouraging the re-experiencing of these badly experienced past situations. The reappearance of the initial symbiosis with the mother, the birth trauma, the primitive relationship with the father, the paranoid–schizoid and depressive positions of suckling, the outcroppings of "psychotic nuclei", would be indispensable conditions for true progress. Out of this arises the illusion, so often contradicted by experience, that reaching the pathogenic archaic situations, by means of drugs or by systematically favouring analytic regression, suffices to obtain progress. But this loses sight of the fact that re-living a trauma is useless if it is not complemented by working-through, if the trauma is not reintegrated into the course of a history, if initial traumatic situations of the subject's life are not differentiated from the historic myth of his origins. The necessary working-through discards the magic eagerness to be able to shorten the analytic process by short-circuiting it.

Freud's (1926d [1925]) discussion of Otto Rank's ideas of the birth trauma and of the technical conclusions derived by the latter from this theory (the birth trauma as basis of all ulterior pathology, its working-through in treatment permitting rapid "cures" by economizing on analytic process) expresses in prototypical form all the criticisms we could make to several later attempts in the same direction as Rank's.

The time of the session is a parenthesis that suspends the time of life, an unhurried time, which sometimes seems to close in upon an atemporal present or a circular time, and which sometimes produces repeated or new events. In reality, it is the optimal experience for the direct observation of the genesis of temporality and history. The analytic process rewrites in some measure the subject's history and at the same time changes its meaning. The moment when we can observe this change, in which the subject simultaneously re-assumes a piece of his history and opens up his future, is the moment of "insight".

Analytic work takes place in the here and now and in the past, in the dialectics of the closed and repetitious temporality of neurosis and fate and the open temporality of "insight".

IV. The mainspring of the analytic process:
interpretation and insight

No one would question it: the specific mainspring of the analytic process is the interpretation. The analyst does many things, apart from interpreting: he maintains or imposes the setting, gently or not; he chooses the point that must be interpreted, he internally tries out hypotheses, and so forth.

From the beginning, Freud described the mainspring of the process as a dialectic: interpretation is necessary when the analysand's "free" association stumbles on an obstacle, expressing the appearance of a resistance in him. The model of these fertile moments of the process would be: resistance–interpretation–remembrance.

As the analytic procedure goes beyond the limits of memory and forgetting, the obstacle takes on new forms, and the interpretive solution produces broader effects, which we will group under the heading of "insight".

Thus, we are faced with two enigmas: what is this strange power of the interpretive word? What is "insight", its result?

The first enigma clears up somewhat if we differentiate two

aspects of this power. The first refers to the word in itself, to the fact of speaking, of interpreting, or of associating; the second refers to the word as carrier of meanings, expressing "what one wishes to say".

The classic papers of Luisa Alvarez de Toledo (1954, 1962) have taught us that, in addition to its semantic value, the word acquires concrete value, most particularly in analytic work, in terms of fantasied action: shooting arrows, throwing rocks, poisoning, suckling, caressing, and so forth. This is sufficient to lay aside all comparisons of the analyst's interpretation with a translation, much less with a simultaneous translation. Even if we consider only its semantic value, the analyst's interpretation is somewhat similar to the spells of a sorcerer's apprentice, calling up all kinds of demons in addition to any that have been summoned. Because of the polysemy of words and sentences, it is often difficult to determine, among the forever multiple meanings of what we say, which meaning has been chosen and understood by the analysand. We all know from experience that, in certain treatments, the analysand systematically understands something different or even the opposite of what we meant to say, and we also know, if we think back over our interpretations, that often our interpretation has been much more meaningful than what we consciously meant to communicate, and that one of its second meanings is the one that has been truly operative. Thus, someone speaks of these "significant inventions . . . which are the only thing capable of curing". There may be interpretation when we invent something, when our work approximates the poet's, when we manage to go beyond utilitarian language, the means of communication. In this, the element of surprise proves indispensable.

Every interpretation, in the one who pronounces it and in the one who listens to it, is necessarily polysemic. It would be a crass error (not infrequently committed) to think that the *precision* of the interpretation, a precision fundamental to any scientific statement (but an interpretation in the analytic process is *not* a scientific statement: its "truth" resides in another place), allows us to avoid the confusions implicit in the polysemy of the statements.

Quite to the contrary, we think that the analyst's search for theoretical precision in formulating interpretations is the direct opposite of what we ask of the patient: to associate—as far as possible—"freely". Therefore, we should distinguish between two moments in the act of interpretation: the moments of searching, similar to what children in the country do to catch crickets (they scratch the ground at the entrance to its hole with a straw: the curious cricket comes out of its cave, which is just the moment to cage it). In our process, this "caging" would be the second moment of the interpretation: an aspect of the unconscious comes to light and is captured by new meanings, analyst and analysand then concur on the meaning of the interpretation. The first moment plays on ambiguity and polysemy; the second momentarily reduces them.

It is evident that the analytic power of the word is indeed strange, since in the psychoanalytic literature it is described in two diametrically opposite ways. Some take its aspect as rupture, referring ultimately to Freud's (1905a) "*via di levare*". To analyse means, etymologically, to un-bind, to un-tie, to break some "false tie", to reveal a self-deception, to destroy an illusion or a lie: Dora, the "beautiful soul", believes that she is the innocent victim of her family's dirty tricks, and Freud reveals her as their unconscious accomplice.

Others, Melanie Klein more than any, consider it a unifying and integrating power: reducing splitting, permitting the synthesis of the object, broadening and enriching the ego. Freud himself, beginning with his initial model (resistance–interpretation–remembrance), conceives of the power of the interpretive word as permitting the recovery of a piece of repressed history. The "*levare*" of the interpretation allows for a "*porre*" from another place (from the analysand's unconscious).

In the movement of the analytic process, rupture and integration go together, the analyst not having to add even a pinch of his own salt. The strange power of the interpretation consists—among other things—of unbinding ourselves from the strange power of certain captivating words of our fate. It is to Lacan's credit to have emphasized this, but this power does not stop here: its reach is greater, just as Lacan himself admitted as from 1963, when he introduced the idea of analytic work, which would be possible using words about the "*object a*"—that is, about something inexpressible, something beyond words.

Finally, if we wish to place a limit (in our opinion) on Lacan's contribution, we must draw it at the point when we are forced to the "second look". We concur with him in recognizing that analytic work does *not* consist in the unflinching exhaustion of "imaginary petting" (i.e., regressive experiences between two persons without physical contact), but it is not limited to a disruptive power. The mainspring is in the evocative power of the word in so far as it produces "insight".

If we wish to remain loyal to the description of our experience, we cannot avoid our obligation to discriminate between two categories of what we call "insight".

Naturally, this categorization aims to describe two extreme, ideally distinct forms of "insight", when in reality they are more often found as mixed forms. The first corresponds to what Freud described as the lifting of repression and the conscious emergence of the repressed. In this relatively simple case, the analyst is only involved in the analysand's resistance as a transferential screen and in his capacity or difficulty in understanding and interpreting this precise moment of the process. The same unipersonal approach to "insight" may be held, although with greater difficulty, in the case of the reduction of splitting.

The second category of "insight" can appear only when the analyst reverts to the "look towards the field"—that is, when the dynamics of the field become obstructed and its functioning paralysed, indicating the presence of a bastion.

In this case, the interpretive process is more complex; it aims first for the analysand to realize that the bastion exists by pointing out its most conspicuous effects: delaying of the process, stereotyping of the analysand's discourse, the feeling that "nothing's happening". From here one may go on to the stereotyping of the reciprocal roles the analysand attributes to himself and to the analyst and then to the fantasies contributing to the structuring of the bastion, whose roots lie in the subject's personal history. This breaking up of the bastion implies returning to the analysand those aspects that he has placed in the analyst by projective identification, without any need for a "countertransferential confession". To do so would eliminate the structural and functional asymmetry of the field, introduce interminable confusions for the analysand, and remove the analyst from his specific function.

The rupture of the bastion means redistributing those aspects of both participants involved in the structuring of this bastion, but this redistribution takes place in a different way in each of them:

conscious and silent recovery in the analyst's case; conscious and expressed in the analysand's.

We may characterize the bastion as a symbiotic phenomenon, in so far as both participants in the analytic situation use transference and projective identification and reciprocally "castle" subject and object. Therefore, any rupture of the bastion is a de-symbiotization. The touchstone indicating that the rupture has taken place lies in the change in feelings, the analyst's as well as the analysand's, in the restoration of movement in the field, in the understanding of the obstacle at the point when it is overcome, in the analyst's spontaneous passage from the second look to the first look that is appropriate to analytic work functioning with no resistance other than the patient's own.

An extreme form of the bastion is found in a pathology of field and of process beyond symbiosis: that which we could describe as parasitism. It is revealed through its countertransferential aspect: the analyst feels as though he were "inhabited" by the analysand, the prisoner of a worry that extends beyond the sessions (either for fear of a self-destructive or criminal act of the analysand, of the imminence of a psychotic "outbreak" or of other, less dramatic situations). These parasitic situations (equivalent to micro-psychoses in the analytic field) tend to lead either to a violent rupture of the analytic situation or to its rechannelling by reducing splitting and by returning the projective identifications to the analysand.

Not all analytic fields reach these pathological extremes, but they all do tend to create bastions, as the Freudian concept of "transference neurosis" implies.

Thus, the mainspring of the analytic process appears to be the production of resistances and bastions and their respective interpretive dissolution, the generator of "insight".

This description owes much to James Strachey's (1934) classic paper, "The Nature of the Therapeutic Action of Psychoanalysis": to his idea, rooted in direct clinical observation, that the mainspring of the process resides in certain moments of "mutative interpretation" in which the entire situation is knotted—past and present, transference and reality, feeling and comprehension—and unknotted, by means of discriminative interpretation that produces the mutation of insight. Aside from some details with which we cannot agree (the idea, taken from Radó, of the analyst's position as auxiliary superego, among others), what was, to our mind, lacking in Strachey's description was the analyst's effective and affective (not only interpretive) participation in this process—something that Michael Balint was acutely aware of and which he expounded in many of his later papers without, however, formulating it in terms of field.

The fertile moments of interpretation and "insight" punctuate the analytic process, described by Pichon-Rivière (1958) as a "spiral process", an image that expresses the temporal dialectics of the process. "Here, now, with me" is often said, to which Pichon-Rivière adds "just as there, before, with others" and "as in the future, else-where, and in a different way". It is a spiral, each of whose turnings takes up the previous turning from a different perspective, and which has no absolute beginning or given end. The superimposi-tion of the spiral's curves illustrates this mixture of repetition and non-repetition that may be observed in the characteristic events in a person's fate, this combined movement of deepening into the past and constructing the future that characterizes the analytic process.

V. Dialectic of process and non-process

Not all analysts have come to realize that the analytic process is an artefact. Not even Freud's clearest warnings (the military metaphor, in which Freud explains that the process of re-conquest is not played out in the same places where the battles of invasion have been fought; the chess metaphor, where he explains that, apart from the openings and the end, the intermediate plays are unpredictable) can prevail against the tendency to think of the analytic process in terms of a "naturalist" model (gestation of a foetus—growth of a tree). The non-parallelism between the pathogenic and the analytic processes is the inevitable evidence to begin with. If analysts have been able to speak of a "typical cure", of "variations of the typical cure", of certain "phases" of the cure, it is because they have a pre-conceived idea of the development of a treatment as part of their scheme of reference. This idea functions as a Procrustean bed and determines the effective course of a good number of treatments, except in those cases where the patient refuses to comply with the pre-established phases.

We cannot avoid, neither can we renounce our function as "directors of the cure": we are an integral part of the process and this process is essentially intersubjective. This is not to say that we can or must use this directive function in an arbitrary fashion. We are victims of an "incurable idea", the idea of curing (Pontalis, 1981), but what we must do is avoid mistaking the very nature of our work and accept, without feeling intellectually shocked, the fact of the enormous variety of *positive* analytic processes.

To take an example: we consider that Klein's (1935) description of the "depressive position" as a concrete moment in an analytic process (the patient, through the interpretation of his persecutory anxiety, approximates his persecuting to his idealized objects, unifies the split-off parts of his "self", realizes his participation in the conflict, feels sadness and hope, etc.) formulates a structure that can be observed time and again in treatments, at moments of change and progress. If we set this discovery up as a general rule, taking the access to the depressive position as if it were a basic standard for the evaluation of an analytic treatment, then we are seeking (like apprentices of Procrustes) that every treatment should achieve this goal. We may even come to think (manifestly contrary to experience) that "whoever doesn't cry doesn't get cured" and even, thinking of the analyst, that "whoever doesn't cry doesn't cure".

Like the fur-covered wire monkeys used in animal psychology experiments on the rearing of monkeys, the analyst who is "programmed" with a prejudice with regard to the analytic process "manufactures", if he can, orthopaedic patients who are more or less similar to "cured" human beings.

What are we left with? Total uncertainty? Exaggeration aside, we do have indicators that a process or a non-process exists in an analytic treatment, and fortunately we take these indicators into account, *even though they do not fit* into our theoretical scheme of reference. We will not now refer to the most frequently mentioned indicators, such as the disappearance of manifest neurotic symptoms, or the patient's progress in different areas of his life (his access to greater genital pleasure, his acquisition of new sublimatory activities, etc.), not because we undervalue their importance, but because they are more or less distant consequences of the process and not its immediate and essential expression.

The indicators of the existence of the process, and those of the non-process, do not correspond to each other exactly as the positive and the negative, as the front and back of the same drawing. Here too, our eagerness for symmetry could deceive us.

One is surprised sometimes to find that the initial indicator Freud described for the existence of an analytic process—the patient's recovery of forgotten (repressed) memories—has fallen into disuse in many descriptions of the process. Can it be that it is taken for granted? Is it that many forget about memory? Is it that *hic et nunc et mecum* is becoming a prejudice and is eliminating temporality? We think that the overcoming of infantile amnesia continues to be a valuable indicator of the existence of a process and that, inversely, the especially prolonged persistence of infantile amnesia marks the end point of the process and often concerns a psychotic episode in childhood from which the subject has recovered at the cost of the erasure of part of his history and a restriction of his person.

Free access to childhood memories goes hand in hand with the possibility of associating freely—that is, with the richness of the narrative, the easy access to the different areas of the subject's existence, and the variability of languages he uses to express himself, especially his capacity for using dream language to allow himself and to allow us access to his unconscious. Fluency of discourse is not enough to indicate the presence of an analytic process unless it is accompanied by affective circulation within the field. Alternating moments of blockage with moments of affective mobilization, the surge of a wide range of feelings and emotions that harmonize with the narrative, the transformation of transferential and countertransferential affects, all indicate to us the presence of the process. This indicator is not, however, sufficient by itself as evidence of the existence of the process: affective movement is often only a simple stirring, and affective permeability becomes instability. Pure feeling does not cure, contrary to the beliefs of some nonanalytic psychotherapists, advocates of the psychological jolting techniques in fashion in certain circles. Only the convergence of the two indicators (variation in the narrative and circulation of affect) informs us fully as to the existence of the process. An invaluable compass for approaching affective circulation is Klein's (1948) categorization of the different forms of anxiety (persecutory, depressive, confusional anxiety). The dialectic between the production and resolution of anxiety and the qualitative transformations of the latter stakes out the process.

If our description of the mainspring of the analytic procedure is correct, the appearance and frequency of moments of "insight" are logically our most valuable indicator. But we must first differentiate between true "insight" and the pseudo-"insight" that the subject uses to deceive both himself and us with regard to his progress. The series of "discoveries" is bound, in these cases, to conceal absence of process.

True "insight" is accompanied by a new opening in temporality, most especially in the future dimension; the process in course begins to have goals, and plans and feelings of hope appear. The circular temporality of the neurosis opens up towards the future.

But one of the most important indicators of the process is the analysand's active work as he cooperates with the analyst: an effort to be sincere as far as absolutely possible, to listen to the analyst and to say "yes" as well as "no", to allow himself to regress and progress. This becomes evident to us when the analysand says: "in the last session we found something interesting", and when we share this sentiment.

Some manifestations of the analytic non-process are more difficult to discover than those of the process: aside from the multiple forms of hindrance, non-process is seen in the appearance of all the positive indicators of process, used to dissimulate its non-existence. Non-process usually disguises itself beneath all the positive indicators of process (cooperation that is actually submission, "insight" that is pseudo-"insight", circulation of crocodile tears, etc.), with which the analysand intends to "placate" his analyst in order to avoid greater dangers.

These disguises give themselves away as such through their stereotyping, which converges them with the indicators of non-process. The danger intrinsic to every psychoanalytic treatment is stereotyping (of narrative, of feelings, of the respective roles, of interpretation). When this stereotyping is disguised as movement, something remains stereotyped: the kind of anxiety being shown or concealed. In its simplest and most obvious form, stereotyping is revealed in certain moments of those treatments where the process has become a sort of circular movement that analysands may describe using the metaphor of the *noria* [water wheel]: the donkey going round and round is the patient, wearing blinkers, who, thinking he is advancing, always returns to the same place. If, as we may think, the water wheel does not involve only the patient, we can imagine (remember?) the analyst going the rounds of his own theories without finding the way to break the cycle for himself or for his analysand.

In certain cases, the non-process may be expressed in the form of an apparently well-channelled movement: those treatments that "run on wheels", where the analysand arrives punctually, associates, listens, approves the interpretation, even gratifies his analyst with quite visible therapeutic results, giving him the impression of a job well done. In the analyst, the alarm signal may be that "this treatment is going *too* well", together with the feeling that "nothing's happening here". Generally, the sign that inspires the second look in the analyst is the treatment's tendency to externalization, and the awakening of intense anxiety in the analysand by the mere idea, sent up as a test balloon by the analyst, that "analysis is terminable".

The subjacent situations are of very diverse natures, but common to all is the existence of a "bastion", in the strict sense. This may be, for example, a concealed "perverse field" (described by us elsewhere), in which analytic activity itself serves as a screen for the analysand's perverse satisfaction (voyeurist, masochist, homosexual, etc.). It may also be an anti-death pact, sustained by the analysand's fantasy that "as long as I'm in analysis, I won't die" and by the analyst's corresponding fantasy, "if I terminate it, he will die".

Just as non-process may be concealed beneath the appearance of process, so process may also take place surreptitiously. The surreptitious processes may sometimes be seen in patients having great internal obstacles to their own progress, or who wish to carry out an old revenge against their primary objects, or who fear to provoke the wrath of the gods or some counterattack from Fate if they show their improvement.

The process is achieved through the successive resolution of the obstacles opposing its movement: these are well known, but not all obey the same mechanisms.

These obstacles may be considered resistances if we adopt the definition of resistance formulated by Freud in *The Interpretation of Dreams*: "whatever interrupts the progress of analytic work is a resistance" (1900a, p. 517).

We are quite familiar with those resistances that are classic expressions of defences and alterations of the ego. Any more-or-less experienced analyst knows how to categorize them and possesses technical resources to deal with them. They are material for our comprehension and interpretation, an intrinsic element of the process, a dialectic part of it. Their resolution is our daily task.

Far more serious are those resistances that, more than a—foreseeable and familiar—obstacle, place analytic work in grave danger, compromise the process, and may come to interrupt it, to detract from it, and finally lead to results that are completely the opposite of those intended. Of course, they are in the same range as the "classic" resistances: we might say that they begin where the latter end, ranking in order of their gravity all the way to the extreme pole of reversal of the intentionality of the process. Among these phenomena, we can distinguish what is commonly called "uncontrollable resistance", the "impasse", and, finally, the negative therapeutic reaction. Many analytic texts use these terms as if they were comparable or interchangeable. However, we consider that a more precise use of terminology would be useful in view of the technical implications.

The essential difference between these processes and the classic resistances resides in their intensity and durability. They are not elements of the process that appear and are resolved, giving way to other movements: they are far more stable, lasting obstacles manifestly accompanied by the relative or total incapacity of the analyst to deal with and resolve them. The analyst is much more involved, and the gravity of the phenomenon is precisely that the analyst becomes powerless to manage it. We think that what we have called "bastion" is subjacent to all these phenomena: they can only be understood in terms of field.

One commonly speaks of the resistance–counter-resistance dyad. This dyad leads to the bastion: a collusion between the patient's and the analyst's resistances, which we consider to be a crystallized formation within the field that stalls its dynamics. Analyst and analysand go round and round an obstacle without being able to integrate it into the process.

The so-called uncontrollable resistance, seen in a unipersonal perspective, is a resistance that tends to become chronic and may finally interrupt the process. If it goes on too long, it arrives at the situation that today is called "impasse". The analyst feels technically involved in the "impasse". He searches in vain for the technical recourse that would allow him to resolve the situation of stagnation. The "impasse" is resolved through the "acting out" of the patient, who leaves the treatment, or of the analyst, who tends to introduce technical innovations. However, sometimes the analyst hits upon the recourse that allows him to save himself and his patient, and if the treatment is interrupted by one of the participants, the patient generally leaves, having preserved the achievements attained up to this moment. The situation of "impasse" can occur at any moment in an analytic treatment. On the other hand, the primary difference between "impasse" and negative therapeutic reaction, remembering Freud, is that the latter tends not to occur at the beginning of an analysis, but after a certain time and in an seemingly successful treatment. It is a negative response to effective achievements of the patient, or to interpretations that the analyst considers adequate: the patient begins to go back rapidly along the road he has travelled, arriving finally at a suicidal situation or a suicidal accident. He generally does not interrupt the treatment: rather, he clings to it to the catastrophic end. The "impasse" may be brought to an end without major catastrophes; the negative therapeutic reaction is, by definition, catastrophic.

We think that a pathognomonic sign of the negative therapeutic reaction is the parasiting of analyst by patient. The analyst is not only concerned scientifically or technically, or even affectively, by the patient, as in the "impasse", but feels totally invaded by the patient. The "impasse" is comparable to what is sometimes called transference–countertransference neurosis. The negative therapeutic reaction may be thought of as a transference–countertransference psychosis: analyst and analysand come to make up a "*folie à deux*". Precisely because it is at the extreme end of the range of obstacles in the psychoanalytic process, it appears much more clearly to us as a specific product of the analytic field. By examining this extreme end, we can understand that the analyst is, to a greater or lesser extent, actively involved in all the phenomena that are manifestly serious obstacles to the analytic process. For this reason, we maintain that, subjacent to all these obstacles, lies a bastion.

When Freud defined the analytic procedure as the repetition of the initial neurosis and the resolution of this neurosis at the level of the transference, he pointed out the two poles of repetition in the technique: the first, inertia or "entropy", or the second, a moment of the processes or part of progress. The introduction of the concept of field emphasizes a double position: that is, in each of the participants in the process, of the repetition compulsion. The analyst also has his ways of repeating: he may enter into collusion with the analysand, unconsciously captured in the fantasy of the field, he may enter into the stereotyping of the analysand when he transforms the sessions into a ritual, he may attempt to break up the repetition by force: can this be the key to understanding the pathology of certain technical innovations, certain undue "terminations" of analysis? But perhaps the most deceptive form of repetition in the analyst has to do with his enclosure in his own scheme of reference, especially if it has acquired a certain degree of systematization and rationalization and has tended to become a routine. The analyst's ideal could be the ferret, which never surfaces where it is being awaited, or the hidden prize of the treasure hunt.

The more rigid the analyst's scheme of reference, the more prone he is to accepting the role of "subject supposed to know": that is, the more he becomes an accomplice to the paralysing stereotyping of the process. For this reason, it is recommended that we pass through multiple schemes, harvesting for ourselves from several, though avoiding confusing eclecticisms: clinical practice is more varied than our schemes and does not cheat us of opportunities for invention.

As anti-repetition and anti-stereotyping procedure, analysis must constantly fight against the bastions being created, and must try to destroy them as they are built up. Some bastions can appear to us as extremely proteiform, others as barely crystallized, and yet others as hard and paralysing for the analyst. *There is process so long as the bastions are being detected and destroyed.* In this sense, the two aspects of the interpretation (rupture and integration) are clearly complementary.

The bastion is always re-born in renewed forms: it is the most conspicuous clinical sign of the repetition compulsion—that is, of the death instinct. When the bastion as such is broken down, this expresses the triumph of the process over our intrinsic thanatic dullness—called in the past "adhesiveness of the libido"—and this victory, though momentary, is perhaps the essence of the joy given us by our analytic work.

5

The mind of the analyst: from listening to interpretation

Madeleine Baranger

There is no such thing as perception without an object, or without another subject. It is only by an effort of abstraction that we can ask ourselves what passes through the mind of the analyst between listening and interpretation. The analyst's internal process which leads him to interpret belongs from the beginning to an intersubjective situation, however structurally asymmetrical it may be.

Similarly, analytic listening is directed in advance towards an eventual interpretation, whose content is not yet known at the time of listening but which gradually takes shape up to the moment when the interpretation has to be formulated to the analysand. The intersubjectivity of the analytic dialogue, while describing an essential aspect of the processes with which we are concerned (what happens in the analyst), conceals—and sometimes reveals—

"La mente del analista. De la escucha a la interpretación" (paper presented at the 38th International Congress of Psychoanalysis, Amsterdam, 1993). Published in Spanish in *Revista de Psicoanálisis, 49* [2], 1992: 223–237. First published in English in *International Journal of Psychoanalysis, 74,* 1993: 15–24; reprinted by permission.

another intersubjective type of structure, just as the visible–audible is superimposed on the invisible–unheard of. This second structure, sometimes called the "intersubjective field", underlies as something unsaid or unsayable both the analysand's material as presented and the analyst's formulations; in the latter, it determines both the content of the interpretation and the feeling-conviction that the interpretation must be formulated.

Context of the interpretation

Unlike the "wild" interpretations that may be "played with" in everyday life, a psychoanalytic interpretation does not arise by chance or in isolation. It belongs to—and is part of—a context whose coordinates are fixed by the patient's demand, the analyst's expectations and the contract defining the analytic situation.

The patient—and even the "training" analysand—asks for analysis because he is suffering from a certain malaise and hopes to improve his conditions of life and pleasure. It matters little at this point whether he brings along a conscious conflict—with his wife, with his children's growing up, with his boss or his workmates—or whether he has been "sent", for instance by his partner or, in psychosomatic cases, his doctor. Either of his own accord on the basis of cultural information or because of what he has been told, he has decided to try out psychoanalysis as a way—sometimes, indeed, a last resort—of solving his conscious and unconscious problems.

We know only too well that this decision may be fairly ambivalent or be based on expectations of magic actions. Yet we cannot rule out the possibility that he has decided to come and ask for something, even if he himself does not know exactly what he is asking for, but he does suppose that the analyst has the knowledge and the instruments to produce beneficial effects in him.

The analyst for his part, in making his own decision to accept this subject for treatment, will have done so in the conviction that he can alleviate his suffering or malaise, and that specifically psychoanalysis is the appropriate way, or one of the appropriate ways, in which he can help him. No analyst undertakes the psychoanalysis of a patient without this minimum of expectation. This is the ethical dimension of psychoanalysis. It implies in the analyst a much more precise expectation than the patient's: that his words will be the factor that will give rise to the desired effects.

The terms of the contract, which are minimal, are intended to organize and protect the new relationship, from which ultimately positive changes are expected. First of all, the contract lays down the material conditions of this intersubjective relationship—the place, frequency, and length of the sessions—which constitute the framework for the analytic work. The regularity or deliberate ir- regularity of this framework of time and space is the hallmark of two completely different kinds of analysis and crucially determines the structuring of the field and the internal work of the analyst.

The functional conditions determine the roles assigned to ana- lyst and analysand, which are asymmetrical. The patient is bound by the "fundamental rule" (Freud, 1905a) to say everything that occurs to him, but without acting out. It is assumed that his associations will betray signs of, or information about, his unconscious.

The analyst takes responsibility for and directs the process by his silence or interpretation in response to what the patient says. In the analyst, the unconscious is involved in a different way. According to Freud (1911–15 [1914]) and others, it functions as a resonance box for the patient's unconscious; this idea was subsequently de- veloped in a way that viewed the countertransference partly as a product of the patient's projections (the Kleinian school's concept of projective identification). The resonance box is an inadequate metaphor; and projective identification and possibly counteriden- tification also have their shortcomings. Both concepts attempt to circumvent the active participation of the analyst's conscious and unconscious personal history, to the extent that he may understand and formulate something that he has experienced in the events of his life and his fantasy.

The concept of "field"

The conscious and unconscious work of the analyst is performed within an intersubjective relationship in which each participant is defined by the other. In speaking of the analytic field, we are referring to the formation of a structure that is a product of the two participants in the relationship but which in turn involves them in a dynamic and possibly creative process.

The psychology of the last part of the nineteenth century, whose concepts were broadly adopted by Freud, had an objectivizing tendency. Freud's "complementary series" (1910a [1909]) were descended directly from this tendency. However, in laying the foundations of analytic technique, he gave up the opposition between an observing eye and an observed object. Freud thus implicitly accepted a new conception of the intersubjective relationship, which was to be made explicit by phenomenological psychology in the concept of the field, particularly in the work of Maurice Merleau-Ponty (1945).

Freud's discovery of the countertransference (1910d) was an advance compared with the objectivizing approach. But even if we take account of the countertransference together with the transference, or regard the transference–countertransference as a unity, this is not the same as what we mean by the concept of field. Let us start with intersubjectivity as a self-evident basic datum. Freud described one aspect of this intersubjectivity in referring to communication from unconscious to unconscious (1911–15 [1914]), which he stated to be bi-directional. The field is a structure different from the sum of its components, just as a melody is different from a sum of its notes.

The advantage of being able to think in terms of a field is that the dynamics of the analytic situation inevitably encounter many stumbling blocks that are not due to the patient's or the analyst's resistance but reveal the existence of a pathology specific to this structure. The work of the analyst in this case, whether or not he uses the field concept, undergoes a change of centre: a second look (Baranger, Baranger, & Mom, 1983 [chapter 4, this volume]) is directed at one and the same time to the patient and to oneself functioning as an analyst. It is not simply a matter of allowing for the analyst's countertransference experiences but of acknowledging that both the transference manifestations of the patient and the analyst's countertransference spring from one and the same source: a basic unconscious fantasy that , as a creation of the field, is rooted in the unconscious of each of the participants.

The concept of basic unconscious fantasy is derived from the

Kleinian concept of unconscious fantasy, but also from the description given by Bion in his work on groups (1952). For instance, in discussing the basic hypothesis of "fight and flight" in a group, Bion is in our view referring to an unconscious fantasy that does not exist in any of the participants outside this group situation. This is what we mean by the basic unconscious fantasy in the field of the analytic situation.

The field is thus structured on three levels: (a) the functional framework of the analysis; (b) the analytic dialogue; and (c) the unconscious dynamic structure underlying this dialogue.

Viewed as movement, the field manifests itself as the analytic process.

The analytic process

As the analysis proceeds, it becomes possible to follow the steps of a process. From this process, both analyst and analysand will emerge changed, although in different ways and to different degrees. The interpretation, the analyst's instrument par excellence, is both part and agent of this process. This is why I contrasted it with "wild" interpretations, which do not belong to any process. The process takes place within a history, the history of this analytic relationship, which has its ups and downs, its moments of progression and phases of stagnation—and sometimes interruptions. In other words, the interpretation is bound up with this or that particular moment of the process; it will not be the same—even if it change only in form and not in object—at the beginning, after a fairly long period of analysis and towards the end.

The interpretation tends to gather together and put into words something that is occurring at a particular moment in the process: the unconscious fantasy underlying and structuring the present situation of the analytic field. This fantasy is a development and combination of—and sometimes a discontinuity in—everything that has occurred and possibly been interpreted since the beginning of the treatment.

I use the word "discontinuity" to refer to a phenomenon that every analyst will have encountered with his patients, sometimes spectacularly and on other occasions on a small scale: something that was developing more or less predictably appears to change course. The analyst feels that he is encountering "someone else". The change concerns not only the manifest themes of the analysand's discourse but also the unconscious conflictuality that the analyst seeks to interpret. The analysand even seems to have moved to a different position in the analyst's nosography. The process seems to have reached a "point of inflection". Not every change in the process or in the patient can legitimately be described as a "point of inflection". A process without changes would not be a process. We may speak of a "point of inflection" when there has suddenly been a mobilization (whether or not in relation to observed interpretation and insight) of the analytic field and a restructuring of the underlying basic fantasy. The point of inflection marks the opening of access to new aspects of the history.

The idea that the history of the analytic process repeats the steps in the patient's history is mistaken. It is, however, true that obstacles in the work of historicization correspond to decisive moments in the life of the patient, when he was obliged to mutilate his own history at the same time as he mutilated himself. The history of himself which the patient has brought—sometimes very poorly—changes, enriching and building itself in the analysis. Interpretation—whose aim is to reconstruct this history—becomes necessary when the analyst perceives what we call the "point of urgency".

The point of urgency

What takes place in the analyst's mind between listening and interpretation could be described as the search for the point of urgency.

This concept is originally to be found in Klein, who considered that the onset of the feeling of anxiety (in the analysand) called for interpretation. However, anxiety is often not experienced consciously. Klein then speaks of latent anxiety, replaced on the phenomenal level by other verbal or behavioural manifestations (silence, logorrhoea, bodily tension, or insistent repetition of material).

We agree with Klein that anxiety is frequently a sign of the proximity of some unconscious material that is about to emerge, and thus it guides our encounter with the point of urgency. However, it is hard to conceive of latent anxiety performing the same function, as we do not know where it is. This leads us to a widening of the concept of anxiety which many would consider improper.

Among our own ranks, the term "point of urgency" was used by Enrique Pichon-Rivière. His idea differs from Klein's in its central focus. He defines the point of urgency as the moment in the session when something is about to emerge from the analysand's unconscious.

Taking Pichon-Rivière as our basis, we consider the point of urgency to be a moment in the functioning of the field when the structure of the dialogue and the underlying structure (the basic unconscious fantasy of the field) can come together and give rise to an insight. The analyst feels and thinks that he can and must interpret (formulate an interpretation to the analysand).

The point of urgency is not generally known at the beginning of the session, although the course of the process itself may have given the analyst a hypothetical idea of what is about to emerge. The current events in the life of the analysand also guide us towards the probable activation of specific fantasy nuclei (e.g., the death of someone close to the analysand, a birthday, etc.). The analyst's first interventions, which are most often not interpretive, are aimed at probing the possible directions for the search.

The search for the point of urgency may succeed or fail. Freud (1937d) taught us that the analysand's verbal acceptance of the interpretation is not enough to validate it, just as its rejection does not mean than it is necessarily false. The true indicators of its correctness are the opening of the field and the dynamicization of the process.

Analytic listening

We define the term "listening" in its widest sense, as the normally preferential attention we direct towards the patient's verbal discourse. But we also "listen to" his tone of voice—lively or depressed—the rhythm and pace of his delivery, his attitudes, movements and postures on the couch, and his facial expressions, in so far as we can see them from our vantage point.

Freud recommended the adoption of a state of "evenly sus-pended attention" (1912e). The aim of this recommendation is that the analyst should be open to whatever arises, without preju-dices of any kind and without systematically seeking confirmation of any project. An analyst who plans a treatment on the basis of his knowledge or theoretical interests runs the risk of becoming blind and deaf to the patient's manifestations. The attitude of analytic listening is diametrically opposed to the mental posture of the ob-server or experimenter in the physical and natural sciences. The latter plans his observation and experiment on the basis of his expectations, which depend both on his general knowledge of his discipline and on an idea or invention that he considers may cause his science to progress. He works with preconcepts that organize the same observations, in order to verify or falsify them. The psy-choanalyst, on the other hand, must beware of mentally obstructing access to the unforeseen, to "surprise", which is precisely what he hopes for as the emergence of the unconscious.

Yet it is not a passive or ingenuous form of listening. It is guided by the analyst's entire listening resources. Analytic theo-ry, which need not be formulated, provides him with an implicit framework to accommodate his discoveries. Aulagnier's concept of "evenly suspended theorization" (1979) can appropriately be applied to this.

The analyst must steer a course between two contrasting dan-gers: the forced application of a pre-existing theory, which will ulti-mately lead to spurious interpretations, and the whole complex of chaotic theories. The analyst's scheme of reference is what guides both the search for the point of urgency and the formulation of the interpretation.

This scheme of reference is the quintessence, condensed and worked out personally by each analyst, of his theoretical allegiances, his knowledge of the analytic literature, his clinical experience—es-pecially his failures—what he has been able to learn about himself in his analysis, and his identifications with his analyst and supervi-sors—as well as the theoretical fashions that periodically sweep through the psychoanalytic movement.

The degree of coherence and elaboration of these different influences varies considerably from analyst to analyst. Some have a fairly conscious and synthesized scheme of reference—the danger in this case is that it might become rigid and not be open to anything that does not fit in with itself. But even analysts who declare themselves to be exclusively "clinical" operate with an implicit scheme of reference, even if it lacks this degree of rationalization or coherence.

Knowledge of the patient and his history acts as a backcloth to the current drama.

Above all, the history of the analytic relationship and of the process are present in the analyst's mind, with the analytic situation in its totality, in its planned and spontaneous (unconscious) dynamism. The process is governed by the analyst's desire (to know? to understand? to help? to discover?) and the memory of the various moments in it.

We consider it extremely worrying that the concept of "memory of the process" is lacking from the majority of psychoanalytic contributions. It is well known that the analyst's hyperamnesia, often willingly accepted by patients, is nothing but the counterpart of the relative amnesia of the patients, as Mijolla-Mellor (1990) points out.

What does the analyst listen to?

What defines analytic listening and distinguishes it from any other kind of psychotherapy is that it attempts to listen to the unconscious. Freud defined the work of analysis as "making the unconscious conscious". However, the very content of the concept of the unconscious is not unambiguous in Freud's work: as we all know, the unconscious of 1915, whose correlate is repression (1915d), is expanded in the paper on splitting of the ego and the mechanisms of defence (1940e [1938]), albeit without forfeiting its validity. This opens the way to the recognition of many forms of rendering unconscious besides forgetting.

Different concepts lie behind the same word, "unconscious", in all the main analytic schools. When Klein refers to the "deep layers of the unconscious", she means an organized mass of very archaic unconscious fantasies present and active at every moment of life. The result is the idea, which we consider to be erroneous, that they can be reached directly by interpretation.

Lacan, on the other hand, says that "the unconscious resists any ontology" (1973)—in other words, that the unconscious is not a thing. If we agree with Lacan on this point, accepting that "making the unconscious conscious" does not mean moving something from one container to another, which would ultimately leave the unconscious half empty, must we suppose that what we are seeking is a new sense? On the level of our listening, does the latent content lie behind the manifest content, or is the latent content a second sense of the manifest content? We are caught between an impossible ontology and the threat of interpretive arbitrariness. But perhaps this antithesis of thing and sense is badly stated, and we should formulate the problem in different terms.

The analyst listens to something other than what he is being told. To imagine that he seeks a latent content that exists behind the manifest content would be to reify something dynamic. The unconscious is not behind but is elsewhere. The listening of the analyst consists in decentring the patient's discourse, stripping it down in order to find a new centre, which at this moment is the unconscious.

The three factors involved are: (1) the patient's explicit discourse; (2) the unconscious configuration of the field (unconscious fantasy of the field), which includes the activated aspect of the transference/countertransference; and (3) what corresponds at this point to something unconscious in the analysand, which must be interpreted.

It is by virtue of the mediation of the unconscious configuration of the field that the analysand's unconscious can express itself and the analyst can find an interpretation. We thus avoid the risk of arbitrariness: it is not just any sense that is appropriate, and not just any interpretation that is valid.

This is best illustrated by the use of the analysand's account of his dreams: among the many possible and plausible interpretations of the dream, we choose the one that corresponds to the context lived by the patient, on the one hand, and the current moment in the process, on the other. The account of the dream is addressed to us and involves us, even if we do not appear directly or indirectly in any of the images reported.

The puzzle with which the analysand presents us in telling us his dream has to do with the unconscious configuration of the field, in the same way that we choose the interpretation in accordance with this mediating configuration. The dream and the interpretation spring from the same source, and can therefore correspond.

If the interpretation has been correct—that is, if there have not been too many barriers on the part of the analyst to understanding the configuration of the field—the interpretation has a chance of gaining access to some part of the analysand's unconscious. It will be access to a single isolated point, experienced by both participants as insight, and it will be followed in the analysand by a new process of rendering unconscious, which, however, will leave behind something new to be contributed to the construction being performed by the analytic process. We are therefore not seeking a thing, and we are not listening to a different sense, but are following the trail of something that (or someone who) is unattainable but always present, whose presence has helped to structure and mould the subject's history and continues to do so at every instant of his life.

Interpretation

Not everything the analyst says is interpretation. An interpretation is sometimes preceded by verbal interventions intended to facilitate the patient's communication and to demonstrate the listening presence of the analyst. Not everything that is understood is communicated as an interpretation. The analyst withholds many things that he understands until he considers it appropriate to communicate them. Spontaneous interpretations that occur to him may and perhaps must be kept back until it is possible to integrate them into a wider understanding of the field.

The interpretation proper is preceded by exploratory and preparatory interventions that are indicative of the progressive processing carried out by the analyst and his patient. These interventions should not be confused with a simultaneous translation of the patient's material. The interpretation arises at the moment when the analyst considers that he has understood the point of urgency and worked out how to make it accessible, at least in part, to the patient's understanding.

Sometimes the patient himself, if working in unison with his analyst, is capable of integrating the elements previously communicated and of arriving at his own interpretive formulation. We agree with Freud in distinguishing between interpretations of this kind and "constructions", which are intended to present a plausible picture of the subject's history.

An interpretation is what attempts to throw light on and make convincingly understandable a current aspect of the field of the analytic relationship and hence of the unconscious of the patient involved in it. This mention of the field—of the transference–countertransference—implies that an interpretation is always given within the transference—an idea that is often confused with that of formulating any interpretation in transference terms.

This confusion leads to an indeterminate broadening of the concept of transference and blurs the difference between genuinely transferential phenomena, which are the repetition with the person of the analyst of past links and situations [*mésalliances*], and the patient–analyst link as structurally defined by the contract. If we regard everything as transference, we in fact lose sight of the transference. This forcing of the transference leads ultimately to interpretations that are off-centre with respect to the point of urgency and may tend to indoctrinate the patient.

Strachey's historic paper on "The Nature of the Therapeutic Action of Psychoanalysis" (1934) describes a certain type of interpretation, including transference and something resembling a construction, but we do not consider that it can be taken as a general model of interpretation. In our view, there are truly "mutative" interpretations that have no explicit reference to the person of the analyst.

We referred above to "withheld" interpretations. They are withheld not only pending a wider understanding, but with a view to having the maximum effect at a specific moment in the session and the process. This is the problem of the timing of the interpretation.

A comprehensive interpretation is not normally given at the beginning of a session, as it would then be liable to be unconvincing and to have a blocking effect. Instead, what is appropriate are interpretations of the different kinds of obstacles in the way of the patient's communication and of the opening of the dialogue.

Towards the end of a session we often think of an interpretation that "we leave for tomorrow" lest its effect be too disorganizing and the patient not have enough time to elaborate it in the session. With other patients we are confident enough to open up a new field for their understanding, in the belief that they can continue the work of elaboration by themselves.

However, towards the end of a session we perhaps tend more to give momentarily "conclusive" interpretations, which take account of the work performed in the session and fix a moment in the process in detail.

Everyone agrees that it is inappropriate to give just any interpretation at just any moment in the process. We do, however, believe that it is impossible to predict an order in which interpretations should be given in a particular treatment—for instance, progressing from superficial to deeper interpretations: the patient does not present his material in the form of superimposed layers, but in accordance with the vicissitudes of the regression and progression of the process.

At any rate, the concept of the depth of an interpretation turns out to be ambiguous: is what is deep equivalent to the most archaic, or does it refer to what is most remote from consciousness at a given moment?

In our view, an interpretation is not deep unless it is recognized by the analysand as something of his own. Only the analyst's empathy, acquired and honed by all his prior experience, gives him the sensitivity that enables him to decide whether a given interpretation can or cannot actually be received by the patient. After all, we are not, of course, speaking to the unconscious, or to the subject of the unconscious, but to the patient to the extent that he can be conscious of himself. The unconscious has no ears. It is only through words and the secondary process in the patient that we can bring him closer to his primary processes and his unconscious.

All the processing that leads to the interpretation does not generally take the form of an explicit deliberation in the analyst's mind, but is spontaneous, except when the analyst is in doubt: can I say this or not? The same doubt is a signal of a difficulty in the field or an obstacle in the process, inviting the analyst to take a "second look" (Baranger, Baranger, & Mom, 1983 [chapter 4, this volume]) at the field and to undertake some conscious and reasoned reflection about what he should do. This process, which may be called "metabolization", usually takes place in silence.

Different forms of interpretation

The formula "making the unconscious conscious" might suggest that the process concerned is unequivocal. However, the effect of appropriate interpretations suffices to show us that interpretation may aim at two different targets, at least: ones whereby the analyst seeks to reintegrate a split-off aspect of the patient, and ones that irrupt into a system of reassuring representations or illusions, giving rise to anxiety. The former combine aspects and experiences of the patient that are not unknown to him in the sense of being repressed and unconscious.

They may, for example, relate a specific childhood experience (described by the patient) to an event in his present-day life. They normally give rise to relief and even to the pleasure of discovery and understanding. The latter, because they open the way to the unconscious, arouse worry and anxiety in the patient and potentially in the analyst, who may then feel like a sorcerer's apprentice. The disruptive intention and the synthesizing intention follow each other in the analyst's mind and act dialectically. Without disruption, the analysis would be idyllic and ineffective. Without unification, it would leave the analysand in a psychological quagmire.

A third form of interpretation, which is particularly important in certain types of patients (e.g., psychosomatics), consists in supplying words to describe experiences that never had any. In this type of interpretation, the analyst proceeds *per via di porre* and not only *per via di levare*, as Freud demanded in referring to neurotics (1905a).

The language of interpretation

An important part of the mental work of the analyst in arriving at the interpretation is the choice of an appropriate formulation in order to be understood by this particular patient at this moment.

The first difficulty in the analyst's way is the universal polysemy of language. However, in our view the analyst's art lies in transforming this difficulty into an instrument. The analyst can never be sure that the patient will understand what he interprets in the same sense as the analyst understands it.

We know from experience that the patient often picks up as an interpretation a fragment of what the analyst has said, sometimes even only a word, and apparently nullifies the analyst's interpretive intention. Yet often this "bad listening" on the part of the patient also induces in the analyst something that corrects his vision and helps to open up the field.

This does not mean that misinterpretations by the patient due to his resistance do not exist. At any rate, the latter show the analyst that his interpretation ought to be centred differently or aim at a different level. For this reason many analysts' aim of seeking the maximum possible precision in the interpretation seems to us to be wrong: this precision may have the consequence of blocking instead of enriching the analytic dialogue.

Nothing could be more precise than an interpretation formulated in such abstract, theoretical terms, with a metapsychological vocabulary. We are all agreed that such interpretations may be exact but are ineffective.

The analyst should instead, as Aulagnier (1986) points out, concern himself with the representability of the interpretation—that is, make sure that his words can evoke for the patient thing-presentations and concrete affects. Key-words with this power of evocation come to be established in every analysis. They differ from patient to patient, and their value is determined by the patient's own history or the history of this particular analysis.

This common vocabulary of the treatment is chosen not at random but because, in addition to their evocative power for the patient, some words have for the analyst himself an effect of resonance in his own fantasy world and his own history.

The creation of this common language is a phenomenon that occurs in each analysis, but it may become a trap: abuse of, and confinement within, an allusive language may create the illusion for both analyst and patient that they are in communication and speaking about the same thing, whereas in fact each continues with his own theme, and there is no meeting between them. The analyst must not be carried away by the appearance of agreement and must remain alert in order to keep the channels of communication open. The use of the improper common vocabulary may eventually result in sterile repetition.

However, not all repetition is sterile. One of the problems the analyst faces before enunciating his interpretation is that it has already been given in some form or another to this patient. He may be loath to repeat it in case the patient retains it intellectually in his memory without the desired insight.

Again, insistence on an interpretation sometimes gives rise in the patient to an apparent conviction, insight having been replaced by indoctrination. Yet we know from experience that the interpretation is often obliterated in the patient or that he has only been able to accept a part of what was said.

It is in the nature of the unconscious to close up again after it has partially opened. We therefore believe that one should not be afraid of repeating an interpretation, possibly formulated in a different way. Again, by virtue of the progress of the process, interpretations are complemented with fresh nuances and are deepened by the contribution of more concrete material. We know at the beginning of an analysis that the patient will bring us an Oedipus complex. However, it is only at the end that we will have an exact idea of the individual form in which this complex has manifested itself in the patient's life history.

Conclusion

The analyst's mind functions so that his interpretation can act as an agent of transformation: it starts from a current context situated between two histories: the one brought by the patient and the one that is constructed during the process. The analyst looks for the point in the session that will mark the urgency of interpreting and the possibility of understanding an aspect of the field and of opening up the dynamics of the process. For this purpose he follows the thread of the basic fantasy of the field and tries to overcome obstacles so as to allow a reconstruction within his patient.

Summary

The analyst demands two somewhat contradictory attitudes of himself: on the one hand, he listens and interprets, on the basis of his theoretical knowledge, experiences and scheme of reference, and, on the other, he must open himself to the new, the unforeseen, and the surprising.

His work, from listening to interpretation, is situated within a context that includes the history of the treatment as well as the history of the analysand, which is in the process of reconstruction. This context determines the moment of the interpretation (which may vary): that is, the point of urgency of a given session.

This point denotes the moment when something emerges from the unconscious of the analysand and the analyst believes that it must be interpreted. It is something that occurs within the intersubjective field, which embraces both participants and has its own, partly unconscious, dynamics. This configuration or unconscious fantasy of the field constitutes the common source from which both the discourse of one partner and the other's interpretation spring.

The moments of blockage in the dynamics of the field, the obstacles in the analytic process, invite every analyst to take a "second look" at the field, focusing on the unconscious intersubjective relationship that determines it.

Focused either on the analysand or on the field, the interpretation can perform its two dialectically complementary functions: it may irrupt into the disguises of the patient's unconscious, or it may allow him to synthesize and reconstruct his history and identity.

6

The infantile psychic trauma from us to Freud: pure trauma, retroactivity, and reconstruction

Madeleine Baranger, Willy Baranger, & Jorge Mario Mom

We might feel somewhat surprised by Freud's statement that neuroses in which the (infantile psychic) trauma factor is relatively more important in comparison with the other two great aetiological factors in psychopathology (strength of the drives and ego alterations) suggest a better prognosis than the rest. For this reason, it seems necessary to clarify the concept of trauma that Freud is using in "Analysis Terminable and Interminable" (1937c). In addition, most interpreters of Freud take his manifest attempt to revalue the economic approach in this text at face value. But to what economy is he actually referring?

In other words, does the "trauma" of 1937 refer to the trauma of 1895 and the metapsychology of 1915, or is Freud referring, in 1937, to the concept he broadened, particularly in 1926 (*Inhibitions,*

Published in Spanish as "El trauma psíquico infantil de nosotros a Freud: Trauma puro, retroactividad y reconstrucción" (*Revista de Psicoanálisis, 44* [4], 1987: 745–774). First published in English in *International Journal of Psychoanalysis, 69*, 1988: 113–128; reprinted by permission.

Symptoms and Anxiety), and other contemporary papers? One might be tempted to draw parallels between the three aetiological factors mentioned and the three approaches to metapsychology. Thus, the trauma would correspond to the economic approach, the strength of the drives to the dynamic approach, and the ego alterations to the topographic–structural approach. We consider that this temptation must be vigorously resisted and that the elucidation of the question on the meaning of the word "trauma" in the text that concerns us is linked to the concept of the economic approach advocated in it.

Only by clearing up this point can we situate the various developments of the concept of childhood psychic trauma within post-Freudian analytic thought and situate ourselves within that evolution.

Vicissitudes of the concept of psychic trauma in Freud's thought

All Freud's commentators agree that the concept of psychic trauma evolves considerably as Freud elaborates and modifies the theoretical edifice of psychoanalysis; they also agree on the meaning of this evolution: progressive broadening of the connotation of the concept; a growing movement away from the medical concept of trauma as a brusque breaking in on organic homeostasis or as injury; increasing diversity and complexity of traumatic situations; more complex metapsychology.

On all these points we agree with Laplanche and Pontalis (1967) and with Sidney Furst, who edited the really "basic" book that assembles, together with his own contribution, a number of articles that enrich our understanding of the concept of infantile psychic trauma (1967). Of course, our reading of Freud is not exactly the same: the differences arise, not from the thorough study of Freud's texts that we've all done, but from questions of emphasis—that is, from the fact that we obviously read Freud *a posteriori.*

At the beginning, before 1900, Freud, with Breuer or on his own, works on the trauma as related to the aetiology of the transference neuroses (especially hysteria) and shapes a metapsychological description whose form is predominantly economic. At that time, the psychic trauma is equated to the infantile sexual psychic trauma. The "abandonment" of the seduction theory leads to the growing predominance of fantasy life in the production of traumas and of their pathogenic effects. Later, exploration of children's sexual life in the years following the initial period opens up a wide range of quite varied situations that are virtually traumatic; these lead to a reconsideration of the metapsychology of the trauma that Freud presented in his *Introductory Lectures on Psychoanalysis* (1916–17).

At the same time, the urgencies of the world's catastrophes reactivate Freud's interest in war neuroses and in traumatic neuroses in general. The concept of "actual" psychic trauma, isolated, likened to a break-in, seems to recover its place beside infantile sexual trauma, while the economic conception of trauma takes on new vigour.

But Freud continues to elaborate his second topology and to deepen his study of the sources of anxiety. *Inhibitions, Symptoms and Anxiety* (1926d [1925]) marks the final restructuring of the concept of trauma as related to anxiety and the definitive replacement of this concept for that of traumatic situation, which includes both the interaction of internal and external situations and also the interstructural nature of all traumatic situations.

This brief overview of the evolution of Freud's trauma theory invites us to specify some of its multifaceted aspects. As we know, Freud's observations are initially an extension and modification of Charcot's traumatic theory of hysteria. Freud himself situates his thinking in this respect:

> The content of the memory is as a rule either a psychical trauma which is qualified by its intensity to provoke the outbreak of hysteria in the patient or is an event which, owing to its occurrence at a particular moment, has become a trauma.
>
> In cases of what is known as "traumatic" hysteria this mechanism is obvious to the most cursory observation; but it can be demonstrated also in hysteria where there is no single major trauma. In such cases, we find repeated minor traumas or, where the factor of disposition predominates, memories which are often indifferent in themselves magnified into traumas. A trauma would have to be defined as an accretion of excitation in the nervous system, which the latter has been unable to dispose of adequately by motor reaction. An hysterical attack is perhaps to be regarded as an attempt to complete the reaction to a trauma. [1892–94, p. 137]

It is true that *Studies on Hysteria* (Freud, 1895d) presents both the aetiology of this neurosis and also the mechanism of its cure from a largely economic approach: the trauma is excessive excitation that cannot flow off along motor paths, nor be integrated associatively, nor "worked over" by memory work. The resolution of the trauma implies catharsis, abreaction of the "strangulated energy". However, we note that although he rejects the importance of Breuer's "hypnoid states" in the aetiology of hysteria, Freud is far from limiting himself to an economic conception. "Draft K", sent to Fliess in 1896, clearly shows the importance placed upon the dynamic and topographic factors in the aetiology of hysteria, as well as the complexity of the process of symptom formation:

> The course taken by the illness in neuroses of repression is in general always the same: (1) the sexual experience (or series of experiences) which is traumatic and premature and is to be repressed. (2) Its repression on some later occasion which arouses a memory of it; at the same time the formation of a primary symptom. (3) A stage of successful defence, which is equivalent to health except for the existence of the primary symptom. (4) The stage in which the repressed ideas return, and in which, during the struggle between them and the ego, new symptoms are formed, which are those of the illness proper: that is, the stage of adjustment, of being overwhelmed or of recovery with a malformation. [Freud, 1950 [1892–1899], p. 222]

We are far from the isolated trauma caused by breaking in and flooding by energy coming from the exterior, carbon-copied on to the traumatic neurosis: most often, this is a series of repeated traumas whose memory requires repression (forgetting). In all cases, quite a particular type of trauma is involved, the type that affects infantile sexuality, specifically the seduction of the child by an adult or by an older child. The trauma itself sets off a complex defensive dialectic, and the cure of the symptoms it produces cannot be formulated exclusively in energetic terms either: the abreaction, aside from its emotional aspect, implies memory work, the re-establishment of associative links, and reintegration into the ego of what has been split off.

Freud's "renunciation" of the theory of infantile seduction has been widely commented on, since he realized that part of the memories that arise in the treatment of hysteric patients could not be considered to be true memories of events that really occurred but were instead fantasy constructions invented afterwards by the patients. In the letter to Fliess on 21 September 1897 (Masson, 1985), Freud confesses to his friend that "I no longer believe in my 'neurotica'" and that he is vexed at the time, to the point that he even has doubts about his own discoveries on the transference neuroses. In fact, what this discovery places in doubt is not the whole theory on hysteria but the content of the concept of trauma: there are cases where the "infantile seduction" corresponds, not to material reality, but to psychic reality; even in cases where the reality of the child's seduction is beyond doubt, the element of fantasy is nonetheless of predominant importance. Several years later, Freud saw it retrospectively in this way:

> The same clarification (which corrected the most important of my early mistakes) also made it necessary to modify my view of the mechanism of hysterical symptoms. They were no longer to be regarded as derivatives of the repressed memories of childhood experience; but between the symptoms and the childish impressions there were inserted the patient's *phantasies* (or imaginary memories), mostly produced during the years of puberty which on the one side were built up out of and over the childhood memories, and on the other side, were transformed directly into the symptoms. It was only after the introduction of this element of hysterical phantasies that the texture of the neurosis and its relations to the patient's life became intelligible. [Freud, 1906a, p. 274]

Therefore, it would be a mistake to speak in terms of Freud "abandoning" the theory of infantile seduction; we could think more precisely of a deepening of the concept of infantile sexual trauma that recognizes fantasy life—that is, psychic reality—as the protagonist as compared with the truly experienced events and the pathogenic effects that we can confirm. Freud's disillusionment with the protagonistic role of seduction opens the way to a more complex theory of trauma that emphasizes its internal aspect, but that at the same time does not renounce the "real" basis of the traumatic sexual situations, now seen in the form of universal and paradigmatic situations. On the other hand, later analytic experience confirms the very great frequency of fully verifiable infantile seductions in analysands, hysterics as well as others.

Nachträglichkeit

In addition to the indispensable participation of fantasy in the constitution of trauma, another point that attenuates and limits the economic aspect of the latter is the universality of the *a posteriori* [*Nachträglichkeit*], a Freudian concept to which many commentators have given less importance than we consider it deserves. Laplanche and Pontalis have underlined its prime importance in the genesis of the infantile psychic trauma, as well as its implications for all of psychoanalytic thought. Even in the case of a simple event, an isolated, infantile seduction for example, although the trace of this event remains in the psyche, it does not in itself constitute a trauma in the sense that it produces no pathogenic effects until conditions of maturation or new and quite ulterior events retroactively convert the first event into trauma, at which time its pathogenic consequences will appear. Freud describes this process as early as 1895 in his unfinished "Project" and arrives at the conclusion that "a memory is repressed which has only become a trauma *after the event.* The reason for this state of things is the retardation of puberty as compared with the remainder of the individual's development" (1950 [1895], p. 413), which involves "*posthumous primary processes*" (p. 416).

Here *this is not simply a deferred action* nor a *cause* that remains latent until it has occasion to appear, but a *retroactive causation* of the present on the past.

The introduction of the *Nachträglichkeit* indicates those moments when Freud leaves aside the model of mechanical causality and linear temporality on the past→present vector for a dialectic concept of causality and a "spiral" model of temporality where future and past condition and signify each other reciprocally in the structuring of the present. The analysis of the "Wolf Man" shows us the prototype of how this re-signification of the trauma (primal scene) is produced in relation to the entire analytic process, although the direct memory has remained unreachable.

This causality and this temporality are the ones that sustain the possibility of a specific therapeutic action in psychoanalysis: if this retroactivity in the constitution of the trauma did not exist, there would be no possibility of modifying our history: that is, our treatments would have no future. Thus we arrive at the explanation for Freud's statement in "Analysis Terminable and Interminable" that the neuroses having the best prognosis are precisely those that are due especially to the trauma as an aetiological factor: the same retroactivity that acted in the constitution of the traumatic situation can also be used, through interpretation, to undo what it has constituted, to reintegrate the elements of the traumatic situations into new temporal dynamics. If we were to abide by linear categories of causality and temporality, we would be deprived of all therapeutic efficacy.

Complemental series

The synthesis Freud makes in his *Introductory Lectures on Psycho-Analysis* (1916–17) gives him an opportunity to resituate the trauma theory within a wider set of concepts that have remained under the title of theory of the complemental series, summarized by Freud in his well-known aetiologic scheme. On the first level of the scheme, "sexual constitution" and "infantile experience" are summed together. In fact, the "sexual constitution" is no more than the precipitate of prehistoric experiences whose most conspicuous example is the Oedipus complex. The second level is the sum of "disposition due to fixation of libido" and "accidental (adult) (traumatic) experience". On the third level the neurosis is produced.

In the series, then, we find trauma at two different points: in the prehistoric experiences (the great trauma of the murder of the father and of castration) and on the level of the accidental adult experience that produces the trauma retroactively.

We are not hiding from ourselves the fact that in this text, while he insists on the constitution of the trauma at two separate times, with retroactivity of the present on the past, Freud attributes this retroactivity to a libidinal regression to the fixation point of the infantile experience, the libido abandoning its ulterior positions. It would, however, be convenient to examine the precise nature of this regression. At first sight, it seems to support a mechanistic view of the theory of the complemental series, and it is generally understood in this way. But another interpretation is appropriate if we think, for example, of the analysis of the "Wolf Man". In this perspective, the regression of the libido would more likely express a re-signification of the infantile experience, the libido's turning from actual interests to the infantile interests that then appear to be a consequence of this process.

War neuroses

Freud's interest in traumatic neuroses was strongly stimulated by the flourishing of war neuroses, beginning in 1914. His *Introductory Lectures* (1916–17) already reflect this interest and Freud's need for renewed thinking that would place the psychic trauma precipitating the war neuroses in relation to the infantile psychic trauma of the transference neuroses. In the former, which is isolated (that terror, that bombing, etc.), the breaking-through and the emotional flooding that characterized the first concept of trauma appear in a far noisier and more evident form, along with the consequent temptation to understand it in predominantly economic terms:

> The traumatic neuroses give a clear indication that a fixation to the traumatic accident lies at their root. These patients regularly repeat the traumatic situation in their dreams; where hysteriform attacks occur that admit of an analysis, we find that the attack corresponds to a complete transplanting of the patient into the traumatic situation. It is as though these patients had not finished with the traumatic situation, as though they were still faced by it as an immediate task which has not been dealt with; and we take this view quite seriously. It shows us the way to what we may call an *economic* view of mental processes. Indeed, the term "traumatic" has no other sense than an economic one. [Freud, 1916–17, pp. 274–275]

This last affirmation is categoric and contradicts all that Freud has been elaborating in the previous years, but he himself goes on to nuance it: "The increments of stimuli have not been able to be 'worked off' in the normal way."

Later reflection by Freud on war neuroses lead him to a somewhat paradoxic evolution: on the one hand, to a further deepening of the economic approach in *sensu strictu* and, on the other, to the discovery of the death instinct. To the former, Freud introduces the economic concept of "barrier against stimuli" whose rupture would provoke the trauma.

> We describe as "traumatic" any excitations from outside which are powerful enough to break through the protective shield. It seems to me that the concept of trauma necessarily implies a connection of this kind with a breach in an otherwise effica-cious barrier against stimuli. [Freud, 1920g, p. 29]

This breach causes considerable disturbance "in the functioning of the organism's energy", but "the mental apparatus" is also flooded by great quantities of stimuli.

Todestrieb

The war neuroses, which had led Freud to re-evaluate the economic approach, are increasingly linked with the transference neuroses, and the trauma at their origin becomes more complex and more similar to the infantile psychic trauma.

> It might, indeed, be said that in the case of the war neuroses, in contrast to the pure traumatic neuroses . . . what is feared is nevertheless an internal enemy. The theoretical difficulties standing in the way of a unifying hypothesis of this kind do not seem insuperable: after all, we have a perfect right to describe repression, which lies at the basis of every neurosis, as a reac-tion to a trauma—as an elementary traumatic neurosis. [Freud, 1919d, p. 210]

In the same vein, he declares that "'war neuroses' . . . may very well be traumatic neuroses which have been facilitated by a conflict in the ego" (1920g, p. 33). The study of the traumatic neuroses and of the war neuroses, together with reflection on other lines of think-ing, leads Freud to introduce a new concept whose fate will be to modify the theoretical edifice of psychoanalysis and, particularly, the trauma theory: that of the death instinct. In fact, the typical dreams of the traumatic neuroses provide the prototypic example of psychic phenomena that escape the mastery of the pleasure principle.

But it is impossible to classify as wish-fulfilments the dreams we have been discussing which occur in traumatic neuroses or the dreams during psycho-analyses which bring to memory the psychical traumas of childhood. They arise, rather, in obedience to the compulsion to repeat, though it is true that in analysis that compulsion is supported by the wish (which is encouraged by "suggestion") to conjure up what has been forgotten and repressed. [Freud, 1920g, p. 32]

These dreams, independent of the pleasure principle, are part of an attempt, Freud says, to master the excessive stimulus retroactively, by developing the anxiety that was lacking at the moment of the trauma, thus revealing a function of the psychic apparatus that is more primitive than the establishment of the pleasure principle. The existence of the compulsion to repeat, which appears in many phenomena, leads Freud to search for the ultimate basis of the psychic conflict in the struggle between the libido and the death instinct. We will return to this point later.

From the trauma to the traumatic situation

Freud makes his last great contribution to the theory of the psychic trauma in 1926 in *Inhibitions, Symptoms and Anxiety*, which correlates with his elaboration of the last theory of anxiety and the establishment of the distinction between automatic anxiety and anxiety as signal.

All Freud's elaboration since the early introduction of the concept of trauma has been aimed at substituting the notion of isolated trauma with that of the traumatic situation. But only when trauma was tied in with the theory of anxiety does the concept of traumatic situation receive the full emphasis it merits. The exploration of infantile sexuality through the analysis of adults, as well as the analytic observation of children like Little Hans, had led Freud to make an inventory of traumatic situations that are present in the evolution of any person, over and above the different forms individual history may take. Castration, whether by direct or fantasized threat and the perception of the lack of penis in women, constitutes the "greatest trauma of his life" for the male, as Freud writes in 1939. The Oedipus complex itself, strongly linked with the castration complex, constitutes in itself a traumatic situation. In the same way, weaning, the loss of the faeces, mourning, the birth of younger siblings and so forth, constitute paradigmatic traumatic situations. We will not take up the birth trauma; Freud has shown quite convincingly what can and cannot be accepted of Rank's theory in this regard: although birth is objectively a separation from the mother, it cannot be considered as the prototype of traumatic situations of separation because "birth is not experienced subjectively as a separation from the mother, since the foetus, being a completely narcissistic creature, is totally unaware of her existence as an object" (1926d [1925], p. 130).

We are struck by the importance, in *Inhibitions, Symptoms and Anxiety*, of the traumatic situations centred on experiences of loss—of the mother, of the mother's love, of the object's love, of the superego's love, and so forth—experiences that immerse the subject in a state of helplessness, in a state of total motor or psychic impotence in the face of irruptions of stimuli of external or internal origin. The key words in this basic work are: "helplessness" [*Hilflösigkeit*] and "overwhelming". The basic traumatic situation is the situation of "helplessness", and all traumatic situations refer to this one. The interrelation between traumatic situation–danger situation and anxiety appears extremely clearly:

> Let us call a situation of helplessness of this kind that has been actually experienced a *traumatic situation*. We shall then have good grounds for distinguishing a traumatic situation from a danger-situation. . . . Taking this sequence, anxiety–danger– helplessness (trauma), we can now summarize what has been said. A danger-situation is a recognized, remembered, expected situation of helplessness. Anxiety is the original reaction to helplessness in the trauma and is reproduced later on in the danger-situation as a signal for help. The ego, which experiences the trauma passively, now repeats it actively in a weakened version, in the hope of being able itself to direct its course. [Freud, 1926d (1925), pp. 166–167]

It is observed that the distinction between external traumatic situations due to the effective absence of the object, the increment of external stimuli, and so forth, and of the internal stimuli due to the increase in the tensions of needs or in the drive tensions, tends to disappear since, whatever the origin of the traumatic situation, it leads to an "overwhelming" of the ego, which is unable to handle this traumatic situation that reactivates its primitive state of "helplessness".

Within the articulation: traumatic situation–"helplessness"–automatic anxiety–anxiety as signal, the operation of the economic aspect diminishes by degrees until it nearly disappears or becomes quite metaphoric when we come to the level of the inter-structural tensions (fear of losing the superego's love, for example).

Freud's introduction of the hypothesis of the death instinct could not fail to influence all the theoretical edifice of psychoanalysis, since it is a question of the very foundation of psychic conflict. However, we believe that *Inhibitions, Symptoms and Anxiety* apparently refers little to this hypothesis and that, specifically, Freud does not concern himself with linking the hypothesis of the death instinct with the trauma theory. But we think that the linking of trauma to the death instinct is adjacent in this work and even appears from time to time. Proof of it is the footnote:

> It may quite often happen that although a danger-situation is correctly estimated in itself, a certain amount of instinctual anxiety is added to the realistic anxiety. In that case the instinctual demand before whose satisfaction the ego recoils is a masochistic one: the instinct of destruction directed against the subject himself. Perhaps an addition of this kind explains cases in which reactions of anxiety are exaggerated, inexpedient or paralysing. [Freud, 1926d (1925), p. 168, fn. 1]

Neither can we forget that the dreams that are characteristic of the traumatic neuroses provide Freud with the most obvious example of psychic phenomena that obey not the pleasure principle but, rather, a repetition compulsion that develops independently of this principle; nor that the trauma, since its first conceptualization, appears in an essentially repetitive way (in hysterical attacks). The characteristic of tending to repeat itself, independent of the pleasure the repetition may provide, is relevant to the nature of every traumatic situation, to a greater or lesser extent. In fact, precisely some of these repetitions led Freud to search for the ultimate basis of psychic conflict in the death instinct. Among the many manifestations of the death instinct, we find, in addition to the dream repetition of the trauma in the traumatic neuroses, children's play, the fate neuroses, the failure-neuroses ("Those Wrecked by Success" [Freud, 1916d]), and, above all, the transferential repetitions of the past "clichés" in the analytic situation, with special emphasis on the traumatic aspects of the Oedipus and castration complexes. The negative therapeutic reaction, aimed at the failure of the analytic treatment—whether because of unconscious guilt feelings or as a manifestation of that remnant of death instinct that can neither be diverted to the exterior nor integrated into the superego nor bound by the libido, and which goes on leading a "mute" existence within the subject, constitutes what is perhaps the main evidence in support of the Freudian concepts of primary masochism and death instinct.

By all logic, we cannot conceive of the existence of any traumatic situation without the participation of this instinct. If, like Freud, we admit that the function of the libido is to bind [*bändigen*] the death instinct, we must admit that the traumatic situation, by altering the dynamic equilibrium of the drives, contributes to unbind what the libido has bound, and that this frees a certain quantity of death instinct. Freud maintains that we almost never find pure instinctual impulses, but instead fusions of both instincts in different proportions. The trauma influences these fusions, provoking an *Entmischung* or defusion, which, in turn, activates the compulsion to repeat on the one hand and, on the other, demands new libidinal cathexes and new defensive measures of the ego (inhibitions, avoidances, phobias, etc.).

> The effects of traumas are of two kinds, positive and negative. The former are attempts to bring the trauma into operation once again—that is, to remember the forgotten experience, better still, to make it real, to experience a repetition of it anew, or, even if it was only an early emotional relationship, to revive it in an analogous relationship with someone else. We summarize these efforts under the name of "fixations" to the trauma and as a "compulsion to repeat". [Freud, 1939a (1937–39), p. 75]

As for the negative effects of the trauma, they pursue a diametrically opposite goal: that nothing of the trauma be remembered nor repeated.

> These negative reactions too make the most powerful contributions to the stamping of character. Fundamentally they are just as much fixations to the trauma as their opposites, except that

they are fixations with a contrary purpose. The symptoms of
neurosis in the narrower sense are compromises in which both
the trends processing from traumas come together, so that the
share, now of one and now of the other tendency, finds prepon-
derant expressions in them. [Freud, 1939a (1937–39), p. 76]

In so far as the trauma is constituted "at two times", the second
movement operates in a regressive direction, on the one hand giving traumatic meaning to a situation that was only potentially so
and, on the other, initiating a movement of the libido that tends
to abandon its forward positions and to regress to former stages.
In this way another defusion is produced that segregates the erotic
elements that had bound the destructive elements characteristic of
the sadistic phases and reactivates the latter elements, requiring of
the subject new defensive efforts.

The conditions in which the two fundamental instincts come
together, or those in which these fusions are altered or broken,
present "the most rewarding achievement" that investigation could
reach, thinks Freud, and he also admits, in cases where this binding cannot take place, the existence of a "tendency to conflict" that
"can scarcely be attributed to anything but the intervention of an
element of free aggressiveness" (1937c, p. 244).

The "rock" and the archaeology of the trauma

It is well known that Freud never renounced the search for the basis of traumatic situations in the facts of reality, and only resigned
himself to attributing them to psychic reality when all possibility of
finding it in real events had been discarded. The efforts he made
to corroborate the primal scene by memory, witnessed by the Wolf
Man and deduced by himself, are evidence of this preoccupation.
In fact, the infantile psychic trauma is not as universal in the events
of individual histories as in their fantasies: not all have perceived
the primal scene between their parents, not all have been threatened with castration or madness when caught while masturbating.

This universality of certain potentially pathogenic fantasies requires, then, another basis, which Freud searches for in the archaic inheritance of ancestral traumas that were experienced in
past epochs by humanity. In the complemental series that inter-

vene in the constitution of traumatic situations, the trauma whose origin is external is then situated in two links of the chain: at the beginning of it with the ancestral traumas and in the middle with the traumas (especially the sexual ones) of the infantile life of the individual.

The transcendence of certain imagos in relation to the facts of individual history is only too observable in every analysis and requires a different basis. Freud seeks it in certain mnemic traces transmitted as such from generation to generation, in a manner that is similar to the transmission of the instincts in animals. Just as a chicken is frightened when it perceives the *Gestalt* of a predatory bird of which it has not had the least experience, so any person in analysis will produce representations of a terrible primitive father, just as we can see him in the myths of Uranus or of Chronos or in the ogres of fairy tales. In the face of this evidence from analytic experience, we can only admit that Freud is right and discard the objections that have been made to the idea of an archaic inheritance of traumas.

First the sociological objection: it is true that totemism is not a universal phenomenon, nor is it very primitive: consequently, the murder of the father by the coalition of the sons is far from being universal as a concrete event. Its universality is on the order of myths and, as such, generates an infinity of concrete events that, in turn, provide its feedback: no one knows for sure whether, as Freud deduces, the Jews murdered Moses, but we do know that the French guillotined Louis XVI.

The concept of mnemic trace used by Freud also provokes objections from psychology. Even when disconnected from the early theory of the engram disavowed by progress in neurology, this concept is far from clear. But here too, clinical evidence prevails. We observe the traumatic effects of the Holocaust of the Second World War in the children and grandchildren of the survivors.

Freud is aware—and this is an objection from biology—that all the experiments attempting to demonstrate the Lamarckian theory of acquired characters have failed, but Freud remarks that they do not refer to the same thing as he: in the Lamarckian theory, the acquired characters are inaccessible, while in the case of archaic inheritance, the mnemic traces he refers to (marks left by the past) are in some way accessible.

Freud considers that we cannot, even at the risk of being im-
prudent, abandon the idea of an archaic inheritance involving both
symbolism and also the set of *Urphantasien* that reflect humanity's
past and have become constitutive of the mind to the point that
they compose, according to the felicitous expression of Daniel Lagache, "a transcendental phantasmatic".

That universal fantasies, pre-dating all individual experience,
come down from traumatic events in human pre-history is not the
most extreme point in Freud's hypothesis on the incidence of the
psychic trauma. The very forms of emotions (of the "affects") are
shaped by phylogenetic traumas:

> Affective states have become incorporated in the mind as pre-
> cipitates of primeval traumatic experiences, and when a similar
> situation occurs they are revived as mnemic symbols. I do not
> think I have been wrong in likening them to the more recent
> and individually acquired hysterical attack and in regarding
> them as its normal prototypes [Freud, 1926d (1925), p. 93]

The most conspicuous example would be the relation between the
affect of anxiety and the birth trauma.

Catastrophes theory: Freud and Ferenczi

The universality of symbols and the existence of a supra-individual
phantasmatic oblige us to seek the origins of traumas beyond the
subject's history. We must go even further, since our preformed system of emotional expression, the "affective structures" mentioned
by Freud, presupposes the inscription in the organism of something
similar to "hysterical attack"—that is, marks from phylogenetic traumas throughout the evolution of living beings. Thus we go from
the traumas of individual history to the historic and pre-historic
traumas of humanity, and to a generalized theory to be found in
many of Freud's texts when he applies the analytic method to metabiological speculations, and systematized by Ferenczi (1933) in
his catastrophe theory.

Now we are able to answer the questions we have formulated on
the concept of psychic trauma in Freud, as used in "Analysis Terminable and Interminable". Quite clearly, this is the broad concept of

trauma, just as we find it in *Inhibitions, Symptoms and Anxiety*—that is, of an always complex traumatic situation which brings the internal world as much as the external world into play, which activates a whole phantasmatic, both in its universal aspects and in the forms it has assumed in the individual's history, and which alters the balances achieved in the libido's struggle with the death instinct.

This history in itself does not invalidate the economic aspect of the trauma but does, however, invite us to situate this aspect more precisely, which we will attempt to do by formulating the limit-concept of "pure trauma".

Trauma, traumatic situation, and object

The theory of the generalized trauma, as Freud formulated it in 1926, prevails upon thought. In psychoanalytic terms, the trauma is always an infantile traumatic situation, which not only involves the subject and a breaking through of his barrier against stimuli, but also a life situation ("helplessness")—that is, a world of inter-human relationship and of "object relations", which are not necessarily the same. The conceptual amplification that begins with the "trauma" and leads to the "traumatic situation" carries, however, its danger: the possible adulteration of the concept of trauma and the drawing of an equation between "traumatic situation" and "pathogenic situation".

We consider that Anna Freud—and others—were right to refuse to equate "traumatic" with "pathogenic" and to want to preserve for the traumatic a certain specificity. But which specificity?

It would seem on first view that the thinking of Melanie Klein tends to place less importance on the concept of trauma. This author uses the term trauma relatively little, except in already extant expressions like "birth trauma" and others. However, her explicit and implicit references to *Inhibitions, Symptoms and Anxiety* are quite numerous, and we could say that the Freudian concept of the traumatic situation initially associated with infantile helplessness and the baby's relationship with the presence–absence of the mother, as well as the destructuring nature of anxiety, occupies a position of prime importance in her theoretical constructions. We also know that Klein was one of the first of Freud's disciples to accept the

concept of "death instinct", so intimately linked by Freud after 1920
to the concept of trauma, if our exegesis is correct.

We consider that in Klein the concept of trauma shifted somewhat (which explains the relative abandonment of the term) towards the term of "anxiety situation" which only partly covers the
Freudian concept of traumatic situation.

For Klein, as she herself says (1955), both her theoretical constructions and her clinical work hinge upon the situation of anxiety,
which led her, in her period of maturity, to formulate the theory of
the paranoid–schizoid and depressive positions.

Klein (1952a) places them in a genetic perspective (in the first
year of life and later, in oscillations, throughout all of life). These
are universal and paradigmatic situations (but many traumatic situations were this for Freud too). Also, they may preserve their full
value without any genetic considerations: no one need confuse
psychoanalysis with developmental psychology.

These "positions" centre around anxiety: on this point, Klein
leaves aside certain distinctions formulated in 1926 by Freud (anxiety, real danger, pain because of a loss, etc.). In these, fusions and
defusions of the "instincts" are actualized, together with unconscious fantasies, defensive ego processes, the states and actions of
internal objects, diverse tensions between the structural agencies,
internal and external object relations.

Both normal and pathological development are determined by
the way in which the subject is able to handle these two universal
traumatic situations (or positions) and their ulterior nature in the
genetic perspective. But, quite clearly, what constitutes the dramatic–traumatic nature of the positions, directly present for Klein
in the anxiety that organizes and manifests them, is the struggle
against the death "instinct".

A different conception of anxiety carries a different conception
of trauma. We will return to this.

We see how Klein both confirms certain essential aspects of
Freud's thinking and at the same time departs from it. We would
say that the departure is greater in those authors who focus their
investigation, not on the situation of anxiety, but on the object
relation, insisting on the external nature of it. Michael Balint was
the first to develop the idea that the trauma is situational (taking

up Freud's opinion) and that, consequently, appears as one of the vicissitudes of the object relation.

Balint (1969) underscores the existence of two psychoanalytic theories of trauma. The first, focused on form the economic point of view (excessive stimuli, breaking through of the barrier against stimuli, flooding of the ego by excessive excitation, etc.) and another, structural, theory:

> The new theory starts with the assumption that the trauma, in spite of its appearance, is not an external event; it is produced by the individual himself as a fantasy. It cannot claim easily that the individual was unprepared and was flooded by an excessive amount of excitation because, after all, it was he himself who produced the fantasy; on the other hand, it can claim the existence of very high intensity strains between the various parts of the mental apparatus, for instance, the id which forced the ego to indulge in fantasy-making and the superego which orders that this activity should be suppressed. I hope that it will prove acceptable if I propose to call this new theory essentially structural. [Balint, 1969, p. 430]

According to Balint, trauma requires at least two persons, both in the internal and in the external worlds.

This begins with the mother. Possibly, Balint has brought to light a situational concept of capital importance: that of "misfit" between mother and baby, leading to the "misunderstanding" between them and to an undoubtedly traumatic situation (now, no longer paradigmatic, but particular to this mother and this child). No one would object to our searching in the parents' histories and those of their families for the origin of this "misfit". We might even think that some people are born "misfitted" through nobody's fault.

But in any case, the trauma always involves the closest persons: "Psychoanalytic experience invariably showed that there existed a close and intimate relationship between the child and the person who inflicted the trauma upon him" (p. 31). Even the very early experiences that lead to an alteration in the ego "in essence are also traumas, and should be considered as events in an object relationship, albeit in a primitive one" (p. 433). Balint maintains that in many cases and aside from his general lack of "fit", the individual in his infantile state of weakness and immaturity cannot find help in the adults around him in order to face traumatic situations and, in his desperation, has to call upon any means he can, be they his own or provided by an adult, to get out of these straits. These means are incorporated into his ego structure itself, disturb his development, and constitute the "basic fault" that is the initial model for resolving any type of ulterior traumatic situation, no matter how inadequate and inefficient it may demonstrate it is.

Thus, the "basic fault" constitutes a point of fixation which will have to be resolved in order to allow the subject to discover new ways of facing his difficulties and to attain "genital love".

On a line that is akin to Balint's thinking, Masud Khan has formulated his theory of the "cumulative trauma" which, in addition to its undoubted clinical value, seems to us to be especially illustrative of a certain type of development of the concept of trauma in psychoanalytic thought.

Khan takes as his departure point that "The whole new emphasis on infant–mother relationship, [has] changed our very frame of reference for the discussion of the nature and role of trauma" (1963, p. 44). "Cumulative trauma thus derives from the strains and stresses that an infant–child experiences in the context of his ego-dependence on the mother as his protective shield and auxiliary ego" (p. 46). "These breaches over the course of time and through the developmental process cumulate silently and invisibly" (p. 47). They are neither observable nor identifiable as traumas at the moment when they are produced, and, "They achieve the value of trauma only cumulatively and in retrospect". These concepts of Khan are based in part on ideas of Winnicott, especially the idea of the breakdown or deficiency of the mother's function of administering and regulating external and internal stimuli, arriving at a situation of "impingement" which has a disruptive effect on the ego's organization and integration.

What is most striking in Khan's conception is the shift of the concept of barrier against stimuli, originally an economic concept impregnated with biological connotations, to a relational field, since the protective barrier is situated outside the organism or individual considered.

It was natural that the richness of *Inhibitions, Symptoms and Anxiety* should lead, after Freud, to the development of divergent lines of investigation. It is possible to achieve, at this time, a synthetic formulation that includes these multiple aspects? This is the attempt of Leo Rangell (1967).

We agree with Rangell when he maintains that the concept of trauma is complex and that the trauma always appears as a sequence. We consider it indispensable to differentiate, as does Rangell, the elements that make up the sequence that we call "trauma":

1.   the *traumatic event*, which does not become so (or may remain innocuous) if the other elements of the sequence do not occur;

2.   the *intrapsychic traumatic process*, which we consider poses a problem to which we will return right away;

3.   the *traumatic effect or result*: that is, a state of psychic "helplessness" of sufficient magnitude;

4.   the *painful and unpleasurable affect* (we would feel tempted to say: the anxiety) that accompanies and follows the traumatic sequence.

As for part two of the traumatic sequence, we consider it necessary to remark that Rangell's definition simultaneously includes two theories that might seem either alternative or complementary:

> The dynamics of the traumatic intrapsychic process which ensue lead to the rupture, partial or complete, of the ego's barrier or defensive capacities against stimuli, without a corresponding subsequent ability of the ego to adequately repair the damage in sufficient time to maintain mastery and a state of security. [Rangell, 1967, p. 80]

It seems to us that, on this point, Rangell tends to equate the economic concept of "barrier against stimuli" with the structural concept of "defensive ego capacities"—or at least considers that both concepts are on the same continuum. We by no means think that this problem has escaped Rangell's perspicacity, but that he was sensitive to the theoretical need to maintain, with a limit-concept, the anchorage of the concept of trauma to the economic rupture of a system. At the same time, his concept of "vulnerability to traumas" seems to us a very valuable clinical indicator for the differentiation between what is truly traumatic and what is simply pathogenic.

Referring the trauma to the object—we know that there is no traumatic situation without object, by definition—be they internal objects as in Klein or external objects as in Balint, Winnicott, Khan—broadens our understanding of the trauma's pathogenic role, but inversely tends to fade our concept of trauma. Rangell's synthesis invites us to preserve the concept's specificity: beyond the vicissitudes of the object relation, we must maintain a limit-concept of the economic trauma in pure state. In this perspective, the anxiety-provoking object, because of its absence, its internal or external presence, its hyper-presence, always appears subjectively as the possibility of ascribing the trauma to someone who failed to do what should have been done or did what shouldn't have been done. Let us give thanks to objects for their most primitive function of preserving us from pure trauma.

Anxiety and trauma: the "pure trauma"

All the studies that have been directed at situating the trauma within the framework of the object relation have contributed to widening our knowledge of many traumatic situations, but they all have the tendency to eliminate the specificity of the traumatic situation, equating it with all kinds of pathogenic situations. Thus, they run the risk of obliterating the relation between the traumatic situation and anxiety that is so frequently emphasized by Freud in *Inhibitions, Symptoms and Anxiety*. In our opinion, anxiety is the touchstone that allows us to differentiate what is traumatic from the merely pathogenic situation.

Freud postulated the existence of two very different kinds of anxiety: automatic anxiety, characterized by the flooding of the psychic apparatus by unmanageable quantities of excitation which provokes a state of psychic disorganization; and anxiety as signal, employed by the ego for the purpose of impeding the irruption of the former and of building up more or less adequate defensive symptoms in which anxiety has its place, but is limited, tamed, and integrated into the subject's life.

Klein's anxiety theory, with its two fundamental variants, paranoid anxiety and depressive anxiety, to which we must add the confusional anxieties and the anxieties of disintegration, conceives of anxiety as one of the vicissitudes of the object relation; but within the Kleinian orientation, some authors feel the need to admit the existence of anxiety beyond the object (for example, "nameless" anxiety). The forms of anxiety described by Klein have a previous history, though more rudimentary, of splitting, projection, defence, and so forth centred on the first object relation with the mother and the breast. In this sense, the universe of Klein may be called "optimistic" since, after all, it is preferable to have a relatively localized persecutor against which the subject may take protective measures than to be at the mercy of nameless, placeless dangers whose nature remains unknown.

All forms of psychopathology as well as the "normal" techniques of control are directed at avoiding the appearance of anxiety in this extreme form which is so primitive that we can only describe it in economic terms: rupture of the barrier, flooding by unmanageable quantities, complete helplessness. This form of "automatic" anxiety could be characterized as the initial trauma, the pure trauma, meaningless, totally disruptive. The first thing our analysands try to do is establish a system of names aimed at containing, regulating, localizing this unspeakable danger: "I'm afraid of rats", "exams frighten me", "the functioning of my heart worries me", "I spend the whole day washing my hands", and so forth.

The first task of analytic work aims at undoing the names that help to defend the subject so badly against the occurrence of the pure trauma, and at questioning the histories that justify it so poorly. We attempt to tame the trauma; as far as possible, to avoid, prevent, channel what might come up as a pure trauma. The most available solution for civilized man is to give it a name, try to situate it within a conceptual framework (or one of words) which will place limits on it in some way. We demand more of the trauma, such as we simple human beings know it, than this limiting nomination. We demand some explanation. This is where psychoanalysis is produced, as a scientific attempt to give conceptual and verbal form to what appeared to be neither assimilable nor understandable, but pregnant with pathologic effects.

We demand that this trauma not be "pure"—purely economic— but, instead, a trauma that is inserted in a human history which, though it may be absurd, is at least a history. From this angle, which we do not consider the only one possible nor the only one we use, the analytic process necessarily implies historicization. The brute event (accident, massacre, war, holocaust), in its effects on the individual who is our patient cannot have meaning if it remains incidental and foreign. Faced with this ill luck, the individual reacts with pure repetition (the compulsion to repeat), and the analytic process allows him to go from repetition to historicization (Lacan, 1973).

Psychoanalysis establishes itself against the pure trauma. This does not mean that historicization is an arbitrary process. As analysts, we cannot propose to anyone any history that is not his own. If at some point we try to substitute the "authentic" (that is, what is remembered beyond screen memories, what is reconstituted beyond what the subject can remember by analytic work) for a piece of our own mind that is not adopted by the analysand with complete conviction, we are closing the process and inviting the subject to substitute a delusional conviction ("my heart may fail at any moment") with an insufficient history ("incestuous masturbatory activities cause lasting damage to the heart", Dad used to say).

We cannot function with the concept of a definitive history. We all know that analysands come with one history (sometimes remarkably poor) and "end" with a different, much richer history, with much subtler figures, moments of happiness and unhappiness, parents who are "good" and "bad" depending on moments and situations. The history we are left with can never be considered as an absolute term, as the "truth" substituted for the lie. This endlessness of the historicization process is what finally makes the analysis "interminable". We could even think that analysts provided with more sophisticated concepts might (decades after our death and possessing the relevant documents) reveal to us the ante-penultimate word in our history.

We can think of the subject of the "pure trauma" as a subject without history. There are subjects with a history, but a history with a huge hole in it, who can teach us something about this: they suffer from "actual neuroses". Others, it seems, totally lack history, and their lives have gone by without obstacles or notable events, either in their anamneses or in their memories of the people who cared–uncared for them during their infancy and childhood: such are many cases of schizophrenia.

The concept of "actual neurosis" that Freud held on to until the end of his work, long after he had left behind the first concept of "libidinal stasis", might appear after 1926 as if it were an archaeological artefact within the theoretical edifice of psychoanalysis. One of us was even able to see it this way. However, when examining it in the light of the concept of trauma, Freud's persistence seems much wiser: the actual neurosis has something in common with the pure trauma, in that it has no meaning. If it is a psychoneurosis, we will be able to act as analysts, we have things to discover, repressions to lift, memories to remove from forgetfulness. But there is a limit: the meaninglessness of a pure force that is not exerted. Freud was doubtless right in declaring that, in the last analysis, all neuroses are traumatic neuroses. Building on this affirmation: the psychoneuroses are traumas with history. The actual neuroses are traumas that have not been historicized or, more precisely: blank areas not historicized nor easily historicizable in subjects whose individual history, however, is fairly substantial. What is "actual" of the neurosis is not biological, but is the impenetrable wall within the subject that opposes the historicization of some sectors of his existence. It is what may remain in him, present and unintegrable, of the pure trauma.

The histories that appear at the beginning of an analytic treatment may abound in "traumatic" events or may be very poor. Often, this poverty only reveals the flaw in the process of historicization—that is, of construction of the traumatic events. In this case, we find ourselves before patients who are closer to the "pure trauma", without history, and the work of temporal restitution that awaits us is more arduous and subject to chance.

Trauma and the death instinct

In *Beyond the Pleasure Principle* (Freud, 1920g), the articulation between the concept of trauma and that of the death instinct is raised. We think that the problem of the trauma turns upon three points: the death instinct; aetiology, and the *a posteriori*; repetition and temporality. Seen through the death instinct, it can be described as a thanatic invasion; through the *a posteriori* of the analytic process, it appears to us as a construction; through repetition and temporality we see it as an attempt to overcome the former and open up the latter.

Thus, we have disorganizing, invading, and paralysing traumas and, at the opposite end of the spectrum, traumas constructed in an open temporal historicization. In the middle, we find more or less failed attempts to bind the thanatic invasion with repetition. We do know that Freud arrived at his formulation of the hypothesis of the death instinct especially because of repetitive phenomena, understandable when we consider the proximity between these phenomena and this instinct. But repetition itself is not the death instinct but is instead the first attempt to master it.

Both psychoanalytic accidentology and the study of traumatophilia—particularly in the form of sexual compulsion—evidence the predominance of repetition as the most elementary attempt to bind the death instinct and prevent it from reaching annihilation.

The psychoanalytic study of "having accidents" by Julio Granel (1987) on the subjective and unconscious processes that precede, accompany, and follow the accident shows that, in many cases, the situation preceding the accident is characterized by an unbearable state of internal tension that cannot be worked over in the form of a representation. The potential and unsolvable drama of the internal world is replaced by a real drama (accident) that can at least be localized. Having an accident is an attempt to "give form to the unformable". For this reason, it often paradoxically leads to momentary relief for the accident victim. We can admit without any doubt that the propensity to have accidents responds to an attempt to bind the death instinct. The active search for sexual traumas, studied by Phyllis Greenacre (1953) in several papers, especially on pre-pubertal girls, although the author does not associate it with the death instinct, could lead us to similar considerations; the search for the external trauma lies at the end of a traumatic series whose first links must be reconstructed if the compulsion to repeat them actively is to be remedied. Accepting the hypothesis of the death instinct, it can be understood that sexual traumatophilia may aim at expelling and binding excesses of unbearable thanatic tension.

The traumatic series that analysands' initial accounts often contain—Freud's first hysterics offer us a good example of this—are a first attempt to historicize, a mixture of real and mythical events, but basically a false historicization, not so much because of its fantasy elements but because of the enclosure its circular temporality produces. It is something like a "stuttered history". In contrast, analytic historicization, operating by a retroactive movement, tends to replace this false history with a truer one and, at the same time, to re-open temporality while future, present, and past dimensions interact dialectically.

The traumas of the initial account act as the beginning of a new traumatic series, not only because new traumas are discovered or, rather, constructed, but because the traumas that effectively correspond to real events change their meaning and their reciprocal location. What differentiates repetitive traumatophilia from analytic historicization is a change in the concept and in the way of experiencing temporality. Midway between the memory of a traumatic event and the trauma constructed in the analytic process, we find an attempt to assimilate and overcome the trauma, which largely fails in its aim to bind, and which we call the screen memory.

The screen memory, as it appears in the analytic process, is found to be a link in the historicization during which the traumas are constituted. An analysand relates the following: he sees himself at the age of 5, in a corridor behind his mother's consulting room, watching her embracing a man, and he "feels relieved" when he sees that the man is his father. This innocent memory, clearly alluding to the traumatic primal scene, allows a whole aspect of the patient's history to surface: his surreptitious observation of the examinations that were done in the consulting room, the mother's infidelities and the ensuing family fights, the importance of the visual component in the patient's infantile and adult sexuality, and, in particular, the silence that governed his entire infantile history before the elucidation of the screen memory. The memory reveals and screens a series of traumatic situations, beginning with his observation of his parents' intercourse and arriving at the discovery of his mother's infidelity.

A psychic "trauma" begins to exist in a psychoanalysis when it is *recognized* as such, either by the analysand or by the analyst. It acquires full status when both realize that this, which before was unnamed, undated, unexplained, played a determinant aetiological part in a series of events and ulterior disturbances. The Freudian theory of the trauma "at two times" remains the crux of our concept of the trauma, both in the presentation of a case and also in its reconstruction, undertaken with the analysand. The trauma is inseparable from the historicization process. If we think of "remembering, repeating, working through", the formula Freud gave for what may happen in an analytic process, we consider that only transferential repetition, once overcome, can lead to the memory (or reconstruction, as in the "Wolf Man") of what is traumatic and to its eventual working-through.

The entire analysis is a *nachträglich* process that stumbles upon unassimilable residues. These residues are the limits that Freud places on the analytic process as therapy in "Analysis Terminable and Interminable".

All that we have discussed on screen memories, sexual traumatophilia, accidentophilia, and so forth can guide us towards the articulation of the specific *Nachträglichkeit* of the analytic procedure with these unassimilable residues. *Analysis could be defined as historicization [Nachträglichkeit] versus death instinct. Nachträglichkeit* is the attempt to constitute the trauma as such within a new historicization—that is, to make it comprehensible. In the two times of the trauma, the first time remains latent until the second time binds it and makes it appear as trauma.

The first time of the trauma (we could say pre-traumatic) acquires its aetiological value from the second time through its reactivation by an event, perhaps trivial but nevertheless datable and nameable, and through the *analytic historicization* that links together the two times. The first time of the trauma remains mute until *Nachträglichkeit* allows it to speak and to become trauma. The mute "pre-traumatic" time of the trauma is as unassimilable, unrepresentable, unnameable, as is the death instinct itself.

The pathogenic effects of the traumatic situation, that is, the symptoms it engenders, are none other than failed attempts to bind by drawing speech from the part of the death instinct that has not been—and never will be—able to become a coherent discourse. The attempt to bind the death instinct by enclosing it *a posteriori* within the construction of an infantile psychic trauma is never totally successful: the essence of the death instinct always escapes traumatic construction. Thus, the measure of the success of this construction confirms Freud's idea, in "Analysis Terminable and

Interminable", that the proportion of traumatic element, when relatively greater, determines a more favourable prognosis for the psychoanalytic treatment.

Progress in analytic theory and technique must be situated at the frontiers of psychoanalysis, in the difficulties that may seem impossible to overcome in order to go farther in the psychoanalytic process (stubborn resistances, impasse, negative therapeutic reaction, etc.) The frontier is not precisely defined, being a large "no-man's land", open both to eventual progress in analysis as well as to spectacular failures. It is a risk zone where the *Unheimlich* reigns, where the dangers have no name, where the analyst cannot go forward without anxiety about his own action—we could say: the zone of the unborn trauma (unborn for both the analyst and his analysand). On reaching this zone, the analyst may be led either to arresting his progress and favouring the transformation of the process into a repetitive circular movement (eternalization of the analysis) or to avoiding the zone of the unknown by hurriedly resorting to other therapeutic techniques of various kinds. The former solution means renouncing the historicizing process of the constitution of the trauma only to use a cruder form of binding danger by repetition. The latter solves the problem with flight.

What we have referred to as the Freud–Ferenczi "catastrophe theory" highlights an intrinsic vocation of psychoanalysis for the trauma theory. Humanity's fate, both in the individual and in human culture, requires the historicization of its traumas if we are to drive back the ever-present unnameable.

The myth of original sin, so absurd and unassimilable in a rationalist *Weltanschauung*, only reveals this truth: we are born sexed and mortal. Our traumatic history helps us to lend detail to this common condition and to order it in such a way as to give some meaning to the "sins" committed—by others against us, by us against others.

Summary

In the works of Freud, the concept of childhood psychic trauma evolves in the direction of increasing complexity. The authors maintain that this expansion corresponds to a new conception of retroactive temporality [*Nachträglichkeit*], which is precisely the one we use in the analytic process of reconstruction and historicization from the present towards the past. We are thus led to differentiate the extreme form of the unassimilable "pure" trauma, nearly pure death drive, from the retroactively historicized forms that are re-integrated into the continuity of a vital flow of time that we "invent" in analytic work.

7

Contradictions between theory and technique in psychoanalysis

Willy Baranger

This paper is a development of a draft version that arose from a long-standing exchange of ideas bringing together four people: Madeleine Baranger, Alberto Campo, Jorge Mom, and myself. The other three persons whom I have just mentioned could well have been the co-authors of this text; they allowed me, however, to add my own developments to our initial draft. As a result, certain conclusions that I have drawn may not be shared by all four of us. Their contribution not only to the overall discussion but also to many points of detail is nonetheless a significant one, and I am grateful to them for it.

My intention here is not to introduce new concepts into psychoanalytic theory but to bring about a closer degree of harmony between those that are already accepted. As with Freud's own work, the theoretical aspect of psychoanalysis has, since his death, developed along many divergent lines, and psychoanalytic technique too has evolved to a considerable extent. This twofold trend has given rise

---

Published in Spanish in W. Baranger & M. Baranger, *Problemas del campo psicoanalitico* (Buenos Aires: Ed Kargieman, 1969). Published in French as "Contradiction entre la théorie et la technique en psychanalyse" (*Topique revue Freudienne, 3,* 1970).

to contradictions between theory and technique that are more and more pronounced, as well as to a great deal of confusion as to certain theoretical concepts. One has only to attend an international congress to realize that, although we use the same words, we do not speak the same language: we do, indeed, find ourselves in a Tower of Babel.

In 1950, Michael Balint defined very clearly what is, in my view, the fundamental reason behind such a situation: "We have only some vague ideas but no exact knowledge about what distortions happen and how much we miss while describing Two-Body experiences (analytic technique) in a language belonging to One-Body situations" (Balint, 1950, p. 124). As is well-known, there are other reasons—however *un*reasonable they may be—for this phenomenon. The reason that Balint proposes is conceptual in its outlook, and in my view the situation can be remedied more easily if we try to reach a "more exact" knowledge of these distortions and omissions.

I shall therefore attempt to define some of the basic concepts that underlie our technique and to show the influence that they have on our theoretical *corpus*; in this way, it will be possible to define several kinds of psychoanalytic theory the methodological values of which are different. Comparing theory and technique in this way will enable us to put to one side certain—outmoded—concepts of "classical" theory and to indicate what, to my way of thinking, would appear to be more productive approaches for future analytic research.

I. The concepts that govern psychoanalytic technique

In describing to an "impartial person" what takes place between analyst and analysand, Freud (1926e, p. 187) wrote: "Nothing takes place between them except that they talk to each other. . . . The analyst agrees upon a fixed regular hour with the patient, gets him to talk, listens to him, talks to him in his turn and gets him to listen." That was how Freud defined the very essence of psychoanalysis: two people talking to each other. Henceforth, the foundations were laid for a new kind of psychology. In a paper that does not seem to have been read as widely as it deserves, John Rickman (1951, p.

151) defines that new psychology as follows: "The example of two-body psychology which has proved of outstanding utility in both theory and practice is the psycho-analyst and his patient in the analytic transference situation." Although a two-body psychology, it is a three-person situation, because the third party is always present: with the arrival of the oedipal dimension, the third party makes a significant appearance, absent physically but present as a person.

As Freud (1905d, p. 226) quite correctly emphasized, "the Oedipus complex is the nuclear concept of the neuroses" (and of "normal" development). It follows, therefore, that the analytic situation, from the analysand's point of view, brings together the following protagonists: the analysand and/or one of his or her various facets; the analyst experienced as a specific function, as a real person or as a carrier for the analysand's many projections or "depositations"[1]; and one or other of the figures that inhabit the analysand's internal world. The fantasy triangle is always present (except in very regressive situations in which two-body reality momentarily corresponds to the fantasy relationship between a subject and an object experienced as a part-object—the contemplation of an idealized object, for example, in a way that wipes out not only persecutors but also the whole world).

If we take these elements of the analytic situation as being self-evident, we cannot ascribe the same value to concepts such as transference, countertransference, psychoanalytic process, analytic situation, Oedipus complex, etc—which quite obviously imply a relationship between two (or more) people—as we would do to others that isolate the analysand as an *object of study* (the entomological point of view, which is shared by classical psychiatry and so-called objective psychology).

When Freud discovered the transference, that was the first step towards the foundation for a bipersonal psychology, simply because he realized that his analysands saw him as part of certain configurations and attributed to him meanings that had to do with their own internal world. Involving the analyst in this way is already a far cry from the role of observer that was his or hers in classical psychology and psychiatry. Analysts are both observers and protagonists in the same situation. Indeed, they are protagonists in two ways: first, by reason of their function of understanding and interpreting, and second, because the analyst becomes the depository of significant figures in the analysand's life, a function that the analyst agrees to take on.

The second step was Freud's discovery of the countertransference. Projection—or, as Melanie Klein was later to put it, projective identification—was no longer thought of as being a one-way process, since the analysand becomes (with, of course, some obvious differences between one direction and the other) the depository of the analyst's projections. A complex structural pattern is thus built up that contains at least two different levels: on the one hand, an asymmetrical therapeutic relationship and, on the other, a transference/countertransference relationship that also is asymmetrical.

The former involves a relatively inflexible setting (place, time, money, the reciprocal functions of analyst and analysand). The latter has, at any given moment, a form or gestalt that is both specific and changing (father–son, persecutor–persecuted, etc.). Together, these two structures form what we could call a bipersonal or intersubjective field.

I am making use here of a concept of the countertransference that is much wider in scope than that generally accepted (Racker, 1960). When first discovered, the countertransference was thought of as parasitizing the analytic situation, and it is still considered to be an obstacle to the psychoanalytic process. In many people's minds, the word "countertransference" implies a pathological response on the analyst's part and, as such, something that ought to be eliminated. In my view, that way of looking at the situation is indefensible. I am not denying the existence or the relatively frequent occurrence of undoubtedly pathological kinds of countertransference, but the label "neurotic response on the analyst's part" tends to make us lose sight of the sheer wealth of reactions (conscious fantasies, feelings, coenaesthetic perceptions, gestures, thoughts, etc.) that are evoked normally and constantly in the analyst in the analytic situation with the analysand. Just as Freud taught us not to overrate the difference between "normal" and what belongs into the neurotic sphere, I would argue that we should include in the term "countertransference" the whole of the analyst's response to the analysand—conscious and unconscious, normal and pathological—at each moment in the analytic process. In this sense, the countertransference is the exact counterpart of the transference and just as worthy of the analyst's study and close attention as is the transference itself.

To summarize: what we call countertransference is the bipersonal domain considered from the analyst's point of view when he or she is included within it. Given its bipersonal nature, that domain is the unique, shared, and intrinsic structure from which the transference or countertransference can be abstracted.

Psychoanalytic observation implies that the analyst can stand back from the situation in which he or she is participating in order to maintain the continuity of the interpretative function and the capacity to understand, in a non-arbitrary fashion, what is taking place within that process. Analysts are therefore both subjects and, for themselves, objects; that is also the case for analysands (for themselves), as long as they do not become completely embroiled in the analytic situation but can gradually come to share their analyst's capacity for observation and understanding (insight).

This is a curious situation, of course, in which the analysand, who is supposed to be an object of knowledge, becomes in fact a subject aiming to gain knowledge, and in which the analyst lets him or herself be included to some extent (i.e., becoming no more than an object) before again being a subject aiming to gain knowledge.

The two situations are certainly not identical: the analyst is in overall control of the context. First of all, it is the analyst who defines the rules and, theoretically at least, whose initial understanding is swifter, although (and this is to their credit) analysts may be able to gain a new understanding from what their analysands have to say. The analyst's words are "truthful", which is what Jacques Lacan quite rightly saw as the essential feature of the psychoanalytic act. The asymmetrical nature of the situation has no *a priori* implications as to the analyst's "mental normality". We all know that, with some exceptions, analysands want to see in their analyst a model of "normality" (or, in some cases, of "brilliant thinking"). Analysts may have to deal with more severe conflict situations than their analysands yet may still be able to say the "words of truth" that will help the latter to understand themselves better.

In any case, the psychoanalytic relationship is one between two subjects, both of whom are trying to understand and to put into words a situation in which they are both involved, albeit differently, as objects.

Consequently, the specific object of study for psychoanalysis is the intersubjective domain of language in the analytic situation.

This is so because what brings about movement in this intersubjective domain produced by the setting that the analyst imposes and by the spontaneous emergence of the transference and countertransference within it is the analyst's interpretation. It is through interpretation that the static field becomes an intelligible process (or at least attempts to become so) and that repetition gives way to working through [*Durcharbeitung*]. Interpretations do much more than simply reflect or give expression to the analytic field: to a considerable extent they contribute to its construction and orientation (that is why attempts to reduce psychoanalysis to an objective psychology are fundamentally flawed). The analytic process is the strict modification of the intersubjective domain by means of words.

II. Some contradictions between theory and technique

In spite of the fact that, ever since Freud invented it, the technique of psychoanalysis has taken the form of a dialogue, most of the concepts that constitute the theoretical *corpus* of psychoanalysis are formulated in one-person terms. That translation from one level to another gives rise to a major methodological misunderstanding and brings several difficulties in its wake.

It could perhaps be said that every scientific observation requires an observer (preferably replaced by an apparatus designed to record phenomena and to reduce to a minimum the observer's sensory participation) and a phenomenon to be observed. In physics, the observer works out a theory and tests it against facts (which also are highly sophisticated) so as either to confirm the truth of it or to prove it wrong. That observer does not enter into any kind of discussion with the phenomenon. Strictly speaking, in objective psychology also, the observer does not enter into a discussion with the object of the observation. Even if the procedure employed is a test, a questionnaire, or a clinical examination aimed at reaching a diagnosis—all of these procedures imply verbal exchanges—the observer's attitude is deliberately objectivizing.

The person being observed is temporally transformed into an object of observation, and his or her behaviour is thought of as being made up of specific items. Clearly, in such a case, expressing what is observed in one-person terms may be justified.

That is not the case in psychoanalysis, however, because the technique of analysis requires not only the analysand's active collaboration (the term "patient" is particularly inapposite, because the analysand plays an essentially "active" role) but also some degree of assent as regards what is being unveiled by the work of the analysis: what we call insight. The analyst's indispensable neutrality, which some think can be carried to the point of complete "asepsis", comparing the analytic situation with that of a laboratory, could be defined as fundamentally "septic". Every time that analysts choose the timing, content, and verbal style of their interpretations, they bring into the situation not only their "scientific" knowledge, terms of reference, understanding of the analysand, and the communication code that the two protagonists have set up between them, but also their voice, with its inflections, their own particular style and, through all of this combined, something that has to do with what they feel at that particular moment. It would be of no avail were all interpretations to be systematically formulated in an unchanging tone of voice (a kind of absurdity that is not entirely imaginary), because that would imply an attempt to dehumanize a situation that is *par excellence* human. Whether they like it or not, analysts are present as human beings as they carry out their work as analysts.

In addition, as Jacques Lacan (1953) has pointed out, the analyst takes charge of the direction of the process that is set in motion, first through the simple fact of imposing a specific setting that enables him or her to work in the best possible way (although there exists a set of general principles, more or less strict, concerning how the setting should be established, each analyst has personal variations on that general pattern that depend on his or her conceptions and personality, as well as on the personality of the analysand), and, second, through the interpretations made to the analysand. My basis for saying this is that, in my view, the analyst's specific aim is to establish and maintain a setting that enables him or her to fulfil the crucial function of interpreting what transpires within that setting.

Even though on that basis the analysand's self-knowledge and potentiality for change increase—the word "cure" is a misnomer—that does not justify expressing phenomena that are specific to the analytic process and situation in terms of a one-person psychology. What in physics or objective psychology is crucial if an item of knowledge is to be classified as "scientific"—that is, proved—becomes in psychoanalysis a kind of pseudo-science: in other words, it is anti-scientific.

That is where the misunderstanding lies—or at least the confusion that reigns whenever we, as analysts, use the word "science". Since we are convinced that we do possess a reliable and productive means of investigation for new knowledge and future discoveries, we call scientific our wish to acquire knowledge that has nothing arbitrary about it. That in itself is legitimate.

There is, nonetheless, one problem that springs immediately to mind: is this new science of the same nature as academic psychology (I mean by that the sectors of psychology that are truly scientific) or as the biological sciences? Or the sociological ones?

Is our science in a position to take on board useful contributions from ideological schools of thought such as phenomenology, structuralism, and so on?

The progenitors of psychoanalysis, in unequal proportions, were: Anna O, who taught Breuer about the talking cure, Breuer himself, who was quick-witted enough to realize the fact (even though his understanding of it was interrupted halfway through), and Freud, who alone had the intellectual audacity to draw theoretical conclusions from it. In so doing, Freud created a new kind of human science, fundamentally different from biology and academic psychology.

That is something that few analysts really understand when they create theoretical premises. Quite the contrary, indeed—the search for continuity between psychoanalysis and other forms of science appears to be much more reassuring. Since most analysts were initially trained in the biological sciences (medicine), there is a powerful temptation to look for some continuity with that branch of science (Freud himself, indeed, did not always avoid falling into that trap, hence the many contradictory aspects we find in his work).

That deeply entrenched search for continuity between psychoanalysis and biology coexists paradoxically with the sometimes frenzied application of psychoanalytic interpretations to phenomena that neither lie within our domain nor correspond to our method of study (cf. the attempt to formulate in biological or even physical terms—entropy—the concept of the death drive, or, conversely, psychoanalytic interpretations of war, the class struggle, etc.).

Although it is true to say that psychoanalysis is *open* to all that has to do with human beings (not only someone who feels ill in his or her body, but also society in general with its ideologies, policies, madness, and reason), it cannot claim to *include* everything that is human. A critical study of Freud's paper "The Claims of Psycho-Analysis to Scientific Interest" (1913j) would show that psychoanalysis can be useful or even essential in a number of disciplines that take humankind as its object, but it cannot replace these. The reader will not have failed to notice that a more wide-ranging problem is involved here: that of the more or less "experimental" human sciences as opposed to those that have more to do with interpretation. Contrary to what Henry Ezriel (1951) explicitly claims—and his point of view is upheld implicitly by most psychoanalysts—psychoanalysis is one of the latter.

I would not wish to conceal the difficulty that lies in determining whether and how the psychoanalytic interpretation of a given human phenomenon is correct or not, as well as to what extent it defines and explains that phenomenon. To argue that "war stems from the death drive" is perhaps true, but the level of abstraction involved in that kind of claim is such that, in the end, it explains nothing at all. To argue that the Oedipus complex includes not only one aspect of what every analyst sees and understands in his or her everyday practice but also something of a mythical experience that transcends individuals is another kind of claim and of truth.

I do not believe that, in choosing a name for one of his fundamental discoveries (the Oedipus complex), Freud happened quite by chance on that of one of the heroes of Greek mythology. The mythical—or, more generally, the ideological—dimension is an integral part of human beings. The linguistic universe in which psychoanalysis exists is also a universe of myth, ideology, the true or distorted awareness we have of ourselves, of other people, of the world of human beings, and of what the future holds in store.

In my opinion, no human science can endeavour to be purely objective without deliberately mutilating itself—it does not simply record a past or present event, it attempts to understand a given situation and its prognosis (its future outcome). The most obvious example is that of pre-election opinion polls. Even in the absence of any deliberate falsification, publishing the results of these polls cannot but influence the electorate. In the same way, the science of history, however objective it endeavours to be, involves some kind of perspective on the future of the society being studied. That is why every political tendency has historians who understand and assess the past history of a given country—or of the world—in terms of the aims to which they aspire or of their vision of a "better" society. To the extent that history goes beyond the simple recollection of facts and attempts to understand and interpret them, it presupposes a whole range of possible goals, each of which can be reached by means of a specific political approach. I am not saying that historians systematically falsify their interpretation of facts to make them correspond to their political intentions (though that may, of course, happen), but that understanding the past and conceiving of possible perspectives based on that understanding are both part of the same dialectic process.

What is true of history is true also of psychoanalysis.

The absolute *hic et nunc* standpoint that seeks to ignore *ab initio* the historical background of the individual in analysis seems to me to be wrong in principle. It is quite true that what comes to be interpreted first and foremost is the unconscious phenomena that appear in the here and now of the psychoanalytic situation; but such an interpretation would come to an abrupt end if it did not both enable the analysand to get back in touch with his or her past and open up new perspectives for the future. "I was like that, and I still am, but I can be different (better, freer from pain)". Not just any "difference" chosen arbitrarily, but one that belongs to the possible paths that are still open.

Each time we formulate a major interpretation, we assume that the analysand has a capacity for self-understanding and the ability to change thanks to that understanding—in other words, to stand back to some extent from his or her past, integrate it, and modify it thanks to that very act. One's past history is particularly viscous.

Interpretations try to unstick the analysand from his or her past insofar as it continues to weigh on the present, thereby modifying it retroactively.

In so doing, psychoanalysis functions according to the principles of dialectic causality. The first confrontation between theory and technique is between, on the one hand, unilateral determinism (that of science in the nineteenth century) as expressed in the theory of "complemental series" (a particularly fragile theory, given that it is based on something we know very little about: the individual's constitution; we know that it does exist, but what it consists of and its importance remain unknown), and, on the other, a technique of interpretation that directly contradicts that principle of causality and the idea of complemental series, unless we decided to include, in the individual's development, the psychoanalytic process as an additional factor between these "series"—an inherently absurd idea.

This calls into question the appropriateness of the genetic point of view in psychoanalysis—its utilization appears to give rise to many mistaken and confused ideas.

The equivalence that some commentators make between the "genetic point of view" and understanding the historical dimension of the individual human being is an example of the kind of unfortunate conceptual confusion that even Freud did not always manage to avoid—for instance, when he introduced his theory of complemental series. It should be pointed out, however, that Freud never included the genetic point of view in his definition of metapsychology. Others, nevertheless, have done so (David Rapaport, for example). They may well have thought themselves justified in making this "addition" (it is, in fact, a distortion) by Freud's description, with Karl Abraham's additions, of the developmental stages of the libido and of the causal relationship between these as regards the defence mechanisms and the neuroses or psychoses that follow on from them (the causal relationship being inherent in the concept of fixation).

According to Hartmann and Kris (1945, p. 17): "The genetic approach in psychoanalysis does not deal only with anamnestic data, nor does it intend to show only 'how the past is contained in the present'. Genetic propositions describe why, in past situations of conflict, a specific solution was adopted; why the one was retained and the other dropped, and what causal relation exists between these solutions and later developments."

It is clear from that quotation that there is an ontological leap from "anamnestic data" to "the past contained in the present"—on the one hand, history, and, on the other, a relationship of genetic causality between past and present.

Rapaport and Gill go even further down that particular path: in their work on metapsychology (1959), when they examine the genetic point of view and formulate it in a series of basic hypotheses, they define the second of these as follows:

> All psychological phenomena originate in innate givens, which mature according to an epigenetic ground plan. [Rapaport & Gill, 1959, p. 158]

They go on to say:

> This assumption underlies, for example, all the propositions concerning libido development, Hartmann's concerning autonomous ego development, and Erikson's concerning psychosocial epigenesis. It is significant because it amplifies Freud's "'constitutional" factor . . . , and brings into focus the biological–maturational character of psycho-analysis as a science, setting it sharply apart from the learning theories whose emphasis is mainly or solely on experience. [Rapaport & Gill, 1959, p. 159]

The eclecticism of that formulation cannot but startle us. It encompasses points of view and models as varied and as contradictory as Freud's concept of the part played by constitutional factors (apparently forgetting that Freud's entire theory of the neuroses was built up in opposition to the constitutional tenets of the time), Hartmann's theory of the "autonomous ego" (apparently forgetting that Freud consistently stated that human beings were in their entirety involved in their conflicts, so that no autonomous ego could ever exist alongside this), and Erikson's epigenetic theory (which entails a basic plan thanks to which individual human beings—by means of the implicit concept of pre-established harmony—at last find fulfilment and happiness in the American way of life). This conception is a theoretical *hippocampoelephantocamel*. It is unfortunate that it presents itself as an expression of Freud's thinking or as a more rigorous definition of metapsychology. As for "bringing into focus the biological–maturational character of psychoanalysis as a science", that hypothesis directly contradicts the first of Rapaport and Gill's propositions, in which they attempt to define the genetic point of view: "a. All psychological phenomena have a psychological origin and development" (Rapaport & Gill, 1959, p. 161). In addition, one can understand the indignation of biologists when the authors affirm "the biological–maturational character of psychoanalysis as a science". What is meant by that statement? Are we talking about an individual's history? About ontogenesis? Biology? Socially determined epigenesis? Or about some kind of cocktail of all these theories?

Should we say that Freud was somewhat forgetful when he omitted to add the genetic point of view to the other three he described: dynamic, topographical, and economic? Or should we not, rather, say that that omission was due to the fact that, for Freud, the genetic point of view and the theory of complemental series were no more than secondary? Or that he realized that the latter theory fell short of explaining the obvious complexity of the neuroses and, even more, of the psychoanalytic process?

At any rate, putting into the same category the genetic point of view and the study of an individual's past history through analysis is completely untenable. The individual *is* his past history, not *determined by* it. In the psychoanalytic process, the individual creates his past history. Even if the "objective" data reported at the beginning of the analysis are the same as those that appear as the analysis progresses (although in fact we know that this is never the case), the two narratives do not have the same meaning. Genetics implies mechanical causality; history does not. If that were not the case, the psychoanalytic process would be completely incomprehensible.

The very expression "historical–genetic" ought to give rise to astonishment in anyone who is even slightly logically minded—because history has meaning, whereas in psychoanalysis genetics does not.

What, then, are we to think of genetic theories in psychoanalysis? Many analysts are tempted, given their experience of analysing adults or children, to look for new "stages" that would modulate with more nuances the schema—obviously insufficient, even though it was initially highly productive—that Freud (and Abraham) put forward as regards libidinal development. Curiously enough, that schema was never completed by similar descriptions of the evolution of the drives linked to Thanatos.

The research model would thus naturally appear to be that of Freud. He discovered the Oedipus complex thanks to his self-analysis (helped to a considerable extent by his analysands), and he proved its existence through the indirect analysis of Little Hans. Thereafter, everyone feels free to discover new stages of libidinal or of thanatico-libidinal development, whether or not they can be said to belong to the Freud–Abraham model. The further back the stages go, the better—because they are more unverifiable. We could think here of Rank and his trauma of birth, or of Jung with his archetypes.

We could think also of Melanie Klein. When, after a considerable number of years of research during which she reworked her theory, she formulated her idea of the two basic "positions", the paranoid–schizoid one and the depressive one (which do not correspond with the Freud–Abraham model—indeed, at times, Klein's conception directly contradicts it), she introduced a new genetic perspective. As far as I am concerned, Klein's schema is at present extremely valuable for the obvious understanding of the analysand that it offers us. I am not, however, convinced of its validity on the genetic level, even though for the moment that aspect does seem to me to be probable—in spite of the conclusions that René Spitz has reached.

It is, all the same, not very important as far as I am concerned to know that during the first three months of life a baby shows traces of the paranoid–schizoid position or that, during the following three months, he or she gradually enters into the depressive position (the reason being, perhaps, that, as the reader will surely agree, we cannot analyse babies of that age, or that, to my mind, the schema itself is sufficiently enriching, independently of any reference to developmental psychology).

The psychoanalytic project does not entail describing the development of human beings from birth (or even earlier, if we could indeed extrapolate in that way): it has to do with understanding what goes on in our analysands, be they children or adults. In our attempt to carry out that task, the genetic point of view often proves itself to be not a help but a hindrance. Individual developmental psychology abstracted from psychoanalysis is equivalent to the imaginary description of the prehistory of humanity that we find in *Totem and Taboo* (Freud, 1912–13): the main point is not whether that description is objectively true or not, but that it opens up new paths towards a better understanding of the analysand's inner world. Contemporary anthropology seems to dismiss the idea that in the prehistory of humankind there was a general occurrence of assassination and cannibalistic manducation of the father of the primal horde by his sons united against him. What we do know, however, is that this fantasy situation appears concretely in the analysis of every group and, more symbolically, in every individual analysis.

Genetic hypotheses would thus appear to be applications of psychoanalysis, deduced from the historical dimension of the individual—it is that dimension which is fundamental.

As for the economic point of view (which does not even correspond to a model drawn from objective psychology, but to one drawn from mechanics, electricity, and even at times hydraulics), it no longer has any relevance to actual experience and, as a result, ought to be dismissed as an archaism.

If the economic point of view is to be abandoned and if the genetic point of view is to be situated differently (i.e., considered as "applied psychoanalysis"), the dynamic and structural (or, as Freud put it initially, topographical) points of view are perfectly coherent with the intersubjective experience that is psychoanalysis. This is true of the dynamic point of view as long as we remove from it any energetic implications (Freud's original hypothesis, that of psychic energy subject to modifications and equivalences) and maintain its basic idea of mental conflict—that is, Freud's fundamental discovery, which in itself (aside from etymology) does not require to be formulated in terms of forces. Since these "forces" are in reality metaphorical, we could think of them as tendencies, as tensions, or, better, as wishes [*Wünsche*], thereby avoiding the halo of mechanistic meaning evoked by the word "force".

The second (i.e., structural) point of view is indispensable if we are to account for the "division of the psychic personality" and for the manner in which it permeates the interpersonal field. While it is true to say that Freud's second description of the personality (in *The Ego and the Id*: 1923b) is to a considerable extent one-person in nature, the discovery of the structuring role of identification (through introjection) is described in many of Freud's writings from "Mourning and Melancholia" (1917e [1915]) on (and even earlier); that description becomes even more systematic after *The Ego and the Id.* This gives rise to the idea of a complex set of intra-psychic relationships of a personal nature (for example, parental authority opposed to the ego's aspirations).

That is exactly what every one of us can observe in the analytic relationship. At times, the only way we can describe a given situation in the analytic field is by using the words that Freud used. For example: the analyst is experienced as a superego (according to whatever aspect of the "real" object has been introjected), and the analysand feels paralysed in everything he or she does by this; or the analysand "is an id", while the analyst takes on the functions of self-observation and control that the other protagonist has delegated to him or her.

The structural point of view that I am adopting here differs in essence from that of ego psychology. For those who belong to that school of thought, "structure" means an organized set of mental functions (that idea can also be found in Freud's writings: he borrowed it from a now outdated form of academic psychology), whereas, for us, it refers to something particularly innovative and specifically Freudian: the idea of an internal world of inter-personal relationships (initially external, then internalized). The contradiction between these two lines of thought (both of which can be found in Freud's writings, right up to the most recent of them) can be seen in the difficulty that ego psychology encounters in trying to account for the concept of the superego in any coherent way.

The concept of metapsychology that I would advocate has, naturally enough, an effect on a certain number of other concepts that no longer belong to metapsychology as such but to psychoanalytic psychology. Roughly speaking, I would differentiate three levels of theorization: the metapsychological level, the most abstract, which brings together the most general points of view and principles; the psychological level, that of concepts that are less abstract and more directly verifiable through observation; and the phenomenalist point of view, which describes experience itself—not in its "raw" form (which does not exist) but as already interpreted. I am well aware of the fact that the frontiers between these three levels are not clearly defined; the foregoing differentiation is only a relative and provisional one.

For example, those "mythical entities" that cannot for a moment be disregarded (Freud, 1933a, p. 95)—the drives—correspond, with reference to this classification, to the second level of theorization (the psychological level), yet they are closely related to the economic point of view of Freud's first metapsychological description of the mind. Their content does, of course, change in *Beyond the Pleasure Principle* (Freud, 1920g), so that they become much more independent with respect to the economic point of view—but in so doing, their biological (or, rather, metabiological, or even metaphysical) content becomes more important, a feature that Freud, with his customary lucidity, did not fail to notice. It was certainly not fortuitous that, in tracing the origin of this concept, Freud turned to Empedocles.

The "indispensable" characteristic of the concept of drive [*Trieb*] must be looked at in more detail. The topic has been studied quite thoroughly in this particular region of the world, especially in a roundtable discussion about which a report was published in 1963 (Bleger, Liberman, Rascovsky, & Rascovsky, 1963). I would like to emphasize what José Bleger has to say on this topic. As early as 1956, Bleger wrote that Freud, by basing his theory of the dynamics of psychological processes on a mechanistic foundation, took the forces in action out of the context of psychological processes and their interplay and saw them as instincts. It was because Freud conceived of them in that way and, in the last analysis, attributed to them the exclusive mainspring behind behaviour, says Bleger, that the theory of the instincts turned into a "mythology" (Bleger, 1956).

I agree entirely with Bleger's argument here and with those aspects of Politzer's (1966) criticisms that they echo. A little later, Bleger went on to say that forces are involved in object relationships, but not in the shape of autonomous entities; they do not in themselves give rise to or maintain behaviour, nor are they accountable for the interplay between its different aspects. For Bleger, this does not mean that we do not require a dynamic theory of behaviour or that we could do away with the concept of "drive" in psychology, but these have to be taken up in a context different from the one Freud used (Bleger, 1958, p. 201). I agree with him also when he says that the dynamic aspect belongs to the phenomena themselves, without our requiring to have recourse to a preliminary and independently existing agent that produces or explains them (Bleger, 1963, p. 151). He went on to say that he did not deny the existence of the drives, but he did not see them as forces that could exist as entities or agents in themselves.

I would perhaps disagree with Bleger on several relatively minor points as regards his conception of these phenomena, but that is not the issue here.

Faced with the bare bones that were, in his time, psychology and psychopathology, Freud discovered something that was alive and human: a thrust, things milling around, a world replete with unfulfilled wishes, conflicts, and repressed urges; something so primitive that it had much more to do with magic, tragedy, and the world of dreams than with physical or mathematical formulae. Something that was human life.

He expressed that discovery by attributing movement, conflict, thrusting pressure to what he called *Triebe*, the drives; that is why many analysts feel that, were we to abandon the idea of drives, we would lose a fundamental aspect of Freud's discovery and find ourselves back in the system of naive robotics that preceded him.

A comparison between Freud and Janet would make this quite clear: I am thinking here of Janet's concept of "psychasthenia". For Janet, this was due to a lack of "psychic strength", whereas Freud saw in it an intrapsychic conflict. The technical (therapeutic) consequences are considerable—nothing can be done about psychasthenia, whereas conflicts can be worked through. The vitality of psychoanalysis as opposed to Janet's out-of-date concept shows how history settled the issue.

How are we to resist the temptation to attribute to biological or psychological forces the workings of this new world that was discovered through its origins in the past history of the individual? The science of mechanics teaches us that nothing can move unless something sets it in motion. We must therefore find something that keeps conflict alive. The drives would appear to satisfy the necessary conditions for this, but the concept is not without major difficulties and ambiguities—in the first place, the hybrid nature of their very definition as a frontier concept between the psychological and somatic domains (i.e., between the demands of biology and the realm of symbols); second, the theoretical relationship with the schema of the reflex arc, which has nothing to do with psychological phenomena; and, third, the ambiguous relationship with schemata that involve economics or biology (some analysts still theorize in terms of homeostasis!).

What keeps the confusion alive is the fact that Freud described in very concrete and convincing terms the "developmental stages" of the drives (although he did stumble somewhat over certain intrinsic difficulties—see, for example, his theory of narcissism). If developmental stages of the libido do indeed exist, then the concept of the drives is a necessary one. However, I am inclined to think that the enormous harvest of genuine discoveries that Freud made as regards various drive-related structures has in fact very little to do with the concept of the drives as such. When considered separately from their developmental sequence (which is debatable, and indeed the subject of debate among analysts), the developmental stages of the drives appear to be more like extrapolations along the chronological axis of significant patterns that we find in the analysis of human beings. Nobody would doubt that the anal structure exists, or that it implies certain fantasies, defences, and behaviour patterns, or that it has a clearly defined relationship with the obsessional neurosis in its descriptive sense. There is, however, some real doubt about whether it can be, in its essence, reduced to a fixation at a given period of libidinal development, even if we include drives related to Thanatos.

Hunger and love, self-preservative (or ego-preservative) drives, reproductive drives (the libido), Eros and Thanatos—all these entities with their binary opposition were formulated by Freud, when all is said and done, simply to account for psychic conflict. The content of the concept evolved as Freud's ideas themselves developed. New models replaced old ones or were condensed together. References to the reflex arc or to processes of charge and discharge gradually faded into the background, while the concept of the drives was filled up with new connotations (although Freud never explicitly repudiated the earlier ones).

I would argue that, looked at in this way, the drives can be thought of as an auxiliary concept; if we do maintain the concept, however, we must respect some fairly stringent conditions:

1. Avoid reducing or impoverishing—as often happens—the concept of the drives by attributing to them only one set of contents among those that Freud proposed: the tension–discharge
   schema, that of the reflex arc, that of the mental equivalent of
   biological needs (this schema ignores the fact that the need to
   breathe, which is more urgent on a biological level than the
   need for food or to reproduce, has only a very scanty "representation" in the mind). None of these simplifications of Freud's
   concept of the drives is justifiable.

2. Avoid attributing to the concept a causative dimension, that of
   a *primum movens* of mental activity: such a step would bring us
   back to the difficulties enshrined in the theory of the complemental series.

3. Drives must not be thought of independently of the situations
   in which they appear: between human beings or intrapsychic
   (intra-personal).

On a descriptive level, we can quite legitimately say that an analysand "has a significant voyeuristic drive"; there would not be much
more to be gained here if we used a term other than drive, as long
as we keep in mind the conditions I have enumerated.

The truest and deepest meaning of Freud's drive theory could
be stated thus: human beings are made up of conflicts, they are
torn between contradictory desires, threatened with breakdown, always unsatisfied, and have various dramatic scenarios being played
out inside them.

In more abstract terms, we could say: drives cannot be observed
independently of internal or external situations, "real" or imaginary,
and do not exist outside these. They are a relatively inadequate expression of the thrusting, conflict-ridden, and intensely emotional
aspect of mental life. They are inconceivable as such outside a relationship with another person (Lacan) or divorced from their fantasy
content; in its simplest form, we could put it thus: "I want to do
such-and-such a thing with this person, and I want such-and-such a
third party to be in this designated position."

If we differentiate it from certain oversimplified formulations
(which can indeed be found in some of Freud's writings), the concept of the drives can be seen to be intimately related to that of

unconscious fantasy. In my view, the content of the latter concept, which plays a significant part in Freud's writings, changed with Susan Isaacs's 1948 paper in which she summarized Melanie Klein's theory on this subject; unconscious fantasy henceforth found itself at the centre of our knowledge of mental life. Susan Isaacs shortened the distance between Freud's concept of unconscious fantasy and direct psychoanalytic experience. It is no longer simply a "scenario" (as, in their 1967 vocabulary, Laplanche and Pontalis put it in their comments on Freud's view) that underlies symptoms, dreams, jokes, or any other mental activity; it is a matrix that gives structure to certain well-defined human situations and in particular that of the psychoanalytic context. As a result, the analyst's task can be defined as that of understanding and interpreting at all times the unconscious fantasy that structures the analytic situation (without, of course, ignoring references to historical or external situations that, when they emerge, activate some fantasy content or other). This becomes quite clear in the supervision of analysts who are in training (it is also the case in those mutual supervisions that often take place between psychoanalytic colleagues who have reached the same level of experience). The analysand, let us say, begins the session with some verbal "material" that could, in theory, give rise to a hundred or so interpretations. Of these, the analyst chooses one axis that seems to be more significant or more urgent. (This choice implies that the analyst understands what has been happening in the preceding sessions, and the analysand's present and past problem complex; it includes the analyst's technical frame of reference, as well as another kind of communication that we usually—and incorrectly—call "from unconscious to unconscious", whereas it involves the echoes stirred up unconsciously in the analyst by the analysand's communications, verbal or otherwise.)

In addition to the content of the interpretation, which, one would suppose, sheds new light on certain issues, the analysand may deal with it in several ways: accept it authentically and take it on board (this is what we call insight); accept it only superficially while rejecting it without saying so explicitly; consider it to be stupid or wrong and run it down quite openly; or nullify it by saying "Well, I suppose that could be the case, but . . .", and so forth.

Whatever the analysand's response, the first interpretation that the analyst suggests affects the way in which the rest of the session unfolds; other interpretations in the course of the session will have a similar effect. Every interpretation contributes to the construction of the session and to the direction it takes—the same is true of the absence of interpretations (when the analyst remains silent). This implies that it is not the analysand alone who determines the unconscious fantasy of a session; it is a situation that acquires its structure through an ongoing dialogue.

In a successful session, the fantasies that underlie the intersubjective relationship can be verbalized; this brings about change, such that another fantasy can emerge. It is only through the sharing of fantasy, encouraged by the contact and dialogue between the two participants, that it becomes possible to have real access to the analysand's internal world, such that he or she can integrate the ensuing modifications.

I would surmise that a true interpretation of a fantasy that emerges in the analytic relationship coincides with one that already exists in the analysand's internal world, thus enabling it to be accessed and reintegrated into verbal discourse. But what is foremost in that experience is the unconscious fantasy that emerges in the analytic dialogue. It is only thereafter that we can formulate some hypothesis or other that refers to the analysand's internal world. If we follow the manner in which the situation actually develops, we would say that a fantasy is above all something that is constructed within the analytic dialogue; it is on that basis that we infer the existence of certain aspects of the analysand's internal world. If we were to think of an analysand's unconscious fantasy as causing the events that occur in the analytic situation, we would be reversing the whole order of how things actually occur.

The unconscious fantasy that unfolds in the analytic situation could be defined as follows: it is the unconscious structure that is created between analysand and analyst during a session, it defines the direction that the transference/countertransference situation will take, and, if it is correctly interpreted, it allows new patterns to emerge. To my mind, an interpretation is correct if the analysand can take it on board—that is, not simply understand it intellectually but integrate it in an authentic manner.

This "creation" is neither intentional nor arbitrary: it is a structure that arises spontaneously, based on verbal and nonverbal communication. It is for this reason that Michael Balint wrote: "The most important field of investigation for this coming theory must be the analyst's behaviour in the psycho-analytic situation, or, as I prefer to phrase it, the analyst's contribution to the creating and maintaining of the psycho-analytic situation" (Balint, 1950, p. 121). The analyst's training and analytic practice itself mean that the analyst can lend him/herself to the building up of this fantasy about the analytic situation and accomplish the necessary to-and-fro movement that enables an interpretation to be formulated; this does not mean, of course, that this to-and-fro movement cannot at times be cut short or deflected by the analyst's own problems, scotomas, theoretical mistakes, and so on, all of which give rise to the pathological effects of the countertransference.

This concept of unconscious fantasy seems to me to avoid the theoretical difficulties that arise in the usual way of formulating that notion—that is, in one-person terms: the need to "biologize", that is to make it hybrid and obscure, the need to "reify" it, that is, to think of unconscious fantasy as being a thing-in-itself that determines mental life with no reference to the actual person involved. It is true that unconscious fantasies very often express bodily demands, but this is because the individual is present in mind and body in the analytic situation: the demands expressed are not those that concern how the body functions as described in anatomy or physiology: they have to do with the subject-as-body, which is neither the equivalent nor the counterpart of the anatomo-physiological concept of the body. In any case, it is a fantasy body, whatever the analysand's knowledge of anatomy or physiology.

The same could be said of the objects that inhabit the analysand's internal world. They first appear in the intersubjective field, with their disguises and their cohort of unconscious fantasies focused on them. In that sense, they can be seen as reference markers around which the analytic field is built up, just as fantasies are the lines of force that give it structure.

At any given moment, the analyst, in addition to his or her function as such, takes on, for the analysand, a specific meaning—that is, represents one or another aspect of an object belonging to the analysand's network of intrapsychic relationships. Analysts in fact contribute to the construction of that network: first because they go along with such representations—and the way in which they do fall in with them has an important impact on the nature of the objects they are called upon to represent. It is well known that some analysts tend to turn themselves into idealized objects for their analysands (cf. Klein, 1952a, p. 233); by failing to interpret that process, they paralyse the course of the analysis, even though they sometimes obtain quite spectacular results. They may also turn themselves into corrupted accomplices, into doormat-analysts, and so forth.

Thereafter, by removing, via interpretation, the showy clothes in which the objects disguise themselves, by calling them by their real name, by describing them at one or another level, by relating them to some aspect or other of the analysand or to figures from his or her past, the analyst to a significant extent actually constructs these objects. The analysand's internal world of fantasies, relationships, and objects is gradually built up within the analytic field and process; when we speak of a person's internal world, we are extrapolating from (or, in one-person terms, translating) something that was gradually built up during the analysis with the help of the analyst's own personality and theoretical *corpus*.

I do not mean that such a construction is in any way arbitrary. Initially, every analysand brings along certain modalities, mental background, a structure, a past history, and a world of internalized objects. All of this can be inferred, however, only from our own construction, when we mistakenly ignore our own participation as architects of that construction. In other words, Mr Z is not the same person if his analysis is with A or with B. The often-quoted cases of successive analyses of the "same" person with different analysts are clear proof of that. That difference may well lead to the spectacular failure of an analysis or, conversely, to its success. This fact is undoubtedly well known, and it has many major technical implications.

The first of these has to do with the "diagnosis" and "prognosis" of someone who wants to undertake analysis. When commenting on psychiatric diagnoses, Enrique Pichon-Rivière quite rightly used to say: "Some diagnoses are made in ten minutes, others in half-an-hour, or ten hours, or a hundred hours". The same person may end up in a psychiatric hospital, in a state of complete dehumanization brought about (with some honourable exceptions) by the hospitalo-concentration camp environment itself, or pick up the threads of a fairly acceptable life, depending on the treatment carried out. Of course, I am not denying that some people have deteriorated so severely physically or mentally that they will be unable to recover, whatever the treatment offered them.

A psychiatric diagnosis—except in cases where it is part of a meticulous research—aims at situating the patient within vast nosological categories that entail, by that very fact, certain therapeutic indications and the necessity—or otherwise—of confinement in a mental hospital (depending on the danger that the patient is felt to represent to other people, the risk of suicide, etc.). There is a reciprocal conditioning between "what are we to do with" the patient and the nature of the diagnosis reached. A psychiatrist has to make decisions concerning the patient, who is therefore viewed in terms of that duty. Progress in psychiatry comes not from improvements in diagnostic procedures but from an increase (and, in particular, a qualitative increase) in the means of action.

These diagnostic/therapeutic categories have little to do with the work of analysis. Of course, there is nothing we can do for someone who suffers from a psychosis the aetiology of which is neurological. In other cases, however, a "ten-minute or half-an-hour diagnosis", even though it may be correct as far as the nosological category is concerned, says nothing about our ability to help the patient. A "quite simple" phobia may take many years of unproductive effort or "be cured" in a matter of weeks without any authentic change having occurred in the analysand. A patient with schizophrenia may make astonishing progress—or remain completely inaccessible. All of this leads to the following conclusion: if we analysts were to continue to use a nosology drawn up in a context and with aims different from our own, we would be seriously mistaken, because that nosology does not in the least correspond to what we can do. Michael Balint put it thus: "To-day, to diagnose a case is always a difficult task; the result is usually an uncertain, rather haphazard, and not even very important label" (Balint, 1950, p. 119).

That is why it is imperative to devise a psychoanalytic nosology: one that is not simply modelled, with some modifications, on psychiatric nosology but oriented towards the kind of action that we can really carry out; this can only be a bipersonal model. If we refer a person to just any analyst, that would be tantamount to acting empirically and somewhat thoughtlessly. Quite naturally, we take into account the impression we have that analyst A would "suit" the analysand-to-be, Z, for such-and-such a reason.

Even though that impression may be empirical and sometimes mistaken, we should not ignore it. I feel, all the same, that much more needs to be discovered about this, and our whole approach must be improved, in an endeavour to define more precisely what kind of person seems able to make better progress with a given analyst. This implies knowing not only how well trained that analyst is and the level of ethical and professional trust we can have in him or her, but also certain features of the person's personality, technique, and ability to establish a fruitful analytic relationship with a given analysand. For the moment, all of this resembles America before Christopher Columbus.

This leads quite naturally to the "micro-neurosis" or "micro-psychosis" of the transference/countertransference relationship. We are prepared for the fact that the analysand's conflicts are expressed directly or indirectly in the relationship with us, thereby creating a situation that may be neurotic, psychotic, or perverse. As regards the perverse situation, I am thinking of circumstances in which normal psychoanalytic activity tends to take on the symbolic meaning of a perverse activity: for example, when the analysand continues to do perverse actings-out in the external world in order to convert the analyst into an obliging and conniving voyeur of these perverse acts. In such cases, in our countertransference, we may become as fascinated as Krafft-Ebing and Stekel were by the perverts whom they studied.

Micro-neurosis, micro-psychosis, micro-perversion of the analytic situation—all of these imply the participation of the analyst, letting him/herself be taken over, within controllable limits, by the pathology at work in the situation. In every case, it implies staying within the boundaries of the "micro" level and ensuring that those limits are preserved. The analyst therefore oscillates between two opposing dangers: on the one hand, seeing him/herself as a neutral observer—and abandoning any attempt at understanding—or, on the other, being drawn into the situation more than need be the case, thereby betraying his or her specific function as analyst.

The setting-up within the analytic field of a micro-neurotic, micro-psychotic, or micro-perverse situation does not depend solely on the analysand's intrinsic pathology (insofar as that concept is meaningful), but also on the analyst's way of understanding and conducting the process, as well as on his or her own propensity to being drawn more into one type of situation than another. An analysand may set up a perverse situation in the course of one analysis and, in a subsequent analysis with another analyst, a quite different kind of relationship (without this being due to any progress that may have been achieved in the initial analysis). It is therefore extremely important for analysts to examine as thoroughly as possible their own range of possibilities of doing worthwhile work as well as the kinds of analysand with whom they feel they can "get on well".

All of this may appear to be not very "scientific"—but it is true all the same.

These considerations may highlight the limits to the effectiveness of each individual analyst, but they do have a positive counterpart: the concept of "negative therapeutic reaction" will have to be looked at anew. Freud defined the concept very strictly (the reaction of analysands who, when they make progress in their psychoanalytic understanding of themselves, manifest an aggravation of their symptomatology rather than an improvement), but it has gradually come to be much wider in scope, so that it includes any analysand who fails to make progress in his or her analysis.

If these premises are true, then a negative therapeutic reaction is not an intrinsic feature of the analysand involved but of the situation he or she sets up with the analyst. An analysand who presents a negative therapeutic reaction with one analyst may not do so with another. From what I personally have been able to observe, I would say that that is indeed what happens in some cases—but in others the analysand does present a negative therapeutic reaction with both analysts, one after the other. In any case, the percentage of analysands who do have this kind of reaction would probably fall if the way in which analyst and analysand chose each other were to be improved.

What I have said about the analytic situation and about the reciprocal choice of analyst/analysand (as long as this does not depend on financial or other practical reasons or any misapprehensions, which is usually the case) has similar implications for the analytic process itself (that is, the way in which the analysis as a whole develops). Freud gave some indication of how difficult the problem is when he compared the analytic process to a game of chess in which we know the openings and end-games but not what occurs in the course of an actual game; he was even more explicit in his paper "Analysis Terminable and Interminable" (1937c). Many analysts have thought it possible to describe the analytic process as if it were a predetermined narrative, with its various phases all set out beforehand. These are what is called "standard treatment" and "variations on standard treatment" (cf. the volumes of the *Encyclopédie médico-chirurgicale* [Encyclopaedia of medicine and surgery] devoted to psychiatry).

In his *Écrits*, published in 1966, which contains a modified version of his 1955 paper "Variations on the Standard Treatment", Jacques Lacan says, without beating about the bush, that he "considers [this title] to be abject" (Lacan, 1955, p. 300).

Perhaps the "abject" quality of the title applies also to the fact that it would seem to indicate that Lacan initially accepted the idea that there does indeed exist a "standard" form of treatment, or that analysis can be looked upon as a natural process, akin to the growth of a plant well looked after by a gardener. The gardener makes sure that the plant has whatever it requires in order to grow, but the plant grows in accordance with its own laws.

That is the concept that underlies the idea that analysis has to go through phases predetermined by the genetic succession of the analysand's developmental stages, lifting resistance and repression layer by layer in much the same way as one peels an onion. Freud had deliberately rejected that idea in his *Introductory Lectures* (1916–1917, pp. 445–456). In the case of "standard treatment", the "phases" are obviously imposed by the analyst, who chooses in the material for interpretation the aspects that correspond to the phase he or she has in mind, putting aside any other aspects that do not fit in with it. Analysands are not slow in grasping this, especially if they want to be "good" analysands and meet the expectations of their analyst. They may, however, prefer to be recalcitrant, wishing to be analysed as they think fit and refusing to be looked upon as some kind of sophisticated onion. In these circumstances, all the analyst can do is to classify the protester as a "variation on the standard treatment". With another initial pattern in mind, the analyst would soon realize that there is no such thing as a "standard" treatment: the so-called "variations" are in fact the rule.

We would nowadays smile at Wilhelm Reich's astonishment (cf. *Character Analysis*, 1945) when faced with "chaotic states" in which the analysand brings a wealth of material belonging to a mixture of all the stages of development, thus making any attempt at interpretation lose its bearings. In saying that, I have no intention of diminishing the credit that Reich deserves for drawing our attention to a fundamental problem.

I do not think that in our psychoanalytic environment anybody would accept the concept of the onion-analysand or be surprised whenever chaotic states in Reich's sense emerge in the course of an analysis.

There is, however, a (more advanced) version of that same principle: I am referring here to a recent book by Donald Meltzer. Having worked with him, I hold him in great esteem and admire his talent as a psychoanalyst. That does not prevent me from being in complete disagreement with him as regards the image of the psychoanalytic process that he gives in his book.

In order to focus properly on the problem, let me quote what Meltzer says: "I have described my tentative reconstruction of the *natural history of the analytic process*, a sequence dictated by the economics of psychic life, as it unfolds in analysis when *adequately presided over and adequately supported* by environmental factors outside the analysis proper" (Meltzer, 1967, p. 32; emphasis in original).

That argument becomes clearer when we compare it with another, taken from the same context: "It is important to bear in mind that this whole concept of the natural history of the analytic process cannot be used in the moment-to-moment work of the consulting room. It is not a tactical conception but a strategic one" (Meltzer, 1967, p. 32).

It is therefore a general concept of the psychoanalytic process, an apparently empirical one. Three points, however, are worth looking into in more detail. First, as we have seen, the economics of psychic life is a concept that seems to have no real content. Second, the so-called "natural history" is revealed when the analysis is "adequately presided over". And, third, it depends on being "adequately supported" by the environment. We could ask ourselves to what extent the unfolding of these stages and their succession are determined by Meltzer's own leanings, with any variations being attributed to inadequate support being offered by the environment (an inadequacy that is very frequent in any case).

I would argue that any "strategy" in fact determines the course of an analysis, except in cases where the other person refuses to go along with this (direct refusal or one attributed to the environment), whenever the analyst has a preconceived strategy in mind. Since we seem to be moving among military metaphors, let me say this: a battle plan may work out as anticipated, if we have correctly foreseen the adversary's movements and manoeuvres aimed at neutralizing our attack, if we have succeeded in thwarting those manoeuvres, and if the unforeseen factors that occur in every battle are not unfavourable to us. It is our strategy that constitutes this pseudo-"natural history", insofar as no unforeseen factors interfere with it. In other words, the psychoanalytic process is indeed a "history", but there is nothing "natural" about it.

When Donald Meltzer argues (1967, p. 33) that "it is not conceivable that any phase can be by-passed, since each phase is seen to have an absolute metapsychological dependence on the adequate working-through of the previous one", our misgivings are at their strongest.

The same thing can happen with the analytic process as with any given interpretation: if the analysand agrees with it, it is valid—but even if it is absolutely correct as to both content and the way in which it is formulated, the analysand may refuse it, or deny it without saying so explicitly. The analysand may deflect the process, just as the analyst may try to impose his or her own schema as to how it should proceed. In my opinion, Donald Meltzer's conceptualization has fallen victim to a theoretical *a priori*: that a "scientific" observer should simply record the empirical facts and try to understand them; the psychoanalytic situation is quite different, because there we both understand *and* create the facts simultaneously. The analytic process is a personal history.

It is personal in its beginnings. Since an analyst must inevitably take on only a very small number of analysands, he or she can usually choose those with whom there is a good chance of working in an efficient way. This has nothing to do with the severity of the case or the psychiatric diagnosis. Even in the case of a relatively mild diagnosis, the person may not be able to be treated by a particular analyst because the two partners are temperamentally incompatible. Someone who has very severe problems may, on the other hand, get on well with certain analysts. The preliminary interview or interviews make it possible to lay the foundations of an agreement that enables an analytic process to begin between the two protagonists. Very often, however, these preliminary interviews are misleading. Every person—analysts included—is a Pandora's box, full of surprises. Given the analyst's training and possible experience, he or she will give rise to fewer unpleasant surprises than will, in all probability, the analysand. This means that analysts are more able to choose their analysands than analysands are as regards a potential analyst—all of this being relative, of course.

When all is said and done, the analytic process that is about to take place between analyst Z and analysand A is completely unforeseeable. It implies on the part of the analyst a perspective, more or less exact, more or less mistaken, that may—or may not—be modifiable, depending on the circumstances, during the actual process. The process is a personal matter all through its unfolding.

This is also the case when the analysis comes to an end. If we agree with Freud that the analytic process is interminable and that from time to time further analysis is absolutely necessary for all analysts, the end of an analysis is in no way comparable to the transformation from caterpillar to butterfly. No butterfly can ever become a caterpillar again, but an analyst (and an analysand) can again be an analysand. That is why the end of an analysis is such a complex process. It does not depend solely on the hopes that the analyst has for the outcome of the analysis of a given person. Some of these hopes may indeed be fulfilled, others not; and, in some cases, others again, thought to be inaccessible, are fulfilled. Nor does it depend on the hopes—magical or reasonable—that every analysand has as regards the analytic process. Ideas about ending an analysis can occur at any point during the process. They may take the form of fantasies of running away, of failure, of manic "recovery", of denigrating the analysis as a whole, and so forth.

Having to deal with such ideas is the daily bread of every analyst; sometimes these ideas are presented as concrete projects for ending the analysis.

From time to time, the analyst becomes involved in the fantasy of ending the analysis that is expressed by the analysand. This is manifested directly through the kind of interpretation made (whatever the precautions taken) and in the analyst's overall attitude. Usually, if we leave aside the unsuitable cases, this corresponds to the analyst's idea that "We have obtained satisfactory results", or "When all is said and done, this is a therapeutic success", or "This analysand will not be able to go any further with me", or again, "There's nothing more I can do, so we might as well call it a day", and so forth.

I am perfectly familiar with the classical descriptions of the process of ending an analysis, once this has been decided upon, as well as with the quite specific features that that process entails. It is nevertheless up to the analyst to decide whether a fantasy of ending the analysis is pure madness or quite acceptable and legitimate—and every analyst makes many errors of judgement as regards that situation (in the case of those who think that they do not make that kind of mistake, I would see that as something very suspicious indeed).

This goes much further than the theoretical ideas we may have about "criteria of recovery" or "criteria for ending an analysis". It implies that two people think deeply about the issues involved, two people who in principle are trying to find a way to share the ending as they shared the work they did together. Apart from situations of unilateral running away or expulsion, or of the analyst unduly holding on to the analysand, they decide together that they will put an end to their work. I agree with Freud when he says that this process comes about when both parties agree that their work together will no longer lead to any benefit. Of course, the classical criteria for ending an analysis are present when that decision is being made, but since they very much represent an ideal scenario, they do not often correspond with the actual results of the process.

According to Balint,

> What we need now is a theory that would give us a good description of the development of object relations comparable to, but independent of, our present, biologizing, theory of the

development of instincts. And for that purpose we need a field of investigation where the conclusions drawn from the theory can be checked and validated, modified or refuted. [Balint, 1950, p. 121]

That "field" is necessarily that of the psychoanalytic situation and process.

III. Psychoanalysis, language, and ideology

Common sense usually contrasts science with ideology, in the same way as truth contradicts error. Unfortunately, I cannot subscribe to that antithesis and assume that "science" covers all clearly established knowledge while "ideology" pertains to any system of ideas that are impossible to prove. In all of the human sciences, it is very difficult to differentiate science from ideology. What, then, are the specific features of psychoanalysis when it is considered to be a science? The fact that it is based on a relationship between subject and subject; that it is constructed simultaneously with observations being made; and that it is conducted in the form of a dialogue. There is also the fact that its specific instrument is interpretation—that is, replacing a lack of awareness or a mistaken awareness with true insight, even though this might be painful for the analysand (if that were not the case, why would interpretations be refused?), together with the idea that this true insight is in itself beneficial for the analysand and the means by which he or she can make progress (if we were not convinced that true insight is beneficial for the analysand, who among us would undertake analysis?)

That is the essential difference between psychoanalysis and all other forms of psychotherapy. These may call upon all kinds of suggestion or other forms of influence, reassurance, holding, and so on—and even interpretation—and, as far as the presenting symptoms are concerned, they often achieve therapeutic results more quickly than can formal psychoanalysis. The aim of these psychotherapies, however, is not the same as that of psychoanalysis (their goal is to save as much time as possible and be as effective as possible in the short term). From a sociological point of view, I would not look down on such goals, even though, in the long term, I would have reservations about the validity of the results obtained. Our aim is different: it entails trying to discover a person's ultimate truth, without the idea of therapeutic urgency being involved. Progress in therapy, although it might satisfy our wish for effectiveness, is meaningless, unless we manage to understand how access to true insight enables a person to change.

We know full well the processes that are involved in the analytic situation, and we know that they come into play also with respect to the outcome of an analysis. This plurality of processes is, however, of value only if they themselves can be understood, formulated, and shared.

The truth that we reach thanks to our interpretative formulation of the events that take place in the analytic situation—a truth that the analysand acknowledges to be his or her own—implies that in the analytic process there is necessarily an ideological dimension. In the first place, the choice of truth as the fundamental value of a process implies a clear ideological stand in the narrow sense of the word (similarly, the choice of therapeutic effectiveness, even if lying is the price to pay, implies another ideological stand, inconsistent with ours). Second, the truth chosen as the axis of the psychoanalytic process is not of the same nature as that of physics or mathematics; it implies that facts and possibilities be taken together—in other words, the existence of a subject with the burden of his or her past history and the (relative) freedom that the future holds out.

Basically, psychoanalysis is a technique of unveiling, a way of revealing the true person behind the character types that the analysand usually puts forward in order to hide from and lie to him/herself. Psychoanalysis, therefore, is a quest for authenticity: it cannot claim to resolve those conflicts that are intrinsic to human beings as individuals or as integral parts of social groups. The "happy executive" would be a caricature of the perfect psychoanalyst.

Behind that caricature, we can see both what many analysands are looking for in the analytic process—that is, the exact opposite of what it really is, and what certain psychoanalytic schools of thought are aiming for—those that have quite casually absorbed the "plague" that, according to historical tradition, Freud brought to them.

That "plague" is, quite simply, the unveiling of the real conflicts that hide behind a whole series of disguises.

Every interpretation has an aim; it is not simply a description. The aim is to free analysands from the burden of their lies, to have them face up to their real problems, and to enable them to take on board their own freedom at another level.

This basic project (not to "cure" people but to make them more human, which entails an attempt to free them from their neurotic, psychotic, or perverse alienation) is fundamentally ideological, as are the means employed to achieve it. A quote from Balint will show how language and ideology are interwoven: "[A very important item . . . will be] the language used by the analyst for conveying his interpretations to his patient. By language I mean the set of technical terms, of concepts, the 'frame of reference' habitually used by the individual analyst" (Balint, 1950, p. 122).

Language is the medium of interpretation. Language is not simply an organized set of words, but a whole technical frame of reference concerning the way in which interpretations should (or should not) be formulated in any given circumstance, and a theoretical frame of reference that provides the basis for what we want to communicate to the analysand. Every word that we utter in the analytic situation is crammed with ideology, as are those that we do not utter but which the analysand expects to hear.

Every time an interpretation is formulated, it brings into the analytic situation an ideological universe—either, as in every case, that of the analyst's own psychoanalytic ideology or, as often happens, that of the analyst's ideology over and beyond analytic technique (what the analyst thinks might or might not be dangerous, progressive, rewarding, etc., for the analysand).

The "words of truth" that the analysand expects from us imply a new understanding on his or her part of a better ideology, one that is more coherent, richer, and—like Ali Baba's "Open Sesame!"—able to open the doors to the analysand's inner world.

Leaving magic to one side, the words we use in our interpretations are our specific way of gaining access to the world of the unconscious. This is what Lacan has to say:

> The unconscious is that part of concrete discourse qua transindividual, which is not at the subject's disposal in re-establishing the continuity of his conscious discourse. . . .
>
> The unconscious is the chapter of my history that is marked by a blank or occupied by a lie: it is the censored chapter. But

the truth can be re-found; most often it has already been written elsewhere. Namely,

1. in monuments: this is my body, in other words, the hysterical core of neurosis in which the hysterical symptom manifests the structure of a language, and is deciphered like an inscription which, once recovered, can be destroyed without serious loss;

2. in archival documents too: these are my childhood memories, just as impenetrable as such documents are when I do not know their provenance;

3. in semantic evolution: this corresponds to the stock of words and acceptations of my own particular vocabulary, as it does to my style of life and my character;

4. in traditions, too, and even in the legends which, in a hero-icized form, convey my history;

5. and, lastly, in its traces that are inevitably preserved in the distortions necessitated by the insertion of the adulterated chapter into the chapters surrounding it, and whose meaning will be re-established by my exegesis. [Lacan, 1953, pp. 214–215]

Here we find hieroglyphics or ideograms, the many forms of writing in which Freud saw the starting point for his art of deciphering dreams and which he himself generalized to include all kinds of mental phenomena.

The specific means we have to accomplish this exegesis and communicate what we have found are the words we use in the analytic process. To quote Lacan again:

Its means are those of speech, insofar as speech confers a meaning on the functions of the individual; its domain is that of concrete discourse qua field of the subject's transindividual reality; and its operations are those of history, insofar as history constitutes the emergence of truth in reality [*réel*]. [Lacan, 1953, p. 214]

David Liberman compared the psychoanalytic experience with communications theory and reached a similar conclusion, although he did formulate his findings differently. For Liberman (1962, p. 52), codification is a process that consists in transposing a series of facts from one form of language to another. When an analyst interprets, he says, this is a process of codification: a certain number of communications, verbal and nonverbal, that have no meaning for the analysand's unconscious, are brought together. The effect on the patient of interpretation consists in an increase in self-understanding which, in terms of communication, signifies an increase in intra-personal communication.

I shall not attempt to point out each time that my own views are in agreement with those of Liberman (this occurs very often, mainly because our views spring from the same source, Enrique Pichon-Rivière's teaching). I would say, then, that the linguistic dimension intrinsic to the extract that I have just quoted from Liberman's book agrees with my own way of looking at these issues. Where we do not agree, however, is with respect to our basic epistemological assumptions, which, in turn, implies differences at less abstract levels: roughly speaking, the difference could be summarized as the antithesis between communications theory and the linguistic model (which is not an exclusive one). This does not prevent us from sharing the view that the psychoanalytic field is bipersonal in nature (Liberman, 1962, p. 14), as well as many other fundamental ideas.

As far as I am aware, these issues and formulations were first brought to our notice by the truly pioneering work of Luisa Alvarez de Toledo (1954). The initial intention of her work was to introduce a new dimension into psychoanalytic technique: the analysis of the fact of associating, as such, by the analysand and of interpreting, by the analyst, as well as the words that pass between them as objects of their communication, over and above the meaning that they communicate. That axis of interpretation has proved extraordinarily rewarding. The reader will, of course, have realized that understanding and interpreting this second level of what is said in certain situations is also expressed through the medium of words. It implies talking about talking—all the while acknowledging that everything fundamental is conveyed through the mediation of words. As Alvarez de Toledo says: "'In the beginning was the Word' . . . and from it all things were born" (1954, p. 311).

The mythical dimension of "the Word" is very close to the technical dimension of the analytic process. Just one step further, and they will be seen to coincide, with the difference that Alvarez de Toledo brings through her work of demystification.

It is interesting to note that she begins with the countertransference.

> Using countertransference emotions in this way, I too was able to observe and confirm that they were related to the patient's unconscious wishes, sensations and emotions (themselves linked to his unconscious fantasies). I noticed too that when I was able to understand my emotional reactions in these terms and to verbalise them internally, they disappeared; through the contents supplied to me by the patient and his entire behaviour, I then succeeded in finding a form of expression that allowed him to become aware of his unconscious wishes and defences. [Alvarez de Toledo, 1954, p. 291]

These ideas are widely accepted in our milieu, because they are true. I think it important nonetheless to emphasize the phenomenon of countertransference understanding, which is created by the internal verbalization of the auto-interpretation of the countertransference, and the ensuing freeing-up of the analytic function of interpreting the situation.

"When 'associating' and 'interpreting' are analysed as such, the primitive identity of act, image and object arises and becomes a reality in the act of speaking and listening to the analyst" (Alvarez de Toledo, 1954, p. 294). The idea is to place oneself at the limit between the processes of symbolization and learning to speak—a frontier where there is no inflexible splitting between mind and body, between the perceived world and the conceived one, between feelings, thoughts, and actions: a world in which an abstract utterance may be of extraordinarily concrete value, even on the bodily level, and in which words have not yet become detached from the emotions.

On the other hand, if we let ourselves be drawn beyond that limit, it is the analytic situation itself that is taken over by splitting. "Where analysand and analyst cannot understand each other in any other way, a regressive form of communication arises between them, mediated by a primitive language corresponding to a primitive level of expression and interrelationship (animals–fear–attack)" (Alvarez de Toledo, 1954, p. 292).

In such circumstances, the benefits of being on the border between symbol and non-symbol are lost; the analyst feels things in an absurd manner instead of understanding, until such time as he or she manages to recover that optimal position that some would call "the analyst's helpful regression in the process" (this restricts the resources of the concept without adding anything new to it).

In my opinion, Alvarez de Toledo's description comes very close to Lacan's idea of the "empty word" and the "full word" in the analytic process, although the two points of view do not match exactly: at a descriptive level, I would say that they are both referring to the same thing, but they integrate it within two different frames of reference.

The process of internal verbalization of the analyst's own countertransference responses is what enables the analyst to stay on that ambiguous but optimal edge between the risk of a kind of communication that would simply be verbal (awakening no echo within the analysand) and that of a transference/countertransference situation that has not been properly understood and is therefore unusable and perhaps even harmful.

I have mentioned only a few aspects of Alvarez de Toledo's work, leaving to one side many other points that are less directly related to the main topic of this chapter.

Deciphering palimpsests may well be a very important activity, but it carries with it no danger. Deciphering someone's dreams or symptoms is, however, dangerous. The words that we utter have a "magic" quality to them, and we are all sorcerer's apprentices who have much to learn about the body we are dealing with—which is not the same as the body that medical science describes, studies, and treats. So, then, what kind of body is it?

The body that anatomy and physiology describe has no place for that essential organ that we call the woman's phantom penis; similarly, the study of the metabolism of our life needs could never account for that hallucinated object we call the lost breast. In psychoanalysis, the body is the one described by Freud: "the whole body is an erotogenic zone" (Freud, 1940a [1938], p. 151). It is a body that must be taken "to the letter", as Serge Leclaire puts it in his wonderful book *Psychanalyser* (Leclaire, 1968, p. 66).

Historically, both medicine and psychoanalysis derive from the social function fulfilled by shamans in ancient times. Civilization had not yet set up for the shaman the dichotomy between body and mind that is current in our conception of the world; psychosomatic medicine attempts to reduce that dichotomy (but this is more of an ideal than something that has actually been achieved). Traditionally, doctors treat bodies that are ill, while psychoanalysts work with people who suffer from conflict situations. Both, however, retain part of the magic function that used to belong to shamans (Valabrega, 1962): taking care of the ills suffered by human beings. Thanks to advances in biological knowledge, physicians can now quite materially take care of many of those ills, but their magic/shamanistic function is still present within their scientific one (for someone who is ill, the doctor is the person who pronounces a sentence of life or death: "With this course of treatment, you will recover your health" or "There's nothing more we can do").

Similarly, for analysands, analysts are the equivalent of shamans. They do nothing concrete, they do not prescribe anything, nor do they forbid the ingestion of any substance whatsoever—but, as far as analysands are concerned, their words are magic. Analysands tend to attribute magic powers to the analyst, and analysts themselves sometimes connive in this: the "ritual" of the sessions is much more than a mere technical convenience, it aims at attributing a special value to the words that are uttered therein.

The analyst's "magic" is simply that of the Word—a kind of magic that is comparable to that of the poet (although the two are not identical). There is, however, one fundamental feature that differentiates the analyst from the shaman or from any modern equivalent of that person: the scientific rigour that all analysts impose on themselves, in the same way as do those who do research in other branches of science.

* * *

The concrete work of analysis—words—is the fundamental reference mark for every theorization concerning psychoanalysis. If we do not acknowledge that essential fact, an insuperable gap will open up between psychoanalytic theory and practice. The only way to move beyond that situation would seem to be—following Husserl's good advice—to go back to the things-in-themselves, to abandon all attempts at expressing the psychoanalytic experience in the language of other disciplines, and to reformulate our theories in our own language.

Everything that occurs in the analytic situation takes place between two people and is put into words by two people. Any abstraction that tends to make one or the other of these two protagonists disappear will also tend to turn their words into silence.

Note

1. I have invented this neologism in order to designate the process by which one person becomes for another the depository of one of the latter's aspects or functions. The analyst, for example, may be the depository of the analysand's superego.

8

Bad faith, identity, and omnipotence

Madeleine Baranger

I. Fundamental rule and bad faith

In his *Introductory Lectures on Psycho-Analysis* (1916–17), Freud defines the fundamental rule of analytic technique as follows:

> We instruct the patient to put himself into a state of quiet, un-reflecting self-observation, and to report to us whatever internal perceptions he is able to make—feelings, thoughts, memories—in the order in which they occur to him. At the same time we warn him expressly against giving way to any motive which would lead him to make a selection among these associations or to exclude any of them, whether on the ground that it is too *disagreeable* or too *indiscreet* to say, or that it is too *unimportant* or *irrelevant*, or that it is *nonsensical* and need not to be said. We urge him always to follow only the surface of his consciousness and to leave aside any criticism of what he finds, whatever shape that criticism may take; and assure him that the success of the

Presented at the Argentine Psychoanalytical Association on 14 April 1959. Published in Spanish as "Mala Fe, Identidad y Omnipotencia" (*Revista Uruguaya de Psicoanálisis, 5,* 1963: 199–229).

treatment, and above all its duration, depends on the conscientiousness with which he obeys this fundamental technical rule of analysis. [p. 287]

Then he describes some analysands' behaviour aimed at avoiding the observance of this rule.

We deal with a phenomenon that presents itself at first sight in the analytic practice as a particular and subtle way of breaching the fundamental rule. However, we shall not deal with the technical aspect of the problem but will refer instead to the fundamental rule solely as a path that may lead us to a possible definition of bad faith and as a first step in our attempt to understand it.

Even though the analysands have accepted the basic commitment of sincerity at the onset of their analysis, they can only keep the fundamental rule partially. There are general reasons to account for this. The spoken material is always a selection: the word is slower than the thought. Besides, what is repressed eludes awareness as well as direct formulation: its emergence in analysis hinders even further the expression of conscious material.

These difficulties have brought about some discredit to free association among analysts. They think, for example, that what is not expressed verbally is expressed in some other way (through gestures, silence, leaving out some kind of material). Since the fundamental rule cannot be totally observed, there is an inclination to do away with it completely and not to give the least importance to the analysand's sincerity or lack thereof. Although it is true that a lie as material is as important as a sincere report, it is not in the same sense, and the fact that there was a lie may be more significant to analyse than its latent content. Both to disregard the patient's sincerity and not to consider verbal material as important seem to me to derive from a feeling of omnipotence in the analyst, since he thinks he can do without the patient's cooperation and can cure him against his will. It is very important to understand nonverbal material: however, the effort of the interpretation should be oriented towards eliciting its verbalization instead of the patient expressing himself in other ways. For example, instead of feeling and talking, a patient moves about in the room, walks, plays with things. This behaviour is his way of expression, but what really matters is to understand that he is expressing his inability to verbalize. Even in the analysis of children, an analysis is not considered finished until the child attains some degree of verbalization of his conflicts. (Klein, 1926)

The difficulty in complying with the fundamental rule is manifested by the analysand's anxiety and suffering when reporting some material. This anxiety may occasionally interfere with communication. Once an interpretation has lessened his anxiety, the patient may spontaneously correct what he had expressed before through silence, omission, or a conscious lie. In these cases, the difficulty is circumstantial and conscious. Some mechanisms of defence or avoidance related to dissociation are more difficult to overcome. Difficulty in communication can become chronic: the analysand reports the material bit by bit and with long silences. Or else, using the excuse of saying everything that comes into his mind, he digresses constantly and overwhelms the analyst with misleading logorrhoea. His anxiety compels him to flee into a flux of words instead of letting his associations flow. A different technique consists in resorting to hypercontrol: the patient brings an already organized story or reports a dream and its associations already analysed and interpreted. A similar technique consists in limiting the material strictly to one subject, cutting all the associative lines that could lead to other subjects and could reduce splitting by interpretation; or the concomitant technique that opens all the associative lines except those leading to a taboo area: this analysand never brings direct sexual material, and when interpretation is about sexuality, he ignores the interpretation and continues with the previous material without giving it any other meaning than the one it had before the interpretation.

A more complete listing would not help us to solve our problem. All these different kinds of avoidance behaviour can be reduced as analysis progresses and free association is attained. All analysands make use of one or more of these techniques at some point. This is due to common reasons: shame, fear of being judged by the analyst, fear of being exploited by the analyst, the need to protect some gratification that the patient himself considers neurotic, fear of direct expressions of love or aggression, and so on. In our opinion, none of these cases means a special character problem.

However, there are cases in which the breach of the fundamental rule and the ways used to avoid it are more serious and pose a more radical threat to the success of the cure. The countertransference impression is that the patient tries to deceive himself and deceive us not because of the circumstantial and common reasons mentioned above but with the intention of spoiling the basis of the analytic process, and as we cannot count on the patient's collaboration, all our efforts are negated by his bad faith.

We do not think of bad faith when a patient lies consciously about his age or when because of a fantasy of exploitation he hides his economic situation from the analyst. On the other hand, it is a serious problem when the patient maintains this lie throughout his analysis and even carefully avoids all information that might contradict what he has already told us. This planned and systematic behaviour—independently from the degree of consciousness—deprives all the material and the analytic process of authenticity. Without coming to this extreme, we may observe in an analysand recurrent behaviour, at moments showing some degree of systematization, with successively different contents. For example, the analysand spends a session reporting, without conviction, trivial problems, and when he leaves, he hands me an envelope with my monthly fees. I realize that he has not included the fees for sessions he has missed. When I tell him so in the next session, he answers that he did this on purpose, to see my reaction. I ask him how it was possible that he came with the envelope ready and this purpose in mind, and he did not say a word about it in the previous session. He answers: " It didn't occur to me. Am I not supposed to associate freely?" or something similar. I believe this is a typical example of bad faith. The patient hides something, misleading the analyst during the session, and uses the words of the fundamental rule precisely to go against its spirit. The caricatures of free association in some patients very often reveal this mechanism.

Another case is those patients who spend weeks talking about their success and their improvement, attributed to the treatment, and they become angry when the idyllic character of the situation is questioned.

Later they admit that they have recently had relationship conflicts or even serious somatic problems with severe catastrophic or death fantasies. They expected a fatal outcome, which would reproach the analyst for failing to save them. Here a more subtle distortion of the analytic situation can be noted: the patient places on the analyst his own bad faith when he assumes that the analyst will be content to please his self-esteem and happily sacrifice the authenticity of the therapeutic process and his own life. This projection of bad faith is found in many processes of underrating analysis.

An even more subtle technique of bad faith can be observed in other analysands. When they receive an interpretation they consider adequate, they hide their recognition, either by saying that they knew this already or by adding some elements that make the interpretation sound insufficient or incomplete. One of them admitted his bad faith in this reaction and said so on one occasion, comparing himself with a child in a Hans Christian Andersen's story: the devil's mirror had been broken, and the child had a piece of the mirror in his eye, which made him see the world as deformed. The devil's mirror not only distorted his vision of the world but also hampered any true communication and authentic response.

Now we have to see whether there are good reasons to think that the phenomena defined as bad faith are really something more than mere dissociation.

The most superficial manifestation of bad faith is found, in our opinion, in the intention to evade the fundamental rule. This results in the choice of the material according to a systematic and planned defence. The patient does not want to accept analytic commitment, although he pretends to do so. He "plays" at analysis but does not commit himself to analysis—that is to say, he remains in an ambiguous position, as expressed by the lack of authenticity in the material. This behaviour seems to aim at radically perverting the analytic situation, reducing the analyst to impotence, and making all material inessential.

The two first examples can be understood as being produced by intense dissociation, and, in fact, there are dissociative mechanisms at work: the patients leave outside the consulting room a predominant aspect of their present situation with the analyst, but they may be not be aware of that. In general, the particular characteristic of bad faith is not found in the degree of consciousness of the deceit. I even believe that a cynical lie has very little to do with what I call bad faith.

But in both cases, dissociation is used to set a trap. The patient uses his right to dissociate, but he does not actually dissociate.

An analysand may at a given moment express only positive aspects of his relation with the analyst, although at the same time dreams or slips unveil negative transference. These aspects are really dissociated, and when they are interpreted, the analysand accepts them only as coming from another ego. They do not merge with positive aspects.

In ambivalence positive and negative feelings can also come together in an effort to integrate object relations constructively.

Yet in the second example the supposedly dissociated positive and negative aspects of transference are both actually present, one conditioning the other, belonging to a more complex structure that has its own goal and mechanisms. In this example the aim is neither to gratify nor to attack me, but to set a trap.

Therefore, bad faith is opposed both to dissociation and to ambivalence. This is a complex technique that implies the presence of contradictory feelings and a restrictive use of dissociative mechanisms and that aims at disguising the urgency point and to divert interpretation. The three examples discussed above share this feature. However, in the third example bad faith acts retrospectively, disguising the impact of the interpretation without blocking it. Perhaps what we come across more often is the devil's mirror is—that is, something that compels the analysand to report only refracted material. We are not referring to the usual partial distortions before the elaboration of the latent content into manifest content, or to processes that may momentarily leave out a part of the situation (dissociation, denial, projection). The whole analytic situation is reported with a distortion—one meant to produce a discrepancy between our perception of the situation and our work on it.

As can be expected, this distortion brought by the patient into the analytic situation also shows an equivalent distortion in his life and in his ego. Bad faith, then, appears as a character trait. But it differs from other character traits in that it is not a partial one, such as greed or meticulousness: it comprises the whole personality and can be a life style. Bad faith appears in what the patient recounts of his life in various ways. The analysand may report episodes in which we see glaring bad faith with enormous ingenuousness and without having the least idea that his behaviour could be understood in those terms. For example, when he talks about family quarrels, he uses, to persuade himself and me, arguments whose falseness he had previously revealed to me, without making any connection between the previous revelation and the present use of this argument. In this case bad faith is supported by especially rigid dissociation.

Other analysands assume their bad faith in a very different way, when this happens outside their relation with me. They report their bad-faith behaviour with pride, showing off and trying to make me their accomplice.

Conversely, others watch out for their bad-faith behaviour, reproach themselves, and suffer for their inability to be authentic.

These are all cases of personal identity disturbance. In the first example, the analysand is not the same when he admits the falseness of his argument as when he uses it; in the second one, he tries to overcome his lack of authenticity, acknowledging it as such and recovering his identity by means of this recognition; in the third one, he suffers because he cannot be one and identical to himself.

But even though any phenomenon of bad faith corresponds to disturbance in personal identity, not all identity disorders relate to bad faith: in most cases it is due to simple splitting processes.

II. Bad faith and identity

The problem of personal unity and identity has always been rather obscure for pre-analytic psychological or philosophical speculation. It is only with Freud and mainly with *The Ego and the Id* (1923b) that analytic thought sees the beginning of a solution to this problem.

The unity and identity of a relatively normal adult personality depend on a complicated and progressive process of ego structuring. The ego is "primarily and first of all a bodily ego", which does not mean, as sometimes it is wrongly interpreted, that the ego is a body, but that the ego is a bodily scheme subjectively integrated.

The ego starts in a stage of no integration and progressively undergoes integration. The same integrating process takes place in the superego: the two processes are parallel.

Ego integration—that is, the solidity of its unity and identity— is lost, to a greater or lesser extent, with regression, as classic psychiatry noted long ago with cases of psychosis. On the other hand, the form and intensity of regression depend on the fixation points of the patient's previous history.

Inherited ego characteristics contribute to character formation ("Analysis Terminable and Interminable": Freud, 1937c)—that is, to identity.

The ego is structured, apart from the biological processes of organic maturation, through successive introjections of the most important figures around the child—mainly his parents—in the course of his evolution. These introjections merge into the ego structure and contribute to character formation, yet in bad faith they provide masks to the ego instead of traits.

In a normal case, ego integration guarantees its unity and identity. Bad faith seems to correspond to a state of inner ego instability. The ego hides behind multiple masks, to the point of failing to differentiate itself from them. This is revealed by the question, "Who am I?" which analysands utter when they become aware of their bad faith. These masks are parts of introjected objects that have not been assimilated between them and with the ego.

Melanie Klein's works (1946, 1952b) throw some light on the genesis of this situation—for us the essence of bad faith—in the evolution of children. It is obvious that any disturbance in personal identity stems from the early paranoid–schizoid position. There, because of the intense use of processes of splitting, projection, and projective identification, the boundaries between ego and non-ego are almost completely erased. The world is structured around the subject's needs—in particular, the need to ward off persecutory anxiety. The subject fails to integrate his object, his world, his bodily scheme, his own ego.

In her recent work "On identification" (1955), Melanie Klein demonstrates, discussing Julien Green's novel *If I were You*, the deep perturbation of personal identity produced by the overuse of projective identification. In other works (Klein, 1957), she stresses another kind of identity disturbance: indiscriminate, greedy, and unstable introjective identification. Both parallel processes reveal and stress ego weakness and the recurrent loss of the ego's own identity.

In bad faith, the essential point seems to be an inner ego situation: a multiplicity of contemporary and contradictory identifications that have not settled down, which makes the analysand feel and stand in for various characters without knowing who he really is.

Analysands who are little aware of this problem ingenuously play successive contradictory roles, boasting of a rigid sexual moral and a scrupulous professional commitment, as well as of their love conquests and their skill to profit from their social status. Here, lack of authenticity becomes clear to the observer, but the subject is not conscious of the multiple characters he is playing.

Yet in most cases these characters are experienced both as an ego and at the same time as a non-ego. They may or may not correspond with the ego. To put it in chemical terms, it is like an unstable combination of various substances. Or, in psychological terms, the ego is not capable of assimilating its characters. To assimilate them would imply discrimination between those aspects of the character that may remain in the ego as a constant trait and those that should be discarded as waste. The subject does not want to synthesize his characters, because this would mean relinquishing their incompatible aspects. This process is analogous to greedy and indiscriminate identification with the objects of the external world, as Melanie Klein describes it in some analysands. Yet in this case, the situation is only internal, and the individual's greed does not allow the person to give up any part of his characters.

In addition, Melanie Klein has shown that the installation of the triangular oedipal situation is a decisive step into non-ego acknowledgment: both parents exist outside the ego, separated from one another, and they gratify each other. Too much envy and greed hamper the establishment of the triangular situation, and the difficulty in assimilating different identification objects is manifested in a primitive way towards the parental couple as object. This is why failure to resolve bisexual identification is found to underlie identity disorders (Klein, 1957). Recent works by Phyllis Greenacre (1958a) and Margaret Mahler (1958; see also Rubinfine, 1958) emphasize this factor in the genesis of identity disorders, although, naturally, they place it much later in the personal evolution than the period of the establishment of the triangular situation of Melanie Klein.

We think that this failure to differentiate the ego internally from the non-ego—the identification objects—goes further and includes the problem of bad faith. In "Being and Nothingness" Jean-Paul Sartre accomplishes a phenomenological description of inauthenticity and bad faith that may help to clarify some dimensions of our problem. I shall not discuss the philosophical side of Sartre's description but refer only to those aspects that may correspond with a psychoanalytic description, while being well aware of the obstacle of using the same words but with different meanings in the two disciplines. There are enough points in common between the two theories to justify this examination. I shall deal with the opposition between the two views, which Sartre stresses, since he uses, paradoxically, his study of bad faith to raise a criticism against psychoanalysis.

We regard bad faith as a constant expression of the personality. Sartre himself states:

> Even though the existence of self-deception is very precarious, and though it belongs to the kind of psychic structures which we might call "metastable", it presents nonetheless as autonomous and durable form. It can even be the normal aspect of life for a very great number of people. A person can *live* in self-deception, which does not mean that he does not have abrupt awakenings to cynicism or to good faith, but which implies a constant and particular style of life. [Sartre, 1943, p. 244]

He also describes bad faith as essentially different from lying. In the ideal lie, the liar has a cynical attitude. He affirms truth within himself, denies it through his words, and denies that negation to himself. The pure liar is not deceived by his lies but intends consciously to deceive others. He plays the comedy of truth. Bad faith, on the other hand, implies the intention to lie to oneself—apparently a contradictory project, since that intention implies consciousness of the deceit. Therefore, bad faith is an intermediate and wavering state between good faith and lying. It is a constantly fading structure. There are also intermediate states between lying and bad faith in which the subject is partially deceived by his own lie. This description corresponds to what can be observed in analysis. In the abovementioned examples it is evident that the analysands do not regard themselves as liars and would angrily reject any accusation of that. Yet can we believe that they are deceiving themselves in good faith? The same difference that Sartre points out between cynical lying and good faith (for us, deceiving in good faith) can be established between lie and repression. From the descriptive point of view, bad faith belongs to conscious and unconscious phenomena: it is a wavering structure. A phobia, for example, belongs to unconscious phenomena in its content: the ego suffers it to a great extent passively. But we are close to bad faith in some analysands who had a perfectly authentic phobia and are now overcoming it. They have already surmounted the deep resistances that maintained the phobia and in the course of their process of cure reach a point where they keep the phobia "without any real need" and use it to continue enjoying some secondary gain.

Or, to come back to the examples mentioned in the first part: such analysands are not fully conscious of their intention to deceive the analyst when they conceal a point of urgency, they do not formulate this purpose (and such a formulation as "I'm going to waste so many sessions of analysis hiding from the analyst the essence of what's happening to me" would sound highly absurd to them, thus doing away with bad faith). But this purpose is not completely unconscious or repressed, as it appears outside and even within the analytic sessions. Nor is it essentially a dissociation, even though the mechanism of dissociation is present. The analysand has all along kept control over the concealed part. Even when it came out in his associations, he has ignored it as being "of no interest" or "irrelevant", and he has only commented on it when he had "insight" into its importance in his global situation, which posed the dilemma between cynic lying and sincerity.

Of course, this phenomenon does not appear in all analysands, nor in the process of cure of any phobia, but only in some particular personalities. This is the essential difference between a phenomenological conception and a psychoanalytic conception of bad faith: while the former limits itself to registering and describing the phenomenon, the latter tries to understand it as belonging to a determined psychological structure.

The behaviour or situation of bad faith is produced, according to Sartre, not by chance, but as an intentional phenomenon: bad faith is an attitude of flight from anxiety. Certainly, Sartre gives this term quite a different meaning from that in psychoanalysis. For Sartre, anxiety derives from the consciousness of Nothingness—

that is, from the consciousness of a void that separates consciousness, or the "being for itself", from the "being in itself", or, more
precisely, from the emptiness or nothingness of consciousness itself. Consciousness is like a "decompression of Being", and it is
always projected towards the world of objects, towards the future,
towards the values it elicits by the mere fact of acting in time. This
same emptiness of consciousness is the measure of its freedom, and
anxiety arises because of this freedom. To assume freedom means
to take a risk, not only by choosing values, but also by "committing
"oneself by this election.

All this seems to be quite far from psychoanalytic thought, yet
who has not experienced in analysis the fear of what is new or
unknown? Who has not realized that his patients were seeking
shelter in their lack of freedom, in bonds they fail to assume or
that paralyse them?

The relation between bad faith and anxiety—this time in psychoanalytic terms—becomes evident. In all cases bad-faith behaviour
in analysis contains the ambiguous avoidance to commit oneself.
The analysand wants to continue in analysis, but he does not want
to take risks. That is why he plays on two gameboards, but without
accepting that it is a double game, because if he did so, that would
seem contradictory. This situation can be a defence from paranoid
anxiety (fearing to surrender to the persecutor), a way to elude the
emergence of depressive anxiety, a plan to avoid human contact (it
may mean the irruption of nothingness or the unknown?) while
maintaining an appearance of contact.

The connection between bad faith and anxiety in Sartre leads us
to consider it as a way of avoiding the basic situation of consciousness: the need to choose and thus to commit oneself. Bad faith includes all the forms that consciousness has of eluding choice—that
is, of surrendering its own freedom. Bad faith implies, in the unity
of one consciousness, the consciousness of anxiety, the endeavour
to elude it, and the negation of this endeavour. Bad faith is the
"being for not being" or, to put it into different words, the purpose
of finding refuge in a particular being to avert the responsibility of
being someone different or someone new. A very well-known form
consists in hiding behind psychological determinism. Sartre gives
the example of a gambler who refuses to admit responsibility for
his previous decision to give up gambling, and now that he is once

again caught in the habit, he claims "to be a gambler and have some complexes".

This relinquishing of one's own responsibility is very often present in patients. They refuse to participate in a process of improvement, believing that it concerns only the analyst, so they remain passive. Surely when this happens, the other gameboard is being used. This defensive technique implies bad faith, since another part of the analysand is witnessing the analyst's efforts as something that does not concern him and is enjoying their futility. "It didn't occur to me. Am I not supposed to associate freely?"

Although it is not necessary, for Sartre, for consciousness to take bad faith as a life style, still bad faith constitutes one of the great recourses against the "facticity" of consciousness. The facticity of the "being for itself" designates its basic characteristic as "not being what it is and being what it is not". In other words: "This contingency of the being in itself which constantly fades and which obsesses the being for itself and relates it to the being in itself is what is called facticity of the being for itself." This facticity points to the fact that a human being always projects himself towards the being in itself he wishes to be, although he will never be in conformity with it. The very nature of temporality makes it impossible for us to correspond to our past characteristics, as they lie behind us, or our future characteristics, as they are still ahead of us. When one attains a new quality or role, one projects oneself towards another time to come, and one cannot be what one has been or what one is about to be. One plays the role of a character (of waiter or professor or grocer) because under no circumstances can one really limit oneself to being only that.

Here we run into the inner problem of our analysands with their characters, but it is different because, for Sartre, the impossibility of being in conformity with oneself is radical and universal, whereas in our analysands this is a particular identity disorder.

The consequence of this radical facticity of the human being is for Sartre the impossibility of contact with another human being, because of his own facticity. The whole of Sartre's theory of relationships with others rests on the experience of the look. The look, in its essence, turns everything he looks at into an object (a lifeless object). There are, then, two basic possibilities of relation between human beings: to look at or to be looked at, to be an object for the other or to regard the other as an object. From this results the inevitable failure of any attempt at human relationship that aims to elude this turning the other into an object: it relies on the contradictory purpose of acting on the other's inalienable freedom. Sartre discusses love, language, sadism, and masochism from this perspective, coming to analogous conclusions in all cases. About love, he states that it rests on a contradictory dual demand: one refuses to be chosen by the other in virtue of passionate determinism (for example, due to a fetishistic characteristic), but one also refuses to be chosen for an unjustifiable reason (hence the common question: " Why do you love me?"). That is to say, each of us, in a contradictory way, wants to be chosen freely by the other as an absolute value. "Lovers, then, are left each by himself in his total subjectivity—nobody can be spared the duty to exist for himself." Flight towards the other complements flight of the being for himself towards an unattainable being in himself.

Whatever our opinion concerning this theory of interhuman relationships, its connection with the "facticity" of consciousness, with the impossibility for the human being to correspond to his characters, draws our attention. Sartre cannot help arriving at a psychoanalytic conclusion: the impossibility of being in conformity with oneself runs parallel with the impossibility of joining others. The lack of authenticity of one's own self corresponds to the lack of authenticity of one's relation with the object.

This is perhaps the most outstanding situation in the abovementioned cases, although it is expressed differently in each case. The majority are aware of this impossibility of contact, and this is one of the most constant complaints, while others suffer from an objective lack of contact without being aware of it. The analysands say that "nobody understands them" or that " are being cheated", although what we can understand from their reports is that they have a great ineptitude for interpersonal relationships. Their attempts to explain the other are generally wrong and reveal an enormous lack of what is generally called psychological intuition. They specialize in "gaffes". Whenever they try to establish contact with someone, they blunder, choosing the wrong person, the wrong moment, or the wrong kind of contact.

Others keep an appearance of affective relations and try to deceive themselves about their authenticity, but from time to time complain again about the impossibility of really giving or receiving.

Finally, with yet other patients this impossibility is closer to Sartre's description. They affirm that sincerity is impossible and think, like Sartre, that bad faith is a constant danger. If they try to get close to someone, they assume a character, and they are never in conformity with what they are communicating. They can receive neither the affect nor the interest that others try to give them, since they feel that this meant for the characters they play and not for themselves.

In spite of differences in terms and basic theoretical assumptions, Sartre's description of bad faith seems to me to provide valid data from the analytic point of view: bad faith is an evanescent psychic situation or structure that oscillates continuously between lies and sincerity; it appears as flight from anxiety and as a rejection of a commitment of ourselves and our objects. It implies lack of authenticity in the ego with its inner characters and with its objects, barring any real contact of the former with the latter.

We are now in a position to gain a better understanding of the specificity of bad faith in identity disorders. There is the same distance between bad faith and depersonalization or disturbance in the bodily scheme of the schizophrenic or schizoid personalities as between bad faith and lying or hysterical comedy. They are neighbouring phenomena, but essentially different.

Schizoid identity disorder is experienced passively, sometimes accompanied by intense anxiety. Bad faith is more active and does not suffer from dissociation but, rather, makes use of it. Bad faith is a way of avoiding suffering or danger, and it becomes suffering only when the subject is conscious of it—that is, when he is able to give it up.

It also differs radically from lying or hysterical comedy. It does not attempt to turn the object into a spectator fascinated by his own ego. If he deceives himself, it is not by the same technique or with the same goal. This is a different kind of lack of authenticity. Bad faith is more carefully planned, systematic, or purposeful.

Therefore bad faith constitutes an identity disorder that may be mixed with schizoid and hysterical elements, but it differs from both. It is characterized by a lack of authenticity in the relationship with oneself and with others—in the first case, because one assumes contradictory characters but never achieves a stable coincidence with any of them; in the second case, the character acts as intermediary between the ego and the other. The very lack of authenticity in the ego prevents real contact, as there is no one there to establish one. Genetically, the two manifestations of lack of authenticity condition each other, and object relation is doomed to be artificial. This artificiality overflows as bad faith, and Melanie Klein describes it as a characteristic of schizoid object relations:

> Another characteristic of schizoid object relations is a marked artificiality and lack of spontaneity. Side by side with this goes a severe disturbance of the feeling of the self or, as I would put it, of the relation to the self. This relation, too, appears to be artificial. In other words, psychic reality and the relation to external reality are equally disturbed. [Klein, 1946, p. 13]

This description holds good for schizoid personalities as well as for bad faith. But as we shall see later, artificiality follows a different process in each case.

The understanding of bad faith as a way of ignoring the fundamental rule and as an identity disorder and Sartre's phenomenological description, all help us to delimit the phenomenon, yet we feel an important element is missing: to understand its purpose and its dynamics.

III. Bad faith and omnipotence

Bad faith has already proved to be a defence against anxiety. To renounce giving and receiving gratification from one's relations with others, the artificiality of object relations, means paying a very high price for something that consequently must be important.

Simple observation allows us to grasp something of the nature of the situations in which bad faith appears. In the course of an argument, for example, the person has run out of valid reasons for defending his opinion. He has been refuted adequately, and it looks as if he has no other choice but to give in—or, rather, to accept being beaten by the other's arguments. However, he appeals to arguments he knows are untrue or irrelevant. He refuses to accept what at this point seems to be reality (the evidence set forth by the other). He might fly into rage, to deny magically his opponent's reasons, and in this was destroy the other. Instead, grounded on bad faith, he maintains the appearance of his arguments. Bad faith allows him to stick to his omnipotence.

We encounter the same process in our patients' bad faith. They need to win over the analysis in the analytic dialogue, and this precludes communication. Triumph serves to deny castration when an interpretation confronts them with this anxiety. On a deeper level, they attempt to grab the interpretation ("I've known this for a long time") in order to elude a situation of oral dependence on the analyst, and they hold on to their omnipotence by reducing the analyst to the mere role of an echo or a mirror. What upsets them is admitting not so much that the analyst has something positive, but that they are lacking in it and therefore they envy the analyst for having it. They have the fantasy that they are absolutely self-sufficient, and this omnipotent feeling finds an obstacle in the fact of being in analysis. So they resort to bad faith and act as if they were analysing themselves. The analyst becomes a tool (the ideal being a cybernetic interpreting machine). The analyst is the technique, they are the thought.

Bad faith and its corollary, omnipotence, produce the dehumanization of both analyst and patient: the analyst is turned into an inanimate object, and the analysand is only omnipotent thought. Omnipotence engenders a lack of communication.

Projective identification leads to an unstable state in which the projected and re-introjected elements are sometimes placed on the analyst and at other times on the analysand, giving rise to fantasies and dreams in which the analyst appears as an omnipotent persecutor and the patient as a poor thing. This ambiguity in the placement of the elements that are intended to be projected in projective identification is a defence against a terrifying fear of contact with the other and even more of transference contact. In the latter there is the risk of a massive re-introjection of destruction. The particular technique of bad faith consists in delivering outdated material and in drawing the analyst's attention towards secondary movements. The analysand misleads the interpretation towards an inessential aspect of the situation and, remaining in constant flight, wears diverse masks, always trying to present empty masks to the persecuting analyst. Bad faith, then, appears basically as a Proteus-like play between divided internal characters intended to sustain omnipotence.

Projective identification already presupposes omnipotence by ejecting at will objects out of the self. Yet, as projective identification is characterized by placing outside oneself aspects of the ego, the external depository objects also acquire omnipotence, leading to a situation of ambiguity, with the concomitant threat of re-introjection of dissociated and omnipotently destructive aspects of the self. Confronted with this situation, the ego struggles to maintain its omnipotence by resorting to bad faith. It multiplies its masks to deceive the persecutor and hides its omnipotence behind the use of multiple features.

It should not surprise us, then, that the analysands who have bad faith as a life style are so difficult to apprehend. They are as slippery as Proteus in Greek mythology. According to legend this sea god, in charge of Poseidon's herds of seals (his ambiguity is already present in his being a shepherd of amphibious creatures), enjoyed omnipotent knowledge of the future, but was unwilling to utter prophecies. To avoid being questioned, he assumed different shapes and transformed himself into any animal or element, such as water or fire.

The legend does not account for Proteus' flight. One may conclude that through his metamorphosis he is protecting his omnipotence.

We should now be more precise about what we mean by omnipotence, as this term carries multiple meanings in psychoanalytic writings, the most common being a general characteristic of primitive, infantile neurotic thought. It is a magical or animist belief that anything you think, will happen. All the other meanings retain something of this. The clearest example of this is the infant's primitive optional hallucination.

Omnipotence also denotes a characteristic of all primitive defence mechanisms. They are "omnipotent" because the subject acts on the promptings of his inner demands without taking either external or internal reality into account. Denial, splitting, projection, idealization, and so on, are all omnipotent.

Omnipotence equally refers to a feeling of elation typical of manic and hypomanic states, with strong denial.

At other times, omnipotence denotes a certain kind of relationship with the object, an omnipotent control through projective identification.

Finally, we can understand omnipotence as a specific mechanism, with its underlying unconscious fantasies, which consists in exalting or magnifying defensively the ego's virtues and powers to shield the ego against persecution anxiety, guilt anxiety, disintegration anxiety, or, in general, against any situation the ego is unable to cope with or elaborate through its own means.

We shall now deal with this last meaning. In our cases, the most evident fantasy of omnipotence is to be absolutely self-sufficient, which is expressed by the ego's total autarchy. Or else, omnipotence relates more clearly to paranoid fears and is expressed via the fantasy of universal command and possession. In both cases—and, I believe, in all cases—omnipotence is a form of avoiding contact with the other and with reality.

The following question arises: Why do the cases described need so badly to cling to omnipotence? And why do they defend their omnipotence by means of this special technique of bad faith?

Bad-faith omnipotence shows characteristics that clearly differentiate it from the type of omnipotence often found in manic or hypomanic states. Freud (1921c) explains the feeling of omnipotence in this case as a phenomenon resulting from the fusion of the superego and the ego, in which the latter takes the omnipotent features of the former, and this leads to a state of triumph. With bad faith, the inner constellation is quite different. Omnipotence is not apparent, because it is hidden behind the masks. Omnipotence does not comprise the whole personality, but only a part of it—surely a very important part. That is, it is limited omnipotence, which has to defend itself and does so through flight.

There is also a radical difference between the omnipotence fantasy of an autistic psychotic child and our analysands' fantasy, although the ultimate basis seems to be the same. In the first case, Rodrigué describes this fantasy as follows:

> The autistic child is an omnipotent creature. In many aspects, he is a despotic sovereign of a static world peopled with those who blindly obey inanimate objects. Their behaviour suggests they only participate in external situations in which the "uniformity" of the environment provides the convenient support for his control fantasies ... due to an overuse of projective

identification, the autistic child considers the external world as a part of himself; he can therefore deny it completely and/or control it. In his omnipotence, he believes people are puppets whose detached parts, as my hand with Raúl, are tools or appendixes they can use for their own purposes. [Rodrigué, 1955]

In our patients, the other's dehumanization and the ego autarchy appear not immediately but later, in a subtle way, when we realize that the contacts have only the appearance of normality. Even the lack of authenticity of the contacts is only relative. In spite of this lack of authenticity, some parts of the ego are capable of communication and in fact have some real contacts. The mask, or the character that serves as intermediary in the communication, is not completely hollow, but surely it is an important and extremely defended nucleus of the ego that escapes communication.

In bad faith two types of omnipotence are found: the mechanism that produces metamorphosis, fantasms, and mirages, and also the omnipotence of the ego's defended part that uses this mechanism. Omnipotence in bad faith is ambiguous.

In bad faith, the subject needs to delude himself at the same time as he is deluding the object, which points to a close proximity between the two. Thus, as in the Proteus myth, he cannot simply refuse to answer his interlocutor and has to dodge him by metamorphosis. If the interlocutor is not discouraged and keeps on asking, Proteus has to give in and answer.

This proximity and this power of the persecutor, his knowledge of what happens in the ego, clearly reveal its superego character. On this level, bad faith looks like an attempt to disregard the superego. Our patients' attitudes concerning ethical issues share this feature, as they accept and at the same time ignore those values. If values are elaborated and rationalized rules of the superego, one is expected to find similar attitudes towards its most archaic forms. This is precisely what happens in the dramatization of dreams, in which bad faith avoids not ethical values, but the persecuting primitive aspects of the superego.

Yet, if the fight of the ego against the superego is, to a greater or lesser extent, universal, the style of fight used by bad faith is a particular one. The ego finds protection against the superego by managing multiple identities. Since the structuring of ego and superego are parallel processes, the ego's multiple identities must correspond to a particular structure of the superego.

Our cases prove that this is the case. All show an intensely marked inability to accept the parents as united and loving each other. In addition, there appears a duplication of the paternal figure. (This phenomenon has already been pointed out in the analysis of "pretenders"—Abraham, 1925; Deutsch, 1955; Greenacre, 1955b—who use a technique similar to that of bad faith.) These patients have gone through traumatic experiences or situations in which intense idealization of one of the parents has given way to intense underrating of the same figure. Their common characteristic is that they were not able to overcome these traumatic situations, which constantly emerge in their complaints, by achieving the unification of the parents' idealized figure and the underrated one. The omnipotent nucleus of the superego that seeks protection in bad faith is what is left of a relationship with a highly idealized object. As the subject fails to unite the contradictory aspects of the superego, he partly identifies with the idealized object to keep its omnipotence in himself. At the same time, he repeats the traumatic situation of deceit. He does not find his identity in himself because he cannot achieve the unity of his superego or the unity of his parents.

The other part of the superego is experienced as terribly destroyed or persecutory, depending on the case, and the proportion of each of them varies constantly. The omnipotence of the mechanism of bad faith proves to be a defence against the unification of the idealized and the underrated aspects of the superego, which produces guilt, depression, and helplessness, as well as a defence against persecution by the "bad" aspects of the superego.

Correlatively, bad faith precludes the intrusion of the reality that brought down the omnipotent idol and triggered the traumatic situation. The infallibility of the object must be maintained at all costs, now introjected and identified with that part of the ego turned omnipotent. Truth would bring about the fall of the idealized object and of the ego identified with it. But the traumatic episodes that seem to have brought about the de-idealization of one or both parental figures belong to a rather advanced stage in a child' life. This process of distortion of the superego being so deep, one can admit that this de-idealization only repeats or prolongs much more archaic phenomena. The subject's lack of authenticity as regards his values, the values themselves, and the superego reflect processes belonging to the paranoid–schizoid position.

Two of these processes—illusion and disillusion—are directly related to what concerns us here. As Rycroft (1955) notes, illusion is a state that depends on the idealization of the object: it is the hope that the object can provide the gratification that in fact it cannot give. In so far as this idealized object is projected into an external object, an illusory gratification is expected. When this gratification fails, disillusion appears in two senses: giving up the illusion that the object can give us more than it really can, or drastically underrating the object and giving up any idea of gratification coming from reality. The latter seems to me essential for the genesis of bad faith.

The inevitable failure of idealization, when the subject is incapable of elaborating it by achieving the synthesis of idealized and persecuting aspects of the primitive object—that is, by an adequate structuring of the depressive position—may give rise to various reactions. I shall refer to only two: in the first, the subject attempts to replace the fallen idol by another idol, which soon falls in turn, and so forth; this happens to be the case with falling in love, followed by disappointment, over and over again.

In bad faith, the idealized object seems to have a different outcome. At the moment of primitive disillusion, the idealized object is introjected and becomes identified with a part of the ego that becomes omnipotent. Consequently, external reality is experienced as radically devalued. Yet the persecuting aspects of the primitive object remain unchanged, either as persecution by an external object or as persecution by the superego.

That is why in bad-faith patients we perceive an inability to appreciate external reality or to find ideals that can yield satisfaction.

In extreme cases, the analysand only learns through novels what it means "to be in love", and he is unable to devote himself to truly achieving a goal he values.

In other less characteristic cases of bad faith, primitive disillusion appears much less radical. These keep the omnipotence of a part of their ego identified with the idealized object, without completely losing the possibility of appreciating aspects of external reality, although these appreciations are not constant and are followed by disillusion. In this sense, these can be regarded as intermediate cases between the two reactions I mentioned before when confronted with primitive disillusion, with a prevalence of the latter. For example, despite the fantasy of absolute autarchy, these subjects are able to fall in love and to have idealized friends. Through analytic treatment they may recover these friends now in a human way instead of the previous idealized one.

Bad faith, then, ultimately points to the psychopathology of idealization. It derives from the ego incapacity to overcome disillusion with the primitive object—the breast—which prevents the synthesis of the object as well as of the ego and the final access to the depressive position. As a part of the persecuting object remains neither synthesized nor assuaged, a part of the ego assimilates the omnipotence of the idealized object and wards off the persecuting object. The ego has lost trust in real or ideal objects of the external world. It faces a distorted and contradictory superego. To retain its omnipotence, the ego can only make use of its own dissociation in order to deceive the persecutors and the superego. To this purpose it uses its masks and characters and, like Proteus, flees from one shape to another to elude his own definition.

9

The dead–alive: object structure in mourning and depressive states

Willy Baranger

Both Sigmund Freud and Melanie Klein consider object structure—with its ego and superego correlates—as an essential dimension of the states of mourning and depression. I will accept here, as a working hypothesis, that there is a fundamental unity concerning the states of mourning, depression, and melancholia, as a fairly successful way of dealing with what Melanie Klein called depressive position.

I do not think I am betraying Melanie Klein's thought when I state that, for her, the nodule of a normal or pathological psychic evolution lies in the way or the ways in which a person manages to face this situation: by partial regression to processes of the paranoid–schizoid position, either by resorting to manic defences, or by remaining partially stuck in mournings that cannot be worked through, or else by progressing towards reparation, discrimination,

Published in Spanish as "El Muerto–Vivo" (*Revista Uruguaya de Psicoanálisis, 4*, 1961–1962: 586–603).

and assimilation. My clinical experience has confirmed the idea that there is a failed mourning at the root of every psychopathological condition—this idea is implicit in the role that projection and introjection free from restraint play in psychic development.

In the states belonging to the depressive series, mourning cannot be accomplished, and the person remains somehow tied to an object that can neither come to life again nor completely die. One could say that a person in a depressive state lives in submission to a dead–alive object, even though this does not appear immediately in a manifest way in his analytic material. Only after some analytic work does this object emerge gradually more and more clearly, so that we can study its structure and characteristics.

I have the conviction, based on several cases of persons suffering from severe depression, that this is a general phenomenon. Before presenting one of these cases, I would like to discuss the different varieties of the dead–alive object, since it appears with different characteristics and having different functions. Some kinds of dead–alive object are close to persecutory objects: we are thus confronted with a series of structures that has, at one end, the dying objects the ego must preserve at any price and, at the other end, objects that arouse in the ego a mixture of depressive anxiety and paranoid anxiety.

I. Varieties of the dead–alive

It is a common experience that in normal mourning it takes us some time to believe that the beloved person is dead. The ego knows consciously that the object has died—however, it reappears alive in dreams and fantasies, and the ego finds itself sharing projects with the dead person, having fantasies of running into him in the street, and so on, as if it could not bring itself to accept his death.

In some forms of slightly pathological mourning, this state persists beyond the normal time of working through, and the dead person keeps on existing "as a separate person, carrying on the function of surveillance and salvation for the subject". In these cases the person keeps the house exactly as it was at the time of the death, refraining from any change in the dead person's belongings, as if he might at any moment come back and take his place among the living. In other cases the dead person acts directly to save the life of the subject in situations of danger, or he communicates with the living "from the afterlife" via tables, a "medium", parapsychological dreams, and so forth. In these cases the dead person tends to acquire superego functions: the person's "bad" actions can make the dead suffer, feel pity, or awaken his vengeful wrath.

A third variety of the dead–alive is found in an object that has been damaged or killed by the living person, and this exercises a moral persecution on him. This is the myth of the silent guest or its modern drama version: *"Amédée ou comment s'en débarrasser"* ["Amédée, or How to Get Rid of It"] by Ionesco.

Sometimes we encounter the fantasy of the dead–alive in decomposition, when depressive anxiety is mingled with too much paranoid anxiety. And the ego is in danger of being dragged into death by the object it loves, dreads, and abhors.

Similarly, there are dead people who are not rotten but "clean" and sometimes even beautiful—a form that appear in many legends as "zombies". These dead persons cannot die completely, and thus they remain hungry and filled with envy towards the living. Their aim is to "dwell" in someone alive and control him from inside. These "souls in torment" become terribly dangerous and vengeful as they are frustrated and miserable. Like the unburied dead in ancient Greek and Latin culture, their greatest pain is not to be able to find peace in death. This reminds us of the legends about men who had been cursed with immortality. An extreme example of this is the vampire, definitely a paranoid form.

Undoubtedly the most important kind is the dying object in depressive states. Here, too, the person is "inhabited" by an almost dead inner object, but the persecution consists only in the demands it makes on the person. It has him enslaved in a pointless reparatory activity, because he will never attain his goal: there will always be something more to be done. This unconscious situation gives rise to depressive anxiety related to external objects, to guilt, to inhibitions, and to other defences we find in depressive states.

I would like now to examine the dead–alive object in a few sessions of a woman patient where, I think, it can be clearly seen.

II. The dead–alive object in a depressive personality

The following fragments of sessions are from the third year of the
analysis of a 29-year-old woman patient who suffered from depression. They show different structural stages of an object clearly sunk
in depression and its corresponding characterological traits. In the
first session this object appears with superego characteristics.

First session

The patient speaks about her lifelong concern with her objects
(mainly her mother) and then remembers a story: "A soldier is
walking across a wood. He finds a tiny old woman lying on the
ground. She looks tired and ill. The soldier feels pity for her and
offers to help. The old lady begs him to carry her along the road for
a while. He agrees. But the old lady becomes heavier and heavier;
the poor soldier is exhausted, he shakes under her weight, but he
cannot get rid of her".

On this level the dying object, through pity or guilt (the soldier
thinks of his abandoned mother), succeeds in getting hold of the
person and enslaving him.

In the following sessions the depressive state deepens, with
much anxiety and crying.

Second session (some days later)

The patient relates a story that has struck her. "This is about a
couple who have a grown-up son. They are given a monkey's paw,
a charm that grants three wishes. The wife persuades her husband
to wish for a sum of money that will allow them to redeem the
mortgage on their house. They do so. At that very moment there
is a knock on the door: their son has been smashed to pieces by a
machine, and the parents can get the life insurance, which is equal
to the money they had wished for before. The mother, desperate,
wishes for the second time: to have her son back. At that point they
hear a knock at the main door and shudder to think what their
son may look like after the accident (in pieces? decayed?). And
they decide to use the third wish to make their son go return the

cemetery. The woman then opens the door, only to see footsteps retreating through the snow.

The session goes on, with different situations of loss and mourning in childhood. She mentions the death of an older cousin of hers, whom she loved very much. She has had thousands of dreams in which she has seen him alive, but now she realizes that she has never been able to see his eyes (as if they had rotted away). She blames herself for her cousin's death (if she had loved him, he might not have gone away and died abroad).

In this session the patient becomes aware of the relationship between different objects belonging to different times in her life (losing her mother at an early age, then losing her nannies, the dead grandmother, her cousin). The dead–alive son in the story is equivalent to her cousin, alive but with rotten eyes (castrated, without sexuality). The dry monkey's paw (castrated and omnipotent) is another representation of the dead–alive object.

Two conclusions can be drawn from this material:

1. The actual mourning for the cousin's death has condensed and crystallized a series of previous losses and mournings—early in infancy—and her cousin, as a dead–alive object, stands for the damaged objects of the infantile depressive position.

2. The monkey's paw (cut off and vengeful) seems to belong to a previous stage of the same object. When the couple accept the charm, they accept responsibility for the damage done to the monkey, which then turns into a moral persecutor.

The third session will be discussed in greater detail because, in my opinion, it throws some light on the inner structure of the dead–alive object.

Third session (immediately following the second one)

"I wonder why these last days I have not been dreaming, considering my anxiety, depression, and mourning, but last night I had a dream. *I saw a little house, it looked like a row house, but I saw only this one. One side was like those ice houses of the Eskimos, an igloo, and the*

other side had an inclined roof, like those tile-roofs. My father was there,
and he told me, 'This beam with the T-shape has slid down and broken. I
have to fix it.' I saw the letter T and thought of the word 'treason'. It was
like a charade where I had to guess."

She associates with the puzzles in magazines that she used to
do as an adolescent with her father, and with her ability to solve
them. Also she mentions a cardboard T cut up into small pieces,
which made it very difficult to put together again. With treason
she associates her fantasy of betraying her people by telling me
her private life.

Afterwards she talks about clearly sadomasochistic anal and urethral fantasies.

She is puzzled by the mixing of these fantasies with the content
of previous sessions, as if all this were somehow related.

She thinks of the dolls' houses her father had given her when
she was a child, which had delighted her. She associates the roof
of the dream house with her father's penis. Then the letter T, a
charade figure that represented the letter D, broken, with something drawn inside that should read, "Within the great defeat . . .".
The T and the teapot. She then tells a joke about Lollobrigida's
"teapots".[1]

I am referring only to what is strictly necessary in order to understand the dream. I have left out, for reasons of space, all that has
to do with the patient's transference situation, although that could
confirm to a great extent what I hold here.

This dream speaks of the patient's desire to gain a better understanding of the essence of the anxiety depression she had felt so intensely during the previous days. Hence the memories she brought
about the puzzles she used to solve with her father (the analyst)
and her fantasies about "insight" as putting together broken and
scattered pieces separated from her experience. This is a particularly "communicative" dream, expressing the patient's desire to do
her best for the analytic work. We can also see in these associations
several memories and fantasies voiced for the first time, and this
has to do with previous interpretations on the nature of the objects
she experiences in her depressive states, adding another dimension
to these interpretations.

The dolls' house alludes to a favourite toy her father had given
her in her childhood (idyllic union with the father). That is why

there appears the association with the father's good penis (inclined roof and tiles).

It is clear that the father's penis appears in two ways: as the tile roof of the "marvellous" little house of her childhood, and also as the broken beam.

As regards the other half of the house in the dream, it is identified with Lollobrigida's beautiful "tits", but made of ice.

The house means, therefore, the imperfect union of the patient's two most primitive objects (mother's breast/father's penis). This faulty union (an awkward house) is due to the contradictory character of the objects it is comprised of: the ice breast and the cheerful tile roof. Yet there is a contradiction not only between the two objects but also within each of them. The roof lies on a T–shaped beam, but broken, displaced, and connected with the patient's "great defeat". The breast is made of ice, but it is also Lollobrigida's tits; and the igloo gives warmth to the Eskimos, but at the same time it conceals the use, disgusting for us, of human urine in their domestic activities. (This interpretation was followed by her comment on a relative's therapeutic use of urine. This was also related to urethral sadistic fantasies during this session: "good" and "bad" urine.)

I think it is evident that the house in the dream represents a prototype of the "series" of objects involved in the patient's depressive states that have already been mentioned.

So far this is the condensation of two objects that are both part objects (as parts of the human body) and also whole objects (loved and hated, "marvellous" but frozen or broken), and the dead–alive object of the previous sessions is not there yet. Let us try to understand this difference.

It is very important to remember at this point how the patient starts the session: the dream is produced *in order* to throw light on the structure of the depressive object, and the object represented in the dream seems to have nothing to do with the objects that had appeared in previous sessions (dead–alive objects threatening death). Just the opposite: a surprising change has taken place. The patient does not cry, does not feel guilty: instead, she develops an intense communication with me in our shared analytic work. And this prevents me from understanding the situation in regressive terms as the repression of guilt and sadness. The patient is ready to "betray" her parents if this can lead her to improvement. This situation is more regressive and more progressive than previous ones. It is more regressive because it heads for an object situation preceding the structuring of the depressive state. And it is more progressive because it unfolds in a context of communication and reparation.

We are now in a position to understand how the object state expressed here by the patient can give rise to clearly and deeply depressive objects that are in general present in her sessions.

I am inclined to think that the object situation expressed in this session is similar to the evolutionary object state prior to the installation of the depressive position.

Depressive feelings of sorrow and guilt are not very important in this dream. The evilness of the ego towards its objects is shown only in her fantasy of "betrayal" and in her concern with her father's broken penis.

Yet if we focus on the latent characteristics (evident in the associations about the dream) of the object situation, they seem to correspond to the characteristics Melanie Klein describes as those pertaining to the depressive position: objects synthesized in an ambivalent relationship with the patient's ego and superego.

Instead of the deep depression of previous sessions, we now have oral-sadistic, anal, and urethral fantasies (sometimes active, others passive). What is found fused in the depressive position is now discriminated in this session: the frozen or damaged objects on the one hand, and sadistic fantasies on the other. When the ego takes these fantasies and relates them to the object, it feels responsible for the damage. Then the object appears as dead–alive, partly murdered by the ego, which is, in turn, overwhelmed by sorrow, guilt, and the compulsion to repair.

Some historical data from the patient's life seem to confirm this description. In the first years of life she had been abandoned by her mother (although not physically), and she chose a mother substitute—a nanny, whom she used to call "Mummy" and whom she lost when she was three. Then she lost another nanny when she was four. A little later she was bereaved of her much loved grandmother. This was a great loss for the whole family, because this grandmother had been the pillar and psychological support of the family.

Throughout many sessions the patient provides a good deal of information about these losses and the attendant death fantasies. The nanny left to take care of her dying mother, and for the patient this was as if the nanny had died. Although they met on many occasions, she could never again feel the love she used to have for her.

This information sheds light on the nature of the "frozen" breast in the dream. The igloo stands for two things: the mother's "dead" breast (the mother of the first abandonment) and her schizoid attempt to "freeze" the object of love, hatred, and frustration. The little house represents her attempt to replace the mother's breast with the father's penis. This is very clear in the anamnesis. But the father's penis is contaminated (due to its origin in a disturbing experience at her mother's breast, to the duplication of the original mother, and to the ambivalence present in the relationship with the father). The distribution of the conflict (between breast and penis) is not enough to lessen it. The penis appears "broken" as the breast, despite its idealization.

One step forward, and we arrive at depressive feelings. Penis and breast join together, libidinal feelings and sadistic fantasies mingle, the ego takes responsibility for the whole situation, objects are shaped through fantasies of rupture and death: the general situation is one of an ego relation with dead–alive objects, and an omnipotent and morally critical aspect of these objects goes into the superego.

This session seems to me to be like a snapshot of the object state previously to the dying of the object.

Of course, the house in the dream also represents, to a secondary degree, the patient's ego in her identification with the abovementioned objects, parts of which have been integrated into the ego structure as characterological traits (feeling of frailty, of ugliness, of worthlessness, etc., of her own ego). The unlucky part (fortunately not essential) of the patient's fate arose from her partial identification with the dying object.

These fragments of sessions show three evolutionary stages of the object involved in the states of the depressive series.

In the first there is the manifest content of the situation, in which the ego is enslaved by an extremely powerful superego that clearly originates as object in the damaged and omnipotent

maternal imago. The second one sends us straight to the latent
nodule of the depressive position: the ego relationship with its
dead–alive object, which has not yet undergone the assimilation
process within the psychic structure—that is, in this case, it has not
been integrated into the superego. The third leads us to a previous
level at which the dead–alive object has not yet crystallized as such
and where ambivalent and contradictory primitive objects appear
with a certain degree of fusion, together with sadistic and libidinal
fantasies corresponding to pre-genital levels.

The heuristic sequence of these object situations in this analysis
may serve to clarify the function of the constitution of the dead–
alive object, if it corresponds (as I think it does, in this case) to a
real genetic sequence in an inverse chronological sense. Depressive
anxiety is thus controlled by focusing and synthesizing both fantasies and libidinal and sadomasochistic impulses.

What puzzles this patient—*coming out of anxiety depression*—is the
mixing (in other cases, this may be manifested by a state of confusion) of these fantasies with the compound objects of the dream
in Session 3. It can be assumed that if her present ego is not too
afraid of these fantasies, her primitive ego has, on the contrary,
had to resort to strong defences to keep the corresponding anxiety
at bay. In order to maintain her sources of gratification and her
relationship with external objects, she has had to isolate an object
on which to centre her sadistic fantasies. She was then confronted
with the danger of the death of this object (a danger confirmed
by actual experiences in her life) and had to invest a great deal
of libidinal interest to avert this danger, at the price of ego impoverishment. Every attempt since then to assimilate the dead–alive
object has meant a release of sadistic impulses; therefore the ego
has tended to cling to the ambiguous structure of the dead–alive
object. Of course, this is not a static situation. There are moments,
or periods, when the dead–alive object diminishes in influence, and
others when it is in full swing, invading the patient's life, structuring
symptomatic depression. So, with ups and downs, and depending
on events in real life, the relationship of the dead–alive object with
the ego and with the superego undergoes significant variations.
On a more developed level of functioning it appears more fused
with the superego, and the ego takes on some of its characteristics
(more fragile, prey to sadism, helpless and poor, etc.), and on an-

other level it appears as independent of the superego, as an object direct from an ego burdened with guilt and sorrow. Each level has a corresponding ego function. On the first level, the ego is relatively free from depressive anxiety and finds defence in its limitations; on the second, depressive anxiety is much more intense, and symptomatic anxiety ensues.

We are aware of the function of the dead–alive object; now we have to examine more carefully the obstacles that hinder it from either dying or living, and which account for its ambiguity.

III. On the rigidity of the dead–alive object and its difficulties of assimilation

In patients like the one I am describing, and in many other similar cases, there is a tendency to create, again and again, situations similar to those described in the sessions above. The question is, why cannot the dead–alive object either die or live? Why does the process that takes place in the course of any "normal" mourning fail with these patients? Of course, Freud was the first to pose this problem and many other authors have done so after him. I will not review these contributions, but only mention some related factors that can, in a way, complement them.

The concept of "the work of mourning" can be a guideline to understanding this problem. According to Freud, it consists in a partitioning of the global death of the object into a series of little deaths or, from the point of view of the ego, into a series of partial relinquishments of all the aspects of the relationship of the ego with the object, of all the memories that kept that relationship alive. Reality testing is decisive in this work.

For further information about this issue I will borrow more case material from the same patient. Some sessions after the last dream mentioned, the patient recounted the following dream: *"Some neighbours came to ask me for help. They were afraid that something, an object, might hurt them. This object was manipulated by someone from another part of the world. I took this object out of the brown trunk of a tree, where it was deeply buried. The object was like this* [shows the shape of a stirrup] *with two plugs, something confusing. Then I saw it turning greener and greener. . . . Then it turned to ashes."*

Her main association referred to a tree that she had, one with dry branches but that was greening, thus bringing hope that it would live and grow. The "neighbours" clearly represented the patient's own family and the "object", in her first description, stands for a paranoid persecutor (dangerous, directed at a distance, cosmic). The tree represents the patient herself with her buried object.

However the "object" does not appear only as persecutor: it is a plug and a stirrup (penis, relationship), and the patient is not afraid of it (this means merely a dream screen). However, the most interesting thing is the destiny of the object. It is turning green and then turns to ashes.

I hold that the patient represents as a sequence—as it often happens in dreams—what is alternatively or simultaneously produced in her psyche. In other words, this dream represents the process of assimilation of the object: its alive part (greening) remains in the patient's tree (ego), while the rest turns to ashes (dead).

This is actually what happens in the process of assimilation of the object by the ego during the work of mourning: part of the dead–alive object is dead and is anally expelled (what is brown), while another part is integrated into the ego and gives it life (libidinal greening). This runs parallel to the reparation process (the patient makes a beautiful tree grow).

Our problem lies in the following: What prevents the assimilation of the object? What turns the work of mourning into a Penelope mourning?

This dream yields a first answer, already formulated by Melanie Klein. It is the intensity of the primitive paranoid–schizoid processes that prevents the resolution of the depressive position. Indeed, in depressive and melancholic states there is always an important mixture of paranoid–schizoid mechanisms and processes. Here, although this patient's problem is at this point in her analysis—essentially the working-through of depressive states—a dream with a paranoid first part arises. It is as if the obstacle and the way to overcome it were appearing together.

Besides, if our description of the constitution of the dead–alive object is right, the isolation of this object and the focusing on it of all sadistic fantasies imply a splitting process, which permits the other objects and the ego in its essential part to continue with its integration. This splitting is different from the paranoid–schizoid one, since it falls on objects more integrated into a relationship with a more developed ego, which also has different intrinsic characteristics: it is less massive and, except in very severe cases, it is more labile.

The process of idealization was first described by Melanie Klein as a defence against the depressive position, although she later related it mainly to the paranoid–schizoid position. The idealization of objects that appear as alive, strong, resistant to any possible damage, emerges in depressive positions as defence against the destruction of other objects. But, differing from what appears in paranoid states, the idealization of the alive object fails to be completely free from ambivalence, and there is always the fantasy of the fragility of the object or of the bond with it as a possible threat to the idealized object.

Furthermore, there is a telling symbiotic relationship of the ego in mourning or in depression with the dead–alive object. When Freud writes that "the shadow of the object falls upon the ego", he also seems to be referring to this process. To put it into oral terms, the object feeds on the substance of the ego: the only way the ego finds to avoid the death of the object. The result is twofold: on the one hand, the ego gives up an important part of its own qualities for the sake of its inner object—and it may also be for the sake of its external representatives; on the other hand, the ego tends to draw upon itself the sadistic fantasies and impulses directed towards the object, which gives rise to a masochistic attitude. This process leads to the impoverishment of the ego and to the already mentioned idealization of the object.

We are bound to recognize the existence, in states of mourning and depression, of two diverse objects, both ambivalent but having different structures. Both feed on the ego and weaken it, both lead the ego to adopt a masochistic attitude, but they have opposite functions. The first, the dead–alive object, has the function of localizing sadistic fantasies and of allowing depressive anxiety to be controlled. The second, the idealized object with life and potency, serves as shelter to the ego as the ego deposits on it part of its own reparatory potential and capacity in order to preserve them from its own masochism and from the danger of its own death. The ego, feeling impoverished and fragile, looks for security in a strong and intensely alive object. This is often observed in transference

manifestations of persons in a depressive position: the analyst becomes a representative of this idealized object, and the patient's
ego partakes in a symbiotic form in the analyst's vitality.

The particular character of depressive idealization has already
been pointed out. This symbiosis also should be carefully differentiated from its paranoid–schizoid counterpart. The latter functions essentially with projective identification, aims at controlling
paranoid anxiety, and eliminates all ambivalence. Here, on the
contrary, symbiosis functions with both introjective and projective
identification, and the projected or introjected parts of the ego
and of the object have undergone the special process of depressive
splitting. That is to say, the idealized object holds fragile or dying
aspects of its own ego together with its potentialities for life. This
can be observed in the transference: even in those moments when
the analyst represents the idealized objects (and not the dead–alive
ones), the depressive patient's fear of losing the analyst or of his
destruction may be intense, and the end of the analysis provokes
acute problems, leading to setbacks.

I am afraid these symbiotic processes of the depressive states
have not been properly assessed so far, otherwise there would have
been awareness that one of the bases of pathological mourning lies
in the ego's previous symbiotic relation with the lost object. The
symbiotic situation itself implies a difficulty in distinguishing that
which belongs to the ego from that which belongs to the object.
When the external representative of the object dies or is lost, it is as
if the parts of the ego placed in the object had also died, and this
naturally hinders its reintegration into the ego even more and ag-
gravates the ego's impoverishment. The new object loss reactivates
the infantile depressive position and increases the ego's difficulties
to overcome it by means of reparatory processes.

Note

1. [*Translator's note:* In Spanish *teapot* is *tetera* which sounds close to
teta—that is, "tit".]

10

The ego and the function of ideology

Willy Baranger

As the purpose of psychoanalysis is not to cure isolated symptoms of neurosis but to modify the life of people entirely, the problems of ideology acquire increasing importance in the process of analysis. Since the ego of a civilized human being is expressed though certain ideological attitudes, the patient's ideology becomes "analytic material" even before we know the exact meaning of this material. It belongs—partly, at any rate—to the ego. It plays a part in psychic balance. We cannot ignore its function or its relationship with the ego.

I. Definition of ideology and the principles of investigation

In most cases we receive the ideology from without (by introjective identification). Therefore ideology has one first form of existence—anthropological or sociological—which we will set aside, for it escapes direct psychoanalytic observation. Neither are we going

First published in English in *International Journal of Psychoanalysis, 39*, 1958: 191–195; reprinted by permission.

to deal with the specific problems posed by each type of ideology.

Above all, we shall set aside the problem of truth. Not because the difference between scientifically "proved" knowledge and an erroneous ideology is not essential. But our purpose is to examine the psychic function of ideology, whether or not it is "appropriate" in its relationship with the ego. The psychoanalytic problem of the adequateness of an ideology should be taken up at a subsequent examination.

By ideology we mean every system of abstract ideas (conscious or unconscious) whose function it is to represent that which is real and man's action upon that which is real.

This is the widest possible definition. It includes scientific knowledge as well as philosophical or religious systems, and ethical, aesthetic, and political conceptions.

It implies a method of examination based on a certain number of principles the fruitfulness of which has been proved by psychoanalytic experience.

1. Owing to the principle of genetic continuity, the most abstract and complex forms of thought are based on the simplest and most concrete forms.

2. The same mechanisms work upon the elaboration of the ideology, be it "valid" or "erroneous" and "neurotic".

3. Fantasies and primitive objects are present and remain active in the most abstract and "objective" of ideological systems.

We shall deal with the subjective aspects of this ideology in its relationship with the ego.

II. Ideology, fantasy, and object

In 1901 Freud formulated the principle of the application of psychoanalysis to ideologies when, in *The Psychopathology of Everyday Life* (1901b), he suggested "translating metaphysics into metapsychology" and considered mythological creeds and superstitions "the projection of unconscious processes". He later extended this principle to other ideologies: religions, moral codes, political opinions, philosophical beliefs.

Every ideology, whatever its "truth" or "validity", is, therefore, in the character of a psychic phenomenon, liable to be reduced to more elementary psychic phenomena. We do not conceive this as the chemical analysis of a compound body and its reduction to simple bodies. The aim is not to exhaust the ideology or to consider it an epiphenomenon of unconscious mechanisms. On the contrary, we intend to prove that from the point of view of the ego ideology assumes an absolutely authentic function.

However, ideology, like every psychic phenomenon, reveals more than it consciously wishes to: in other words, it has a latent content; it expresses unconscious fantasies and object relations (just like dreams, play, the neurotic symptom, or any mental phenomenon).

Freud proved that the ego acquires its ideology through a series of introjective identifications—that is to say, it is itself experienced as an object, and itself represents a series of introjected objects.

We believe that ideology represents an attempt on the part of the ego to integrate these unconscious fantasies and these object relationships in a "world" that is more or less coherent and more or less true to "reality".

So ideology is neither absolutely determined (as it would be in a mechanistic materialistic perspective) nor absolutely determinant (as it would be in an idealistic perspective).

The following example can illustrate these ideas:

The analysis of patient A was at times centred upon an ideological system revealing all sorts of conflicts. It dealt with a discovery that was on the other hand objectively valid. It had come into the patient's mind to connect the stages of phonation with the stages of individual psychic development, which made it possible to diagnose important aspects of their individual history and their structure by studying the individual's phonetic expressions and their inhibitions. A had thus elaborated a test that constituted an accessory method of diagnosis.

In the course of the analysis A realized that her first experience with the "test" had taken place in her childhood. She used to listen to her parents' voices in the adjoining room at bedtime. Without understanding their words, she knew from the tone of their voices what was the state of their relationship at that moment and the nature of the tensions made manifest between them (for the patient, this was the degree of aggressiveness on the mother's part and the danger run by the father in the primal scene). This recollection, having all the characteristics of a screen memory, reveals the fantasy contained in the ideological system and in the test: the control of the danger in the primal scene experienced as the destruction of the father by the bad mother.

But other object relations took part in the elaboration of this ideology. The system allowed A not only to control the bad mother but to become identified with a kindly maternal figure.

Mrs X, a singing teacher, had played an important affective part in A's adolescence. Because of her beauty, her charm, and her kindness, she stood, in A's mind, for the type of sympathetic, "perfect" mother who permits sexual activity. And Mrs X only had to study someone's voice in order to know the person.

In A's case, then, the control of the primal scene was possible by means of an identification with the idealized mother, which allowed her to locate and limit the persecution of the "real" mother.

The system thus came to substitute an object (Mrs X) and to be experienced as such. This situation could be seen clearly in the transference. As the result of a dream in which a man representing me broke into a cabin to steal some papers belonging to A, she realized that she was misrepresenting the content of her discovery to me: she thought I would steal it and publish it under my own name. The more superficial significance of the dream (rape in the genital plane) screens the fear of being robbed of an object that the patient regards as "marvellous", "of too great importance", "a wonderful discovery". The conscious obsession of rape concealed the patient's fear of the theft of an idealized object. This fear was revealed by a typical obsessive behaviour. During a given period she would spend several hours a day writing out her theory. Then she would tear up the written sheets, because the language always seemed "too imperfect for a discovery of such importance". She compared her conduct to "the work of Penelope". The imperfection of the language revealed the desire that the work should be quite beyond reproach (every criticism being experienced as terrible persecution). The ego appeared as the unworthy receptacle of that capital discovery—"a garbage can into which a pearl had been cast"—and the outer world symbolized a double threat: the theft of the idealized object and its devaluation.

Melanie Klein showed that idealization is in direct proportion to the intensiveness of the anxiety of persecution, the idealization and the persecution being the result of the splitting process. The analysis of paranoid anxieties and their weakening, the appearance, in the transference, of depressive anxieties, and the beginning of elaboration allowed A to begin to assimilate the idealized object. In the practical ground she dared to formulate her theory and set it before reality—through coherent experimenting and gradual adjustment of the theoretical formulation.

We find, in this case, not a completed ideological system but a system in the process of constitution. The problem pertaining to the ideological system is therefore mingled with that of sublimation. But the two problems are connected, since every ideological production or participation implies a degree of sublimation.

An all too brief examination of this case leads to the following conclusions:

1. An ideological system expresses unconscious fantasies.
2. An ideological system expresses object relationships.
3. An ideological system is experienced in itself as an object.
4. An ideological system corresponds to a certain stage of elaboration or assimilation of an idealized object.

III. The ego, the ego-ideal, the superego, and the ideology

The ego, in its functions of cognition and action, appears as the privileged centre of the ideological process. At least in its conscious aspects, ideology is controlled by the ego. However, it is absolutely necessary to distinguish, in a given individual, several types of ideology. Some belong above all to the ego, others are in contradiction with it and derive from archaic aspects of the superego (or of introjective identifications, overcome but not assimilated by the ego).

In the evolution of his thoughts, Freud substituted for the concept of the ego-ideal that of the superego (not, however, renouncing the first concept). If the ego-ideal does not constitute a separate instance, there is an important contradiction between the primitive aspects, cruel, irrational, and frustrating, of the superego, and the elaborated aspects, rational, civilized, and gratifying, which we call the ego-ideal. The contradiction between the superego and the ego-ideal is always revealed to a certain extent in the opposition between the conscious ideology and the unconscious ideology of the individual (this gross opposition must be tempered and studied concretely in each case). The distinction between the ego-ideal and the superego might also do as a basis for a very elementary classification of ideologies. Thus very persecutory or highly idealized ideologies—very absolute ones, in short—would be opposed to more relative ideologies, nearer to reality, better synthesized with the experiences of the ego. This would open new perspectives on ideological "distortion". The ideology of minor "distortion" would correspond to the greatest possible degree of harmony between the ego, the superego, and the ego-ideal (assimilation of the successive objects of identification that constitute the superego and the assimilation of the superego and of the ideal of the ego). These three factors—superego, ego-ideal, and ego—acquire internal coherence as they harmonize.

This would also explain the relationship of the ideology with the idealized objects. The more idealized the object is, the less assimilated it is by the ego, the more split up and the more powerful the persecutory objects are. The contact of ideology with reality is obtained by means of synthesis, the object acquiring more "real" characteristics as the ego can defend itself from the persecutory anxieties and elaborate its depressive processes in the form of a reparation.

IV. Function of ideology

Ideology seems to assume three types of function:

(1) A defensive function

Ideology is one of the means of struggling against persecution. Very often the apparent content of the ideological system makes way for the persecutory objects, which makes it possible to distinguish, personify, and control them. We think of the devil in many religious creeds; we think of evil in certain philosophical beliefs.

The breadth of the splitting processes implied in idealization as well as persecution directly influences the more or less powerful hold of the system upon the concrete phenomenon.

From that point of view, an ideological system always expresses one of the essential constellations ruling the relationships of the ego with the superego and the internalized objects. The anxiety of persecution is thus partly located in an object whose persecutory character is intelligible to a certain extent, liable to be assimilated by the ego and much more liable to be controlled.

In the experience, the system is not more rigid than the constellation expressed by it; one same system can be experienced by one individual in a more or less regressive way at different times, that is to say that the extent of the splitting up, of the idealization, of the persecution, implied in the system, can vary considerably.

Obviously the system does not express *solely* the reciprocal internal structure of the ego and the persecuting objects. Elements and characteristics undoubtedly pertaining to the ego are assimilated to the parts of the system ruled by persecuting and idealized objects and form a part of its total structure.

(2) *The function of restoration of the object*

This function acts upon the transposition of the unconscious "object" to the ideological "object".

The process of elaboration performed more or less successfully by the ego in this transposition implies an attempt on the part of the ego to give the object a coherent and viable structure—that is, a certain liberty to modify the object without fearing to destroy it. If this fear is too strong, the ego is not able to assimilate its object and has to shut itself in a sterile contemplation. The object then remains unchanged, and the ego just supplies the marvellous object with a kind of protective cyst or shell.

In this plane, ideological elaboration follows the rule of every sublimation.

In A's case, for instance, the "Penelope work" (a technique of protection from genital and much more regressive threats) persisted until the analysis succeeded in reducing the paranoid anxieties (manifested in phobias), thus permitting less frequent application to splitting and idealization.

But the depressive anxieties played a determining part too in A's difficulties in producing her work. She called herself "the sand-breasted woman" and kept her children at a distance so as to protect them from her destructivity. She felt that she could do nothing for them, that "she could give them nothing" (depressive anxiety). Penelope's tapestry has a depressive meaning too, since Penelope destroys her work with her own hands as she creates it. A felt the same fear regarding her work. She could not "give birth" to it because her ego could not intervene in the assimilation of the idealized object necessary to the birth. Her fantasy was that her work "would come out from her with forceps, all cut into pieces".

As long as the opposition of value between the ego and the object has been radical, the assimilation of the ego and the object has been equivalent to the destruction of the latter, and this provoked an intolerable depressive anxiety. The ego contented itself with protecting the idealized object, encysting it, but without touching it.

Some aspects of the ego (experienced previously as "bad" or "valueless") had then to be able to assimilate the object in order to permit the overcoming of the "Penelope" stage. When this was achieved, there were observed at the same time a weakening of the anxieties, a much more gratifying attitude of A towards her children, the progressive elaboration of her work, and a growing self-confidence in her capacity to produce a valuable work and restore her objects.

We consider that the analysis of the processes of ideological creation in A's case shows:

> that the process of ideological creation corresponds to the restoration of an object threatened or damaged by the aggressive tendencies of the individual;

> that there is a direct connection between the intensity of the depressive anxieties and the difficulties of the ideological elaboration and between the overcoming of the depressive position and the freedom of this elaboration.

(3) *A function of regulating system*

Ideology partly controls the relationship between the ego, the id, the superego, and reality. This does not mean that it constitutes a particular instance such as the ego or the superego, although it cannot be exclusively attributed to one or the other. Every ideology implies and represents a certain conception of what is real, with a given position of the ego within reality.

Ideology seems to be an attempt on the part of the ego to assume consciously the task of reconciling the demands of the superego with those of the id as far as they may be expressed in reality (Freud). This is possible only when the ego is not overcome by the feeling of its own destructiveness or of its own incapacity to restore its objects.

Ideology aims at the integration of the psychic instances and an important sector of reality. It depends in the first place on the parental models identified with the ego and passively submits to them. But as it represents an attempt at the restoration of the object and at the synthesis of the ego, that is an attempt at harmonizing successive and partly contradictory identifications, it contributes a new factor that changes the sense of these identifications. Then there comes into play a selection depending on a more or less consistent synthesis of the objects and instances.

> Patient B, with a philosophical vocation, centred his ethical system upon a notion of "quality". It was not an extrinsic quality of the action or the person who performed it, but an intrinsic characteristic of the ego and its action upon the world. This characteristic served to distinguish two categories of people. In B's world there was a small number of chosen ones with whom relations were possible, and the rest of mankind, having no existence of their own, were reduced to the category of implements. The perception of any sign of meanness or of any "inauthenticity" in any of the chosen ones was enough for B to transfer him to the second category, which was done with a feeling of disillusion and a general decline of affective interests.

> This aristocratic code was connected with several identifications. B laughed at the aristocratic claims of his mother and derisively

compared the high society of his native town (which he only called "Versailles") to the court of Louis XIV. This counteridentification with his mother screened a deeper identification, "quality" being the equivalent, in a higher plane, of his mother's "blue blood".

B had at first been in love with his mother, for whom he had written poems since he had learnt how to write. The discovery that his mother had shown his poems to other people instead of regarding them as a world of wonders reserved for the two of them had caused deep disillusion, followed by affective rupture with her and the destruction of all the poems. This prototypical experience of disillusion (in connection with the previous perception of the primal scene) had marked the end of his affection for his mother (B imagined that he had no relationship whatever with his parents, "that he was entirely self-made"). Nevertheless, B wished to reconstruct his ideal relationship with his mother (more profoundly, with an idealized maternal breast) in love affairs endowed with wonderful characteristics. The objects of this relationship were chosen in a very narcissistic way (the name of the star Sirius designated, in the particular language of one relationship, at the same time B himself, his object, similar to himself, and the particular world they shared).

Disillusion with his mother in the primal scene (in connection with the oral frustration) leads B to reconstruct his idealized object on a more and more abstract plane (philosophic vocation—the fantasy of universal wisdom—fantasies of absolute autarchy and auto-generation similar to divinity). At the same time his internal idealized object is further and further identified with the ego.

The theory of "quality" is the expression of this situation. The ego contrived to keep its idealized object, elaborating it as an abstraction (it possesses it as an intrinsic "quality"). It has partly assimilated it, thus acquiring omnipotence; the persecuting aspects of the superego are denied or reduced to impotence, and contact with reality is produced on the intellectual plane. I am sure that the analysis of B would have been quite impossible without an examination of his theory of "quality" and the processes at its basis. B had remained practically unproductive up to the moment of the analysis of those processes; this allowed him, in a way, to regain contact with the split-up aspects of his objects and his ego; sorrowfully to go through the experience of his own destructibility; to renounce divinity; which was revealed by a lesser splitting in his object relationship and by the acquisition of an effective intellectual productiveness.

The analysis of the theory of "quality" in B's case clearly shows how ideology constitutes an attempt on the part of the ego to take up the internal organization of the instances and insert it into reality. Ideology represents the greatest effort made by the ego to turn its superego into the ego-ideal, to assimilate the ego into the ego-ideal, and to accept certain aspects of the id to integrate them in the world.

V. Ideology and neurosis: technical consequences

Certain forms of neurosis—particularly character neurosis—are located above all in the ideological sector; but an ideological expression of the conflicts occurs in every patient. The ideology may be transformed into a bastion that the patient opposes to the analytic process (B refused analytic contact every time he could perceive— or imagined he could perceive—lack of "quality" in his analyst). Being, by definition, valued (that is, idealized to a certain extent) it serves as a refuge to very important identifications that the patient does not want to bring into play in the course of the analysis, and it is never experienced as a symptom. That is the reason why, in the technical plane, ideology and its bases must be systematically analysed, since they are an essential sector in human experience.

Final comments

Leticia Glocer Fiorini

Throughout the pages of this book, the reader has come into contact with pioneering and anticipatory work of great interest for the field of psychoanalysis: the work of Willy and Madeleine Baranger. This volume gathers together a series of articles that have been profoundly influential in psychoanalysis in Argentina, Uruguay, and the rest of Latin America.

As a brief biographical note, we recall that Madeleine and Willy Baranger came to Argentina in 1946. Willy [1922–1994] was born in Algeria and was a professor of philosophy; Madeleine was a professor of classics in France. They subsequently joined the Argentine Psychoanalytic Association. Afterwards they moved to Montevideo, where they created the Uruguayan Psychoanalytical Association in 1955. When they moved back to Argentina in 1966 they continued with their psychoanalytic practice and publications as well as participating in the institutional activities of the APA. They both received the "Mary Sigourney" Prize: Willy in 1993 and Madeleine in 2008. Nowadays, Madeleine continues working with her clinical practice and publications as well as contributing at scientific and institutional events.

The roots of their training were inevitably part of the ideas they developed in the psychoanalytic field. The ideas of Freud, Klein, Paula Heimann, Racker, Susan Isaacs, Bion, Pichon-Rivière, and Lacan circulate through their works—although they have always been re-elaborated in a personal way through critical judgement—with which they were able to generate innovative proposals. In other words, it is not a question of simply enumerating the presence of a simple coexistence of theories in the work of the Barangers, but one of analysing the theoretical roots that allowed them to produce ideas of their own concerning psychoanalytic theory and clinical practice.[1]

In a recent publication (2004), Madeleine Baranger identifies the sources of their ideas: the authors who inspired them, as well as the psychoanalysts who subsequently based their thinking on similar proposals, some of them without yet knowing about field theory. She thus placed their *oeuvre* within a genealogy, recognizing origins and influences while also describing the projections of their own work in other authors, an infrequent event that deserves acknowledgement. In this way, the anticipatory character of the Barangers' work is combined with its absolutely current status and prospective capacity.

Throughout the book, the reader will have found an itinerary that can be taken in visiting the works included herein. The concept of the analytic field, the focal point of the Barangers' proposal, is inseparable from their analyses of the analytic process and insight as well as from their concept of the bastion in the analytic situation. There is also a guiding thread that connects these proposals with others included in this volume, which reveal their way of thinking as well as their clinical concern. Certainly, we need to emphasize that the Barangers' work always includes the question of ethics in clinical work.

The psychoanalytic field and the "spiral process"

The reader who has gone through this book may define different lines of thinking. In my opinion, there are two intersecting lines that predominate in the Barangers' work: the concepts of the analytic field and the temporal factor, two conditions so intimately related that it is impossible to think about one without the other.

As described in this volume, the concept of the analytic field emerged from the confluence of different sources and disciplines: from philosophy with Merleau-Ponty's studies in the area of phenomenology, from Kurt Lewin's Gestalt theory, and from Bion's and Pichon-Rivière's work with groups.

The introduction of the notion of the analytic dynamic field (M. Baranger & Baranger, 1961–1962) addresses the whole question of intersubjectivity in the analytic situation. It is no longer the analyst interpreting the object of study (the patient) but the formation of a bipersonal field in which the analyst is a participant rather than a neutral and dispassionate observer.

We need to point out that the concept of the analytic field is a theoretical concept that has been broadened and deepened in the course of time by the Barangers in the same way as the psychoanalytic dynamic field is itself a formation in movement in clinical practice. Thus, the original concept of the analytic field has grown more complex, with the notion of the shared "basic unconscious fantasy", which subsequently acquired a structural dimension. On the basis of Bion's studies of small groups, the Barangers focused their thinking in other directions that extended beyond those of transference–countertransference interaction or the crisscrossing of projective identifications between patient and analyst. Bion's "basic assumption" is thought of in terms of a "basic fantasy" in which patient and analyst participate (both, at the same time, based on an initial oedipal triangulation). However, the Barangers point out that the basic fantasy is not a sum or any combination of individual fantasies of analyst and patient but, rather, an original fantasmatic whole, created by the situation of the field itself. *That is, it emerges in the analytic situation, in its process, and does not exist outside the field.* Thus, a third party is constituted, different from the individual fantasies belonging to the patient or the analyst. The concept of the analytic field as a third is therefore inseparable from the notion of the bipersonal basic fantasy. In other words, something new in the relation is generated that is neither one nor the other but includes both. It is true that the concept of the analytic field includes the concepts of transference–countertransference, projective identifications, and counteridentifications, but its totality is not reducible to these parts.

Psychic reality becomes more complex: "a different reality" is structured that is not static but is created from session to session and from moment to moment. This reality is inseparable from the intersubjective field. As a result, the psychoanalytic field has a spatial and temporal structure of its own and its own laws, able to generate the possibility of an event. Here, I take the concept of event as the emergence of something new and different from anything preceding or determining it: something not totally contained in the patient's history. Therefore, we need to emphasize that in the concept of the analytic field, coexisting structural and temporal dimensions converge.

If we think about this proposal in an epistemological perspective, we find categories that allow us to consider the concept of the analytic field in terms of its epistemological grounding. We recall that Green (2003) considers hyper-complex epistemologies a part of the future of psychoanalysis. We can also analyse the work of the Barangers in terms of these epistemologies since they form, as we said, an advanced dimension for their time and are now entirely topical.

The proposals of Morin (1990) regarding "complex thought" allow the development of a model of thought that operates beyond mono-causal determinism, and this applies well to the concept of dynamic psychoanalytic field. From a different vantage point, the ideas of Bakhtin (1963) in the field of literary criticism concerning the polyphonic and dialogic structure of the novel may contribute elements for understanding the concept of the analytic field as a dynamic medium where an interchange occurs including the other's voice in the structure. It points to multiplicity, in the sense that several functioning languages exist at the same time.

In philosophy, it is important to consider the contributions of Deleuze (Deleuze & Guattari, 1980) concerning the configuration and dynamics of the event, as well as the "lines of flight" that de-centre any dualism and strict polarities. It is also of interest to add the proposals by Trías (1991) regarding the "logic of the limit", who theorizes on the limit as a third space that generates its own laws between two categories or sets that come into contact. In these contributions, we see epistemological grounding that allows us to confirm that the proposal of the Barangers is not limited to the logic of a simple dualism between patient and analyst. Neither is it comparable to the interactional, symmetrical version of intersubjectivity. The concept of the analytic field involves the acceptance of a different logic, unlike that of subject–object in immovable positions or that of two subjects acting symmetrically; it is no longer monopersonal or merely bipersonal but a creation emerging from the participants and, in some way, surpassing them.

In this sense, it could be related to the transitional space between mother and baby as formulated by Winnicott (1959)—an "other" space for playing and possible creativity. Other authors have worked on similar ideas, each with specificities and differences: Green (2003) on the analytic object as a third, Ogden (1994) on the analytic third in intersubjectivity, Bollas (1979) on an intermediate zone generated between the subjectivities of patient and analyst, to mention a few.[2]

It is true that we could argue whether the Barangers' concept of the psychoanalytic dynamic field and basic unconscious fantasy responds to a dialectic synthesis generated in the bipersonal field or whether heterogeneous elements belonging to each individual psyche coexist in it. In my view, there are elements in the field belonging to the analyst and to the patient, which are present as heterogeneous elements unable to reach a final synthesis. In this sense, the dynamic field could be considered as based on disjunctive conjunctions that construct provisional syntheses (Deleuze & Guattari, 1980).

This point leads us to another central line that is inseparable from the concept of the analytic field: the temporal factor, always present in the works of the Barangers. The logic underlying the analytic field is the logic of movement, process, situation, and possibility of change. Therefore, there is a great preoccupation with the temporal dimension in clinical work. The Barangers' reflections induce them to think in terms of complex temporalities that appear in progressive and regressive, simultaneous or successive ways in the analytic process. They particularly highlight retroactive signification [*Nachträglichkeit*] as well as the interplay between past, present, and future. Along this line, they focus special attention on the prospective capacity of the interpretation and include the notion of future in the analytic process.

The notion of "spiral process", adopted from Pichon-Rivière, indicates a movement in time that is part of the possibilities for psychic change. It allowed Willy and Madeleine Baranger to think about the complexity of the regressive and progressive phenomena that occur in the analytic process. In the intersubjective field, the "here and now" is conjugated with the patient's history, but neither one nor the other by itself. History is re-signified in the present, while the "here and now" puts pieces of history into reach. The Barangers also emphasize the need to mark a difference between the genetic-evolutional and the historical. On this point, we need to underscore the distinction the authors draw between the facts and their personal historicization. This implies that history is seen as a work of historicization rather than a narration of facts. This alludes to the different temporalities operating in the analysis. The "spiral process" indicates that it is not only a question of the circular, repetitive time of the neuroses and fate, but of the open temporality of insight.

It is precisely the notion of bastion that they develop, inseparable from the concept of the dynamic field, that indicates a halt in the analytic process. In the construction of the bastion, an artificial neo-formation, both patient and analyst participate: that is to say, the resistances of both come together in different ratios. In other words, the concept of bastion includes the analyst and the analyst's countertransference and resistances and the limits imposed by the analyst's ideology and theoretical choices. Therefore, this implies an entrapment in an a-temporal condition encompassing both protagonists of the analytic situation and blocking the insight needed to re-start the process.

The concept of bastion led the Barangers to indicate the need for a "second look" by the analyst, a focus on the field as a whole to defend it from the constitution of a bastion that might support situations of *impasse* or negative therapeutic reaction. They underscore that only once the process is re-started will it be able to advance from a closed temporality to the establishment for the patient of a dilemma between various open possibilities with an anticipatory dimension. The "second look" also motivated them to inquire into concepts applied in excess such as the omnipresence of the transference to the detriment of the historical dimension of the analytic process. As we can see, the debates aroused by their works remain open and fresh today.

An examination of the concepts of psychoanalytic dynamic field and "spiral process" in the Barangers' works reveals: (a) that the analytic process is not a "natural" process that needs to go through pre-conceived stages; (b) the intrinsic degree of connection between temporal and spatial relations, comparable to Bakhtin's (1963) concept of the "chronotope"; (c) that each process is unique and in this sense atypical. It is unique to this patient, this history, this life. It is this characteristic that inspired Willy Baranger (1994) to consider the analytic work as a "handicraft".

In contrast to those who consider that analytic work must be directed to the patient's past, Willy Baranger maintains that the interpretation needs to be placed also in the analysand's future. This influenced him to modify his conception of "material", to distance himself from the sense of deepening and re-discovering more and more archaic "layers" of the analysand's psychic life, and to consider it instead as a set of situations experienced by the patient, in both their prospective and retrospective dimensions. He says: "Analysis does not consist essentially in re-discovering (although this re-discovery is an integral part of it), but in re-structuring, creating, and inventing. It points towards the new, to what is invented in the analytic process: an invention of the patient's own; by us and perhaps ours."

We cannot omit the reflection that the concept of event is present. The configuration and dynamics of the event (Badiou, 1999; Deleuze & Guattari, 1980) contribute elements to support the emergence of something new, in a *poietic* sense.

In sum, the concept of the psychoanalytic dynamic field and process in the Barangers' work incorporates the capacity to generate differences: that is, not only to discover the repetitions, but to create and invent. In this sense it can be thought of as a productive field, rooted in temporalities and in becoming, with ever possible expansion.

Note

1. See De León de Bernardi's (2008) introductory study to the Barangers' paper, "The Analytic Situation as a Dynamic Field".
2. Kancyper (1999) confirms the influence of the Barangers' ideas on Latin American psychoanalysis.

REFERENCES AND BIBLIOGRAPHY

Abraham, K. (1924). A short study of the development of the libido. In: *Selected Papers* (pp. 418–501). London: Hogarth Press, 1942.

Abraham, K. (1925). The history of an impostor in the light of psychoanalytic knowledge. In: *Clinical Papers and Essays on Psycho-Analysis*. London: Hogarth Press, 1955.

Alvarez de Toledo, L. (1954). The analysis of "associating", "interpreting" and "words": Use of this analysis to bring unconscious fantasies into the present and to achieve greater ego integration. *International Journal of Psychoanalysis*, *77* (1996): 291–231. [First published as: El análisis del asociar, del interpretar y de las palabras. *Revista de Psicoanalisis, 11* (No. 3): 267–313.]

Alvarez de Toledo, L. (1962). Psicoanalisis de la communicacíon verbal [Psychoanalysis of verbal communication]. *Acta Psiquiatrica Argentina, 8*: 16–24.

Amado Levy-Valensi, E. (1963). *La dialogue psychoanalytique* [The psychoanalytic dialogue] Paris: Presses Universitaires de France.

Aulagnier, P. (1979). *Les destins du plaisir* [Destinies of pleasure]. Paris: Presses Universitaire de France.

Aulagnier, P. (1986). *Du langage pictural au langage de l'interprète. Un interprète en quête de sens* [From pictorial language to the language of the interpreter. An interpreter looking for sense]. Paris: Payot.

Badiou, A. (1999). *El ser y el acontecimiento* [Being and the event]. Buenos Aires: Manantial.

Bakhtin, M. (1963). *Problems of Dostoevsky's Poetics*, trans. C. Emerson. Minneapolis, MN: University of Minnesota Press, 1984.

Balint, M. (1950). Changing therapeutical aims and techniques in psychoanalysis. *International Journal of Psychoanalysis, 31*: 117–124. Also in: *Primary Love and Psycho-Analytic Technique*. London: Hogarth Press, 1952.

Balint, M. (1968). *The Basic Fault: Therapeutic Aspects of Regression*. London: Tavistock.

Balint, M. (1969). Trauma and object relationship. *International Journal of Psychoanalysis, 50*: 429–435.

Baranger, M. (1956). Fantasía de enfermedad y desarrollo del insight en el análisis de un niño [Fantasy of disease and development of insight in the analysis of a child]. *Revista Uruguaya de Psicoanálisis, 1* (2): 143–182.

Baranger, M. (1960). "Regresión y temporalidad en el tratamiento analítico" [Regression and temporality in the psychoanalytic therapy]. Paper presented at the Asociación Psicoanalítica Argentina. [Published in: *Revista de Psicoanálisis APA, 36* (No. 2, 1969).]

Baranger, M. (1963). Mala fe, identidad y omnipotencia [Bad faith, identity, and omnipotence]. *Revista Uruguaya de Psicoanálisis, 5*: 199–229. [Chapter 8, this volume.]

Baranger, M. (1993). The mind of the analyst: From listening to interpretation. *International Journal of Psychoanalysis, 74*: 15–24. [Chapter 5, this volume.]

Baranger, M. (2004). Field theory. In: S. Lewkowicz & S. Flechner (Eds.), *Truth, Reality, and the Psychoanalyst* (pp. 49–71). London: IPA, 2005. [First published as: La teoría del campo. In: *El otro en la trama intersubjetiva* (pp. 145–169), ed. L. Glocer Fiorini. Buenos Aires: Lugar Editorial, 2004.]

Baranger, M., & Baranger, W. (1961–1962). The analytic situation as a dynamic field. 1961–1962. *International Journal of Psychoanalysis, 89* (No. 4, 2008): 795–826. [First published as: La situación analítica como campo dinámico. *Revista Uruguaya de Psicoanálisis, 4* (1): 3–54.]

Baranger, M., & Baranger, W. (1964). El "Insight" en la situación analítica ["Insight" in the analytic situation]. *Revista Uruguaya de Psicoanálisis, 6*: 19–38. [Chapter 1, this volume.]

Baranger, M., Baranger, W., & Mom, J. (1983). Process and non-process in analytic work. *International Journal of Psychoanalysis, 64*: 1–13. [Chapter 4, this volume.]

Baranger, M., Baranger, W., & Mom, J. M. (1987). El trauma psíquico infantil de nosotros a Freud. Trauma puro, retroactividad y reconstrucción [The infantile psychic trauma from us to Freud: Pure trauma, retroactivity, and reconstruction]. *Revista de Psicoanálisis, Asociación Psicoanalítica Argentina, 44* (4). [Chapter 6, this volume.]

Baranger, W. (1958). The ego and the function of ideology. *International Journal of Psychoanalysis, 39*: 191–195. [Chapter 10, this volume.]

Baranger, W. (1961–1962). El muerto–vivo. Estructura de los objetos en el duelo y los estados depresivos [The dead–alive: Object structure in mourning and depressive states]. *Revista Uruguaya de Psicoanálisis, 4*: 586–603. [Chapter 9, this volume.]

Baranger, W. (1961–1962). La noción de "material" y el aspecto temporal prospectivo de la interpretación [The notion of "material" and the prospective temporal aspect of interpretation]. *Revista Uruguaya de Psicoanálisis, 4* (2): 215–251. [Chapter 2, this volume.]

Baranger, W. (1969). Contradictions between theory and technique in psycho-analysis. In: W. Baranger & M. Baranger, *Problemas del campo psicoanalitico*. Buenos Aires: Ed Kargieman. [Chapter 7, this volume.]

Baranger, W. (1979). Proceso en espiral y campo dinámico [Spiral process and the dynamic field]. *Revista Uruguaya de Psicoanálisis, 59*: 17–32. [Chapter 3, this volume.]

Baranger, W. (1994). La situación analítica como producto artesanal [The analytic situation as a handcrafted product]. In: W. Baranger, R. Zak de Goldstein, & N. Goldstein (Eds.), *Artesanías Psicoanalíticas* (pp. 445–461). Buenos Aires: Kargieman.

Bibring, E. (1953). The mechanism of depression. In: P. Greenacre (Ed.), *Affective Disorders* (pp. 13–48). New York: International Universities Press.

Bion, W. R. (1952). Group dynamics: A review. *International Journal of Psycho-analysis, 33*: 235–247.

Bion, W. R. (1959). Attacks on linking. *International Journal of Psychoanalysis, 40*: 308–315.

Bleger, J. (1956). Sobre los instintos [About drives]. *Revista de Psicoanalisis, Buenos Aires, 13* (4): 367.

Bleger, J. (1958). *Psicoanalisis y dialectica materialista* [Psychoanalysis and materialist dialectics]. Buenos Aires: Ed. Paidos.

Bleger, J. (1961). La simbiosis [Symbiosis]. *Revista de Psicoanalisis,18* (4): 361–369.

Bleger, J. (1963). Mesa redonda sobre la teoria de los instintos [Panel about drive theories]. *Revista de Psicoanalisis, Buenos Aires, 20* (2).

Bleger, J., Liberman, D., Rascovsky, A., & Rascovsky, L. (1963). Mesa redonda sobre la "Teoría de los instintos" [Panel on "Drive theory"]. *Revista de Psicoanálisis, 20* (4): 147–179.

Bollas, C. (1979). The transformational object. *International Journal of Psycho-analysis, 60* (1): 97–107.

De León de Bernardi, B. (2000). The countertransference: A Latin American view. *International Journal of Psychoanalysis, 81*: 331–351.

De León de Bernardi, B. (2008). Introduction to the paper by Madeleine and Willy Baranger: "The analytic situation as a dynamic field." *International Journal of Psychoanalysis, 89*: 773–784.

Deleuze, G., & Guattari, F. (1980). *A Thousand Plateaus*. Minneapolis, MN: University of Chicago Press, 1987. [First published as: *Mille Plateaux*. Paris: Les Éditions de Minuit.]

Deutsch, H. (1955). The impostor: Contribution to ego psychology of a type of psychopath. *Psychoanalytic Quarterly, 24* (4).

Eizirik, C. L. (1993). Entre a escuta e a interpretação: Um estudo evolutivo da neutralidade psicanalítica [Between listening and interpretation: A developmental study of psychoanalytic neutrality]. *Revista de Psicanálise da Sociedade Psicanalítica de Porto Alegre, 1* (1): 19–42.

Eizirik, C. L. (2007). On the therapeutic action of psychoanalysis. *Psychoanalytic Quarterly, 76*: 1463–1478.

Ezriel, H. (1951). The scientific testing of psychoanalytic findings and theory: The psychoanalytic session as an experimental situation. *British Journal of Medical Psychology, 24*: 30–34.

Ferenczi, S. (1920). The further development of an active therapy in psycho-analysis. In: *Further Contributions to the Theory and Technique of Psycho-Analysis* (pp. 198–217). London: Hogarth Press, 1926; reprinted London: Karnac, 1994.

Ferenczi, S. (1933). *Thalassa: Theory of Genitality.* New York: The Psychoanalytic Quarterly, 1938.

Freud, A. (1967). Comments on trauma. In: S. Furst (Ed.), *Psychic Trauma* (pp. 235–245). New York: Basic Books.

Freud, S. (1888b). Hysteria. *S.E.,* 1: 39.

Freud, S. (1892–94). Translation with preface and footnotes of J.-M. Charcot's *Tuesday Lectures. S.E.,* 1.

Freud, S. (1895d) (with Breuer, J.). *Studies on Hysteria. S.E.,* 2.

Freud, S. (1900a). *The Interpretation of Dreams. S.E.,* 4/5.

Freud, S. (1901b). *The Psychopathology of Everyday Life. S.E.,* 6.

Freud, S. (1905a). On psychotherapy. *S.E.,* 7.

Freud, S. (1905d). *Three Essays on the Theory of Sexuality. S.E.,* 7.

Freud, S. (1906a). My views on the part played by sexuality in the aetiology of the neuroses. *S.E.,* 7.

Freud, S. (1910a [1909]). Five lectures on psycho-analysis. *S.E.,* 11.

Freud, S. (1910d). The future prospects of psycho-analytic therapy. *S.E.,* 11.

Freud, S. (1911–1915 [1914]). Papers on technique. *S.E.,* 12.

Freud, S. (1912e). Recommendations to physicians practising psycho-analysis. *S.E.,* 12.

Freud, S. (1912–13). *Totem and Taboo. S.E.,* 13.

Freud, S. (1913c). On beginning the treatment (Further recommendations on the technique of psycho-analysis, I). *S.E.,* 12.

Freud, S. (1913j). The claims of psycho-analysis to scientific interest. *S.E.,* 13: 165.

Freud, S. (1914g). Remembering, repeating and working-through (Further recommendations on the technique of psycho-analysis, II). *S.E.,* 12.

Freud, S. (1915d). Repression. *S.E.,* 14.

Freud, S. (1916d). Some character-types met with in psycho-analysis. *S.E.,* 14.

Freud, S. (1916–17). *Introductory Lectures on Psycho-Analysis. S.E.,* 15–16.

Freud, S. (1917e [1915]). Mourning and melancholia. *S.E.,* 14: 239.

Freud, S. (1919a [1918]). *Lines of Advance in Psycho-Analytic Therapy. S.E.,* 17: 159.

Freud, S. (1919d). Introduction to *Psycho-Analysis and the War Neuroses. S.E.,* 17.

Freud, S. (1920g). *Beyond the Pleasure Principle. S.E.,* 18.

Freud, S. (1921c). *Group Psychology and the Analysis of the Ego. S.E.,* 18: 67.

Freud, S. (1923b). *The Ego and the Id. S.E.,* 19: 3.

Freud, S. (1926d [1925]). *Inhibitions, Symptoms and Anxiety. S.E.,* 20.

Freud, S. (1926e). *The Question of Lay Analysis. S.E.,* 20: 179.

Freud, S. (1930a). *Civilization and Its Discontents. S.E.,* 21.

Freud, S. (1933a). *New Introductory Lectures on Psycho-Analysis. S.E.,* 22: 3.

Freud, S. (1937c). Analysis terminable and interminable. *S.E.,* 23: 209.

Freud, S. (1937d). Constructions in analysis. *S.E.,* 23: 257.

Freud, S. (1939a [1937–39]). *Moses and Monotheism. S.E.*, 23.

Freud, S. (1940a [1938]). *An Outline of Psycho-Analysis. S.E.*, 23: 141.

Freud, S. (1940e [1938]). Splitting of the ego in the process of defence. *S.E.*, 23: 273.

Freud, S. (1950 [1892–1899]). Extracts from the Fliess papers. *S.E.*, 1.

Freud, S. (1950 [1895]). Project for a scientific psychology. *S.E.*, 1.

Furst, S. (1967). *Psychic Trauma*. New York: Basic Books.

Garbarino, H. (1958). La posición depresiva y la melancolía [The depressive position and melancholia]. *Anales de la Clínica Psiquiátrica (Montevideo), 1*.

Gill, M. (1956). *Topography and Systems in Psychoanalytic Theory*. New York: International Universities Press.

Granel, J. (1985). On the capacity to change, the collusion of identifications, and having accidents: Their interrelations. *International Journal of Psychoanalysis, 14*: 483–490.

Green, A. (2003). *Key Ideas for a Contemporary Psychoanalysis: Misrecognition and Recognition of the Unconscious*. London: Routledge.

Greenacre, P. (1953). *Trauma, Growth and Personality*. London: Hogarth Press.

Greenacre, P. (1958a). Early physical determinants in the development of the sense of identity. *Journal of the American Psychoanalytic Association, 6* (4).

Greenacre, P. (1958b). The impostor. *Psychoanalytic Quarterly, 27* (3).

Grinberg, L. (1956). Sobre algunos problemas de técnica psicoanalítica determinados por la identificación y contraidentificación proyectivas [About some problems of psychoanalytic technique determined by projective identifications and counteridentifications]. *Revista de Psicoanálisis, 13* (4): 507–511.

Hartmann, H., & Kris, E. (1945). The genetic approach in psychoanalysis. *Psychoanalytic Study of the Child, 1*: 11–30.

Heimann, P. (1950). On counter-transference. *International Journal of Psychoanalysis, 31*: 81–84.

Heimann, P. (1952). Certain functions of introjection and projection in early infancy. In: M. Klein, P. Heimann, S. Isaacs, & J. Riviere, *Developments in Psycho-Analysis*, London: Hogarth Press.

Isaacs, S. (1939). Criteria for interpretation. *International Journal of Psychoanalysis, 20*: 148–160.

Isaacs, S. (1948). On the nature and function of phantasy. *International Journal of Psychoanalysis, 29*: 73–97.

Jacobson, E. (1953). Contribution to the metapsychology of cyclothymic depression. In: P. Greenacre (Ed.), *Affective Disorders*. New York: International Universities Press.

Kancyper, L. (Ed.) (1999). *Volviendo a pensar con Willy y Madeleine Baranger*. [Thinking again with Willy and Madeleine Baranger]. Buenos Aires: Grupo Editorial Lumen Argentina.

Khan, M. M. R. (1963). The concept of cumulative trauma. In: *The Privacy of the Self* (pp. 42–58). London: Hogarth Press, 1974.

Klein, M. (1926). Infant analysis. *International Journal of Psychoanalysis, 7*: 31–63.

Klein, M. (1935). A contribution to the psychogenesis of manic-depressive states. *International Journal of Psychoanalysis, 16*: 145–174. Also in: *Writings, Vol. 1: Love, Guilt and Reparation and Other Works*. London: Hogarth Press, 1975; reprinted London: Karnac, 1992.

Klein, M. (1940). Mourning and its relation to manic-depressive states. *International Journal of Psychoanalysis, 21*: 125–153. Also in: *Writings, Vol. 1: Love, Guilt and Reparation and Other Works*. London: Hogarth Press, 1975; reprinted London: Karnac, 1992.

Klein, M. (1946). Notes on some schizoid mechanisms. In: *Writings, Vol. 3: Envy and Gratitude and Other Works*. London: Hogarth Press, 1975; reprinted London: Karnac, 1993.

Klein, M. (1948). On the theory of anxiety and guilt. In: *Writings, Vol. 3: Envy and Gratitude and Other Works, 1946–1963* (pp. 25–42). London: Hogarth Press, 1975; reprinted London: Karnac, 1993.

Klein, M. (1952a). *Developments in Psycho-Analysis*. London: Hogarth Press.

Klein, M. (1952b). Some theoretical conclusions regarding the emotional life of the infant. In: *Writings, Vol. 3: Envy and Gratitude and Other Works*. London: Hogarth Press, 1975; reprinted London: Karnac, 1993.

Klein, M. (1955). On identification. In: *Writings, Vol. 3: Envy and Gratitude and Other Works*. London: Hogarth Press, 1975; reprinted London: Karnac, 1993.

Klein, M. (1957). Envy and gratitude. In: *Writings, Vol. 3: Envy and Gratitude and Other Works* (pp. 176–235). London, Hogarth Press, 1975; reprinted London: Karnac, 1993.

Klein, M. (1958). On the development of mental functioning. In: *Writings, Vol. 3: Envy and Gratitude and Other Works* (pp. 176–235). London, Hogarth Press, 1975; reprinted London: Karnac, 1993.

Klein, M., Heimann, P., & Money-Kyrle, R. (Eds.) (1955). *New Directions in Psycho-Analysis*. London: Tavistock; reprinted London: Karnac, 1993.

Koolhaas, G. (1957). El tiempo de la disociación, de la represión, de la reparación [Time of splitting, of repression and of reparation]. *Revista Uruguaya de Psicoanálisis, 2* (1–2).

Krafft-Ebing, R. (1886). *Psychopathia Sexualis*. New York: Bell, 1965.

Kris, E. (1956). On some vicissitudes of insight in psychoanalysis. *International Journal of Psychoanalysis, 37* (6): 445–455.

Lacan, J. (1953). The function and field of speech and language in psychoanalysis. In: *Écrits: A Selection* (trans. B. Fink). New York: W. W. Norton, 2006.

Lacan, J. (1955). Variations on the standard treatment. In: *Écrits: A Selection,*, trans. B. Fink. New York: W. W. Norton, 2006.

Lacan, J. (1958). The direction of the treatment and the principles of its power. In: *Écrits: A Selection*, trans. A. Sheridan, London: Tavistock, 1977; revised edition trans. B. Fink, New York: W. W. Norton, 2006.

Lacan, J. (1973). *The Four Fundamental Concepts of Psychoanalysis. Seminar, Book 11*. New York: W. W. Norton, 1978.

Lagache, D. (1956). Pathological mourning. In: *The Works of Daniel Lagache: Selected Papers*. London: Karnac, 1993.

Laplanche, J. & Pontalis, J.-B. (1967). *The Language of Psychoanalysis*. London: Hogarth Press, 1973; reprinted London: Karnac, 1988.

Lautréamont, C. de (1868–69). *Les chants de Maldoror* [Songs of Maldoror], trans G. Wernham. New York: New Directions, 1943.

Leclaire, S. (1968). *Psychanalyser* [Psychoanalysing]. Paris: Editions du Seuil.

Liberman, D. (1955). Acerca de la percepción del tiempo [About the perception of time]. *Revista de Psicoanálisis, 12* (3).

Liberman, D. (1962). *La comunicación en terapéutica psicoanalitica* [Communication in psychoanalytic therapy]. Buenos Aires: Ed. Eudeba.

Mahler, M. (1958). Autism and symbiosis, two extreme disturbances of identity. *International Journal of Psychoanalysis, 34* (2–4).

Masson, J. M. (Ed.) (1985). *The Complete Letters of Sigmund Freud to Wilhelm Fliess, 1887–1904*. Cambridge, MA: Harvard University Press.

Meltzer, D. (1967). *The Psycho-Analytical Process*. London: Heinemann; reprinted London: Karnac, 2008.

Merleau-Ponty, M. (1945). *Phenomenology of Perception*. London: Routledge & Kegan Paul, 1962.

Mijolla-Mellor, S. de (1990). Le travail de pensée dans l'interprétation [The work of thinking within interpretation]. *Topique, 46*: 192–203.

Morin, E. (1990). *Introducción al pensamiento complejo* [Introduction to the complex thought]. Barcelona: Gedisa, 1995.

Ogden, T. (1994). The analytical third: Working with intersubjective clinical facts. *International Journal of Psychoanalysis, 75* (1): 3–19.

Pichon-Rivière, E. (1956). Communication at the First Latin-American Congres.

Pichon-Rivière, E. (1958). Referential schema and dialectical spiral process as basis to a problem of the past. *International Journal of Psychoanalysis, 39*: 294 [abstract].

Politzer, G. (1966). *Crítica de los fundamentos de la psicología: el psicoanálisis* [Critique of the fundamentals of psychology: Psychoanalysis]. Buenos Aires: J. Alvarez.

Pontalis, J. (1981). *Frontiers in Psychoanalysis*. London: Hogarth Press.

Racker, H. (1948). The countertransference neurosis. In: *Transference and Countertransference*. New York: International Universities Press, 1968.

Racker, H. (1953). A contribution to the problem of countertransference. *International Journal of Psychoanalysis, 34*: 313–324.

Racker, H. (1958). Classical and present techniques in psychoanalysis. In: *Transference and Countertransference*. London: Hogarth Press, 1968.

Racker, H. (1960). *Estudios sobre tecnica psicoanalitica* [Studies on psychoanalytic technique]. Buenos Aires: Ed. Paidos.

Rangell, L. (1967). The metapsychology of psychic trauma. In: S. Furst (Ed.), *Psychic Trauma* (pp. 51–84). New York: Basic Books.

Rapaport, D. (1942). *Emotions and Memory*. Baltimore, MD: Williams & Wilkins.

Rapaport, D. (1951). The conceptual model of psychoanalysis. *Journal of Personality, 20*: 56–81.

Rapaport, D. (1973). *The History of the Concept of Association of Ideas*. New York: International Universities Press.

Rapaport, D., & Gill, M. (1959). The points of view and assumptions of metapsychology, *International Journal of Psychoanalysis, 40*: 153–162.

Reich, W. (1945). *Character Analysis*. New York: Farrar, Straus & Giroux, 1980.

Richfield, J. (1954). An analysis of the concept of insight. *Psychoanalytic Quarterly, 23* (3): 390–408.

Rickman, J. (1951). Number and the human sciences. In: *Psychoanalysis and Culture*. New York: International Universities Press. Also in: *Selected Contributions to Psycho-Analysis*. London: Hogarth Press, 1957; reprinted, with a new Preface by P. King, London: Karnac, 2003.

Rodrigué, E. (1955). The analysis of a three-year-old mute schizophrenic. In: M. Klein, P. Heimann, & R. Money-Kyrle (Eds.), *New Directions in Psycho-Analysis*. London: Tavistock; reprinted London: Karnac 1993.

Rosenfeld, H. (1959). An investigation into the psycho-analytic theory of depression. *International Journal of Psycho-Analysis, 40*: 2.

Rubinfine, D. (1958). Problems of identity. *Journal of the American Psychoanalytic Association, 6* (1).

Rycroft, C. (1955). Two notes on idealization, illusion and disillusion as normal and abnormal psychological processes. *International Journal of Psychoanalysis, 36* (2).

Sartre, J.-P. (1943). L'être et le néant. In: *Existentialism from Dostoevsky to Sartre*, trans. & intro. W. Kaufmann. Cleveland, OH: Meridian, 1956.

Schmidl, F. (1955). The problem of validation in psychoanalytic interpretation. *International Journal of Psychoanalysis, 36* (2).

Segal, H. (1956). Depression in the schizophrenic. *International Journal of Psychoanalysis, 37*: 339–343.

Strachey, J. (1934). The nature of the therapeutic action in psychoanalysis. *International Journal of Psychoanalysis, 15*: 127–159.

Trías, E. (1991). *Lógica del límite* [Logic of the limit]. Barcelona: Destino.

Valabrega, J.-P. (1962). *La relation thérapeutique* [The therapeutic relationship]. Paris: Flammarion.

Winnicott, D. (1959). The fate of the transitional object. In: *Psychoanalytic Explorations* (pp. 53–78). London: Karnac, 1989.

Zetzel, E. (1951). The depressive position. In: P. Greenacre (Ed.), *Depressive Disorders* (pp. 84–116). New York: International Universities Press, 1953.

Zilboorg, G. (1952). The emotional problem and the therapeutic role of insight. *Psychoanalytic Quarterly, 21*: 1–24.

INDEX